W9-CFM-363

SIMPLIFIED BASIC PROGRAMMING FOR MICROCOMPUTERS

GERALD A. SILVER
Los Angeles City College

MYRNA SILVER

1817 **HARPER & ROW, PUBLISHERS, New York**
Cambridge, Philadelphia, San Francisco,
London, Mexico City, São Paulo, Sydney

Sponsoring Editor: **John Willig**
Project Editor: **David Nickol**
Designer: **Michel Craig**
Production: **Delia Tedoff**
Compositor: ComCom Division of Haddon Craftsmen, Inc.
Printer and Binder: R. R. Donnelley & Sons Company
Art Studio: Vantage Art, Inc.

SIMPLIFIED BASIC PROGRAMMING FOR MICROCOMPUTERS

Copyright © 1984 by Harper & Row, Publishers, Inc

All rights reserved. Printed in the United States of America. No part of this book may be used or reproduced in any manner whatsoever without written permission, except in the case of brief quotations embodied in critical articles and reviews. For information address Harper & Row, Publishers, Inc., 10 East 53d Street, New York, NY 10022.

Library of Congress Cataloging in Publication Data

Silver, Gerald A.
    Simplified BASIC programming for microcomputers.

    Includes index.
    1. Basic (Computer program language).
2. Microcomputers—Programming. I. Silver, Myrna. II. Title.
QA76.73.B3S543 1984   001.64'24   83–22561
ISBN 0–06–046162–4

CONTENTS

PART THREE SAMPLE PROGRAMS FOR STUDY   151

APPENDICES

PREFACE

The past decade has seen an explosive growth in home and small-business computers and the use of BASIC. The utility of BASIC has far exceeded the expectations of its creators. Today BASIC is widely used in homes as well as in education, business, industry, and science because of its innate simplicity and ample processing power.

BASIC comes close to being the ideal language for the home computer as well as the classroom. It is easily learned and is suitable for both small and large computers. BASIC is well on its way to being the de facto standard of hobbyists and users of small computers.

This book is an easy-to-understand introduction to BASIC. It gives the reader a firm grasp of the fundamental tools needed to use a computer. This book includes several significant features to help you learn the language.

1. Clear, nontechnical language is used to convey the fundamental concepts of the language. Ideas are presented in terms that the reader will already understand or can grasp easily. Advanced programming concepts and difficult terms have been kept to a minimum and are explained clearly.

2. A nonmathematical approach to the language is used. Although programs of some mathematical sophistication are presented, the reader is not required to learn mathematics as a prerequisite to learning BASIC.

3. The book uses a modular approach. Each chapter is self-contained, discussing a different part of the programming process. Each BASIC statement is presented in an individual unit, with examples, explanatory material, and exercises.

4. The subject matter is introduced as the reader needs it, moving from the simple to the complex. This allows the reader to begin writing working programs early in his or her study of the language.

5. A list of rules at the end of each language unit brings together all the many do's

and don'ts related to each command. This facilitates referencing easy-to-forget details and helps the reader improve his or her programming skills.

6. Learning is reinforced by the inclusion of exercises at the end of each language unit. The reader can immediately apply new knowledge and test his or her understanding of that command.

7. A diverse set of sample programs are carefully documented and explained. They illustrate statement usage, fundamental algorithms, and program logic. The diverse nature of the examples demonstrates the graphic, mathematical, text processing, and interactive capabilities of the language.

8. The reader is introduced to flowcharting and program debugging in the appendices. This will be useful throughout the reader's study of the language.

9. Unless otherwise noted, all programs and examples in this book have been run and tested on Microsoft BASIC. Microsoft is one of the most common versions of BASIC found on microcomputers. However, the reader will find that even if his or her system does not have Microsoft BASIC, virtually all of the programs and examples in this book will still run on his or her system. The language concepts are presented in a generic form, without tying them to specific pieces of equipment or language implementations.

An important feature of this book is the appendices, which are devoted to error prevention, program debugging, and documentation. Many illustrations are included, both to help the reader avoid errors in the first place and to enable him or her to find and correct those that will inevitably occur.

The authors wish to thank the following firms who have kindly provided assistance in preparing this manuscript: Vector Graphic, Inc.; Apple Computer, Inc.; and Radio Shack, a division of Tandy Corporation.

GERALD A. SILVER
MYRNA SILVER

PART
ONE
EXPLANATORY TEXT

CHAPTER 1
INTRODUCTION TO BASIC PROGRAMMING

Let's begin by dispelling a few myths about computers: "You must have an extensive background in electronics, mathematics, or some other technical subject to understand computers." "Computers are complicated, mystical machines, which are only for business or scientific use."

Nothing could be further from the truth! Computers can be fun and entertaining.

Directing the computer to produce the results you want requires only three qualities: a basic skill in typing, a familiarity with a computer language (such as BASIC), and an understanding of programming principles. (And, of course, even the typing skills can often be delegated to someone else.) So if you don't know a bit from a byte, or an arc sine from a stop sign, don't be worried; you can still have a lot of fun with BASIC and your small computer.

WHAT IS BASIC?

BASIC stands for Beginner's All-purpose Symbolic Instruction Code, which is the name of a computer language; for convenience, it is usually called just BASIC. BASIC is one of the many computer languages that have appeared during the past several decades to facilitate communications between people and computers. It is the means a hobbyist or a professional programmer uses to direct a computer through the various steps necessary to get results.

In many respects, BASIC is like a foreign language. A Frenchman who speaks no English must be given directions in French if he is to be expected to understand them. Similarly, since the computer cannot "speak English," the user must learn its language in order to communicate with it.

And, like French, computer languages have rules of grammar, spelling, order, and

FIGURE 1.1 Microcomputer systems are widely used in business applications. (Vector Graphics, Inc.)

so on. If the directions are to be understood by the computer (or the Frenchman), the words and phrases must follow the rules.

When computers were developed in the 1940s and 1950s, it became evident that one of the biggest problems was in human-machine communication. Although the computer was capable of processing problems very quickly and accurately, the actual task of directing it was complex and difficult.

The computer understands instructions in only one language—machine language—which is composed of a combination of 1s and 0s, such as

0110   0010   1001   0001   1010

(A simplified explanation of these symbols is that they represent "on" and "off." They tell the computer which circuits to turn on and which to turn off.) Writing programs in machine language is obviously a cumbersome way for human beings to communicate with machines. In order to simplify programming, interpreter languages were developed. An interpreter is a program that remains in the computer and translates instructions into the machine language which the computer can execute.

The first computer languages were designed for use by professional programmers, scientists, and engineers, and they were relatively complicated. That hobbyists, secretaries, or even grade school children might do programming was never considered. What was needed was a simple language the professional and nonprofessional programmer could use.

John G. Kemeny and Thomas E. Kurtz, working under a National Science Foundation grant at Dartmouth College, developed a relatively simple language, which they named BASIC. Dartmouth students found BASIC easy to learn and use; and before long, many schools, colleges, and business firms became interested in the language.

BASIC uses only about 20 fundamental words. This simplifies the task of learning

FIGURE 1.2 A wide variety of games and hobby programs are available on small computers. (Radio Shack/Tandy Corp.)

the language. Today almost every home and small-business computer is equipped with a BASIC interpreter.

ADVANTAGES AND LIMITATIONS OF BASIC

BASIC is an easily learned language. It includes only a few words and concepts, being composed of readily recognizable English words and algebraic symbols. BASIC is an interactive language, which makes it very versatile.

BASIC is a powerful language, possessing good mathematical and alphabetic capabilities. It is used by the professional and nonprofessional programmer for a variety of applications—for instruction in schools and colleges, for design and engineering by engineers, mathematicians, and statisticians, among others. It is also used by business people for programming inventory, financial, accounting, marketing, and other problems (Fig. 1.1).

BASIC's usefulness is further expanded by an extensive library of ready-made programs. These programs, written by manufacturers or users, are stored in the computer's system library and can be called into use by any user. This saves a user much time and effort, since he or she can process data with these programs without taking the time and effort to write a program.

The libraries of programs vary from one computer manufacturer to another. They include statistical, financial, engineering, and mathematical procedures. Some libraries have many games and demonstration programs, such as Star Trek, Bandit, and Blackjack (Fig. 1.2).

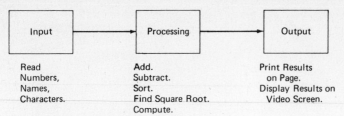

Input	Processing	Output
Read Numbers, Names, Characters.	Add. Subtract. Sort. Find Square Root. Compute.	Print Results on Page. Display Results on Video Screen.

FIGURE 1.3 Data processing cycle.

HOW COMPUTERS "THINK"
AND CARRY OUT INSTRUCTIONS

To solve a problem, a computer must be given a clear set of instructions and the data to be operated on. This set of instructions, called a *program,* is written by a *programmer*, who may be a student, an engineer, or a hobbyist. The data are the numbers or words that the machine is to process.

The program, or set of instructions, directs the computer to perform various tasks in a predetermined sequence. The machine may be directed to read in numbers or words, to rearrange numbers or words, to calculate sums and products, and so on. And it may be instructed to print out the results in a usable form.

The entry of data or information into the computer is called *input,* and the manipulation of data is called *processing.* The communicating of results to the user is called *output.* Figure 1.3 illustrates the input-processing-output sequence.

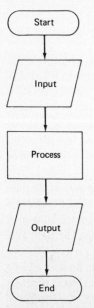

FIGURE 1.4 Batch processing.

The sequence of steps followed by the computer is thus

INPUT → PROCESSING → OUTPUT

In order for the machine to perform these tasks, the programmer must

1. write a program (give a clear set of instructions)
2. prepare the data (arrange the numbers or words to be processed)
3. enter the program into the computer
4. enter the data into the computer

The computer responds by

1. receiving the program
2. receiving the data
3. processing the data according to the instructions in the program
4. outputting results

A computer may output results in many ways. For example, it may type out information on a line printer, punch data into paper tape, display information on a video screen, or record it on magnetic tape.

WHAT IS INTERACTIVE PROGRAMMING?

Programs and data can be processed by the computer in two ways: *batch processing* and *interactive programming*. In batch processing, the program and data are entered into the computer at once and run without any further intervention or direction from the programmer. The computer operates on the data exactly as instructed by the program and outputs the results as directed. This is shown in Fig. 1.4.

In interactive programming, the program and data are entered at once, or in steps, while the computer is executing the problem. The programmer interacts with the computer, giving and receiving information, while the processing proceeds. This is illustrated in Fig. 1.5.

Interactive programming differs from batch processing in several ways. In interactive programming,

1. the program and data can be entered in parts
2. the computer can request more information or data while it is processing the data
3. the instructions in the program can be changed by the programmer during the run of the program to direct the computer to perform different steps than were originally planned
4. the programmer is in direct communication with the computer at all times

Interactive programming has numerous advantages. It provides the programmer with a fast, flexible means of solving a problem. It allows the programmer to process a

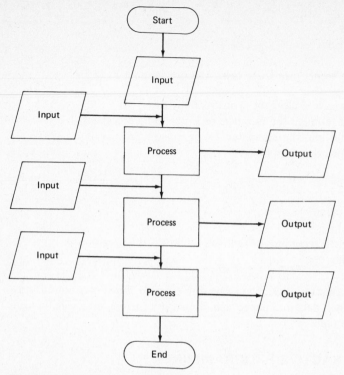

FIGURE 1.5 Interactive programming.

FIGURE 1.6 Interactive programming allows the programmer to alter program flow. (Apple Computers, Inc.)

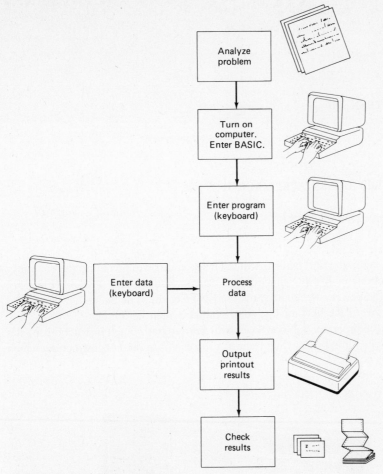

FIGURE 1.7 Computer session.

problem step by step and check each step as he or she goes along (Fig. 1.6). It allows him/her to change instructions during processing and add or delete data or perform other procedures on the data after observing the results of processing.

EXAMPLE OF HOW
THE COMPUTER IS USED TO SOLVE A PROBLEM

Sue Smith wants to determine the average of the scores her classmates have achieved in her English literature class. Sue proceeds to solve the problem in the steps listed in Fig. 1.7.

1. Analyze the problem. After some study Sue writes a program that directs the computer to read the group of 20 scores, find their sum, divide by 20, and print out the answer. It takes Sue about half an hour to write down the set of instructions. Now she is ready to enter the information into the computer. The set of instructions is shown in Fig. 1.8.

```
10 REM PROGRAM AVERAGES 20 NUMBERS
20 LET T=0
30 LET C=0
40 INPUT S
50 LET C=C+1
60 LET T=T+S
70 IF C=20 THEN 90
80 GOTO 40
90 LET A=T/C
100 PRINT
110 PRINT
120 PRINT "THE CLASS AVERAGE IS: "; A
130 END
```

FIGURE 1.8 Sample program (BASIC).

2. Turn on computer and enter BASIC. This step involves preparing the computer to receive instructions in BASIC. Since Sue is using a Radio Shack TRS-80 (Fig. 1.9), she will turn on the power switch and press the ENTER key. The machine will respond by displaying the word READY on the televisionlike screen before her.

3. Type in the program. Sue now keyboards her program. Each instruction she has written down is typed line by line. Sue then types in END as the last instruction, which

FIGURE 1.9 TRS-80 model II microcomputer. (Radio Shack/Tandy Corp.)

indicates to the computer that the program has been entered. Depending upon her typing skill, entering the program may take Sue only a few minutes.

4. Process data. After the program has been entered, she instructs the machine to begin processing by typing in the word RUN. The computer will begin to follow the instructions in her program. It will request her to enter the data to be processed at the proper points in the program. It will add up the scores, divide by 20, and output results. This step may take only a fraction of a second, since the computer is much faster at processing than Sue is at typing.

5. Output results. As soon as the computer calculates the average, it displays the result. Sue has directed the machine to print an identifying line before listing the results. The output looks like this:

THE CLASS AVERAGE IS: 92

6. Check results. Sue now checks her results by manually computing the answer. Once she is assured her program is correct, she can then use the same program to process other data, such as a longer list containing more numbers, with confidence.

EXERCISES

1. Discuss the function of the program.
2. Summarize the differences between batch processing and interactive processing.
3. Summarize the advantages of BASIC.
4. Study the documentation and language reference manuals for your particular machine.
5. Obtain a copy of the BASIC system library of ready-made programs. Make a list of seven or eight programs that you might be interested in running later.
6. Identify the power switch on your computer and determine what steps are necessary to enter BASIC on your machine.
7. Determine whether your computer will output information on a videoscreen or line printer.
8. Study the program Sue used to compute averages, and trace the steps the computer follows in processing her program.

CHAPTER 2

HOW TO RUN A PROGRAM IN BASIC

You've probably already unpacked your computer and are anxious to learn how to program. You may have run a few games and perhaps even a simple computation following the instructions that came with the computer. But what comes next? Perhaps you are beginning to discover that a computer is more than a toy. You would like to learn how to write your own programs, or perhaps modify those provided by the computer manufacturer.

That's what this chapter is all about. You will learn the key terms necessary to understand programming and some of the general practices you need to know to write programs in BASIC. You will be introduced to some of the fundamentals of small computers so you can begin to write programs or play games on your system easily.

Each computer system has its own idiosyncracies. While there are many similarities, you will still need to study the reference manual that came with your computer.

If the program you plan on writing has more than a dozen or so statements, you will need to approach the problem systematically. After you have reviewed the problem to be solved, you must define what information is to be input into the computer and how it is to be processed. You will find it helpful to use a diagram, or flowchart, to aid you in laying out the steps in the program. Appendix A of this book explains the details of how to write flowcharts and develop program logic.

Let's start with a discussion of coding, which is simply writing down the instructions you plan to use. Coding is a little like making an outline of what you plan to say before you write a report for school or business. It can be done on an ordinary sheet of notebook paper. Write down or print clearly and neatly each instruction you will want to enter into the computer. You will learn about the various BASIC instructions in later chapters. You will make fewer mistakes and find programming easier if you do your coding first. Without a coding sheet in front of you it is easy to make mistakes, overlook statements, or key in the wrong information. Figure 2.1 shows a handwritten coding sheet for a short program. Each line on the coding sheet is typed into the computer on a separate line.

You may also want to develop some test data to run through your program so you can compare the results and be sure that the program is processing information accurately. Program testing and debugging is discussed in more detail in Appendix B.

SOME IMPORTANT TERMS TO KNOW

Computing is full of interesting and colorful jargon and phrases. Let's learn a few terms in "computerese."

1. *Program.* A program is a set of instructions that directs the computer through a sequence of steps to solve a problem or produce a desired result. Programs are simply recipes that direct the computer to carry out the steps to solve a problem. Computer programs are sometimes referred to as *software.* Software includes programs, manuals, instructions, and information on how to use a given system (Fig. 2.2).

2. *Hardware.* Computer hardware is the equipment—machines and devices—for processing data. Computer hardware includes the computer itself (Fig. 2.3), line printers, cathode-ray tube displays, and so on.

3. *Input/output.* This frequently used term refers to the devices that feed the information to or from the computer. For example, a keyboard is an input device, since it inputs information to the computer (Fig. 2.4).

4. *Bug.* A bug is an error in a computer program that causes the machine to print out erroneous results. Debugging is the task of correcting errors in a program.

5. *Numeric data.* One or more symbols that represent a fixed quantity, a number.

Examples

2141, 32, 9, 42, 506

6. *Digit.* One of the numeric symbols used to represent data.

Examples

0, 2, 9

7. *Alphanumeric* or *alpha data.* Data in the form of alphabetic letters, special characters (punctuation), digits, or a combination of the three. (Numbers read in as alphanumeric data cannot be used in mathematical manipulations.)

Examples

GEORGE, D-21, PART: 164A4

8. *Alpha string.* A collection of alphanumeric characters treated by the computer as a unit.

Examples

THIS LINE IS AN ALPHA STRING
THOMAS GOULD   PART ZX9312

```
10 REM PROGRAM AVERAGES 20 NUMBERS
20 LET T=0
30 LET C=0
40 INPUT S
50 LET C=C+1
60 LET T=T+S
70 IF C=20 THEN 90
80 GOTO 40
90 LET A=T/C
100 PRINT
110 PRINT
120 PRINT "THE CLASS AVERAGE IS:  "; A
130 END
```

FIGURE 2.1 Program coded in BASIC.

9. *Literal data.* A symbol or quantity in a program that is in itself data rather than a reference to data. A literal can be numeric, such as 10 or 350, or alphanumeric, such as COLUMN 1 or THE ANSWER IS:.

10. *Constant.* A value that does not change throughout the run of a program. For example, the number 10 always represents 10 units. A constant may be alphanumeric, numeric, or literal.

FIGURE 2.2 Microcomputer shown with software and supporting documentation. (Apple Computers, Inc.)

FIGURE 2.3 Computer hardware includes the computer, plus line printers and other devices. (Radio Shack/Tandy Corp.)

Examples

104, PERCENT, PAGE NUMBER:

11. *Variable.* A name or symbol used to represent a quantity. The value of the quantity it represents may change throughout the execution of a program. For example, A may represent the number of units ordered and be equal to 4 at one point in the pro-

FIGURE 2.4 Microcomputer keyboard. (Commodore Business Machines, Inc.)

gram, but later A may change to 6 or 12, and so on. A variable may be numeric or alphanumeric.

Examples

```
T, B1, S$, NN
```

GENERAL PRACTICES TO
FOLLOW WHEN PROGRAMMING IN BASIC

BASIC is a simple language to use, but it has certain rules that must be learned, just as in any language. Something as seemingly insignificant as a misplaced comma can cause a program not to function. Below are some rules and general suggestions you should follow when writing programs. Since there are many versions of BASIC in use, it is difficult to state absolute rules. The guidelines stated below are applicable to most versions of BASIC.

1. Study the reference manual for your computer to learn the specific commands that relate to your machine. Language and system commands differ, so that you must know the correct version for your computer.

2. Begin each statement with a line number. Every BASIC statement must have a unique line number. These numbers may range from 1 to 9999 and must be in sequence. (Some systems may allow the use of up to eight- or nine-digit statement numbers. Still others allow a maximum line number of 63999 or 65535. Your reference manual should be checked on this point.) The computer stores your statements in numerical order, by line number. Line numbers also serve as labels to refer to a specific line.

Many programmers number their statements in increments of 10; for example,

```
10 . . .
20 . . .
30 . . .
40 . . .
```

This allows extra statements to be added easily at a later time. For example, a statement that must be entered between lines 30 and 40 may be labeled 35 (or any other number between 31 and 39). Unless instructed otherwise, the computer will always execute the statements in sequence, beginning with the lowest line number and moving progressively to the largest.

3. Note that each line number should have only one entry. Two statements should not be listed under one line number, regardless of how short they are. Each should be entered on a separate line, with a different statement number.

4. Do not enter a line with more than the maximum number of allowed characters. Most computers accept a specific maximum number of characters on a line. The excess characters will be ignored, usually resulting in an incorrect statement.

5. Press the carriage return key at the end of each entry. The carriage return signals the computer that the line is ready for entry into the system. On some systems, the ENTER key effects the carriage return. On most systems, the RETURN key is used as carriage return.

6. It is good practice to terminate all programs with an END statement. The END statement should be the last physical statement in your program and have the largest line number in your program. Not all machines require an END statement.

7. Begin each program with a REM statement. The REM statement should include the title of the program. The REM statement (short for REMARK) does not affect the program flow; it aids in documenting the steps followed in the program. More than one REM statement may be used in a program. In fact, it is good practice to include REM statements at branches, calculation sequences, subroutines, and so on.

8. Write your instructions on a coding sheet (or piece of notebook paper) before keyboarding. Print clearly. Do not code from memory or hastily prepared notes.

9. Slash certain characters to avoid confusion. Some programmers always slash the alphabetic letters Ø, I, and Z to prevent confusion with the numerals 0, 1, and 2. Other programmers prefer to slash the numerical characters instead of the alphabetic. Which system you follow is not important, as long as you are consistent (see Fig. 2.1).

10. A slashed lowercase b (ƀ) is used to indicate a space when handwriting programming instructions or to show layout on forms, output, and so on. The ƀ is only for the programmer's convenience and should not be keyboarded.

11. You may enter numerical data as either whole or decimal numbers. If the numerical value that results from a calculation is a whole number, it will be printed out as a whole number, with no decimal point indicated. This is the case whether or not the data processed were entered as whole or decimal numbers.

Values read in as whole numbers, with a decimal indicated, will print out as whole numbers without a decimal point. If the numerical value that results from a calculation is a decimal number, it will be printed out with a decimal point. Most BASIC interpreters will print the decimal value showing up to six digits to the right of the decimal. All trailing and leading zeroes will be dropped by the interpreter when it prints out a numerical value. For example,

```
2         + 2        = 4
2.        + 2.       = 4
2.5       + 2.5      = 5
2.5       + 2        = 4.5
5         ÷ 2        = 2.5
2.25      + 2.25     = 4.5
```

12. Negative numerical values should be entered preceded by a minus sign (−). Numbers are otherwise assumed to be positive.

13. The maximum number of digits that the computer will print out depends upon the particular computer system. Some will not print numbers with more than six digits, whereas others may output nine or more. If the number to be printed out has more place positions than the computer is designed to print, a shorthand method of output, called the E specification, is used.

In the E specification, the first six or seven digits will be printed out, rounded off, followed by the letter E and a number. The number following the E indicates what power of 10 the value should be multiplied by. This is easily done by moving the position of the decimal point as many places as indicated by this number. If the number has no sign, or a plus sign (+), move the decimal point to the right, filling in with zeros where necessary. If the number is preceded by a minus sign (−), move the decimal point to the left, filling in with zeros where necessary. For example,

```
2.30000E+11  =    230000000000
1.23457E+9   =      1234567890
-1.23446E-3  =     -.001234456
1.69342E-4   =      .000169342
```

14. The names assigned to quantities (variables) read into storage must follow certain rules. The rules for naming variables vary depending upon the particular computer. Generally, though, the following usually applies:

    a. Acceptable names for numeric values may be a single alphabetic letter (A–Z), such as A, F, G, T, or an alphabetic letter followed by a single digit (A1–Z9), such as A1, G3, J7.

    b. Acceptable names for alphabetic variables may be a single alphabetic letter followed by a dollar sign (A\$–Z\$). Examples are A\$, B\$, K\$. On some systems, two of the same alphabetic characters are used (AA–ZZ), such as AA, GG, RR.

15. Data read in under an alphabetic name cannot be processed mathematically by the computer, even though it contains numbers. It can be moved to new storage locations, assigned to different names, printed out on the printer, and in some cases joined to other alphabetic variables.

16. Data may be input into the computer in either of two ways: in the program, using READ/DATA statements, or from the keyboard, using an INPUT statement.

    a. READ/DATA statements. Each time the computer encounters a variable name in a READ statement, it will assign this name to a value listed in a DATA statement. The first name goes to the first value, the second name to the second value, and so on.

    b. INPUT statement. The required data are entered into the computer from the keyboard. Each time an INPUT statement appears in the program, the computer will stop and print out a ?. The programmer must then enter the data at that point. The computer will assign the variable name listed in the INPUT statement to the value read in. This method allows the data entered and processed to be changed for each run. Both of these statements are described in more detail later in the book.

17. Only characters from the standard character set may be used in programming BASIC statements. These vary slightly from one system to another. Figure 2.5 shows the standard character set used by one system.

18. Many system commands can be abbreviated to only three letters. This does not affect their meanings. Check your computer manual for the abbreviations allowed. Examples are

    CAT for CATALOG
    DEL for DELETE
    BAS for BASIC

Code	Character	Code	Character	Code	Character	Code	Character
0	SPACE	14	,	30	8	54	L
1	!	15	-	31	9	55	M
2	"	16	.	32	:	56	N
3	#	17	/	33	;	57	O
4	$	20	0	34	<	60	P
5	%	21	1	35	=	61	Q
6	&	22	2	36	>	62	R
7	'	23	3	37	?	63	S
10	(	24	4	40	@	64	T
11	)	25	5	41	A	65	U
12	*	26	6	42	B	66	V
13	+	27	7	43	C	67	W
				44	D	70	X
				45	E	71	Y
				46	F	72	Z
				47	G	73	[
				50	H	74	\
				51	I	75	]
				52	J	76	↑
				53	K	77	←

FIGURE 2.5 Standard character set.

CONTROL CHARACTERS

There are two types of shift keys on many computers; shift and control. When the shift key is held down and a key depressed, a shift character is transmitted. If the control key is held down and the key depressed, a control character is transmitted. Some keys can transmit control, shift, and regular characters. Others can transmit only regular and control characters or regular and shift characters.

The control characters are a special set of *nonprinting* characters on the keyboard that transmit special commands to the computer. They direct the computer to perform various operations, such as terminating execution of a program, deleting a partially typed line or a single character, returning control to the operating system, and so on.

The particular function performed by each character varies from system to system. Refer to your language reference manual or computer instruction manual for specific details.

Examples of control characters are

CONTROL/D
CONTROL/X
CONTROL/B
CONTROL/C

To transmit a control character, press the key marked CTRL and then press the appropriate letter (D, X, B, C, etc.).

DELETING AND CORRECTING A PROGRAM

Both novice and advanced programmers expect to make errors when keyboarding a program. The reader should know how to correct a single line, delete one or more mis-struck characters or an entire program, and so on. Following are guidelines on how to perform these operations. Be sure to consult your reference manual on the specific procedures involved for your computer.

1. How to delete one or two characters from a line. If you inadvertently strike an incorrect character, you can delete it without rekeyboarding the entire line. On most systems, pressing the left-facing-arrow key (←) will erase the last character entered into computer storage. When this key (left arrow) is struck, it will print a left-facing arrow, indicating that the last character has been deleted. The operator can then type in the correct character. Pressing the key several times will remove several characters. One character is deleted for each left arrow struck. If you have already entered many characters beyond the point of error, it is probably easier to rekeyboard the entire line.

2. How to delete a partially keyboarded line. If you type a line and then decide not to enter it into storage, it may be cleared from the system if you have not yet pressed the carriage return key. On some systems, the CTRL-X annuls the line currently being typed.

3. How to delete a numbered line that has been entered with a carriage return. After you type a line and press the carriage return, the line is transmitted to the computer and is put in storage. The entire line may be deleted from storage by typing the line number and pressing the carriage return.

4. How to clear the display screen. If the display screen is full of characters and you wish to clear the screen, this is done on some computers by typing the word CLEAR. Check your manual for specific details for your machine.

5. Positioning the cursor. Many computers have a cathode-ray tube display that features a cursor. The cursor points to the place on the screen where new information can be typed in. On some computers, the cursor is positioned by pressing the up and down arrows. On others, the ESCAPE key and the letters A, B, C, or D are pressed. These routines move the cursor up or down, left or right.

6. How to add a line to your program. BASIC is designed to facilitate adding program lines. Choose a line number that will correctly place your new statement in numerical sequence in the program. Enter this line number, the programming instruction, and the carriage return. The system will automatically place the line in the proper sequence.

If you enter several statements with the same line number, the computer will always replace the line in storage with the most recent version keyboarded. There will always be only one statement per line number. If you accidentally type in the wrong line number and erase the wrong statement, you will have to rekeyboard it to return it to storage.

7. How to delete an entire program. On occasion, it may be necessary to delete all lines in a program. One could type each line number followed by the carriage return, but this is slow and awkward. Instead a system command will remove all lines from the workspace. Depending on the computer, words such as NEW, SCRATCH, CLEAR, or DELETE perform this function.

8. Interrupting execution. Some computers have provision for interrupting the execution of a program or the printing out of a listing. Sometimes the BREAK key is de-

pressed. Typing in the word CONT resumes execution. On some systems, the CTRL-C halts execution and CONT resumes it.

DIAGNOSTIC AND ERROR MESSAGES

After you have entered your program, you will want to see if it runs correctly; and one of the advantages of interactive programming is the immediate outputting of results by the computer. If you type in the appropriate system command (usually the word RUN), the computer will attempt to execute your program. If no errors are present, the computer will execute the steps indicated and print out the results immediately.

This rarely happens. Usually, there are several programming or logical errors present. These errors, sometimes called *bugs,* prevent a program from executing properly. To help you diagnose these bugs, the computer prints out error messages. The messages identify the specific line number of the statement and indicate the type of errors present. It is up to you to determine the exact cause of the error and correct it.

One of the most common error messages generated by the system is the ? or the word WHAT?. These messages usually mean that an incorrect command was entered or the computer was in the wrong mode for the command.

Refer to Appendix B for help in correcting errors (debugging). It is also a good idea to have a list of error messages and their meanings available while at the computer. These lists are prepared by computer manufacturers and are often included at the end of their reference manuals.

EXERCISES

1. Prepare a list of statement numbers for a program 10 statements long. Space the numbers so additions can be made later.
2. Determine which method is used to delete a line on your computer. Type in several lines of information and then delete them.
3. Determine which method is used to delete one character from a line. Type in a line of information and practice deleting one or more characters.
4. If your computer has a cathode-ray tube display and cursor, practice moving the cursor about on the screen and adding and deleting information.
5. Determine what method is used to clear all information from the display screen on your computer. Type in several lines of information and practice clearing the screen.
6. Practice writing some simple programming statements by coding them on a sheet of notebook paper. You may wish to copy down one of the programs illustrated in Part Three of this book. Be consistent in your style and in the use of the slash.
7. Practice using the control characters on your keyboard. How do control characters differ from shift characters on your particular computer?
8. Obtain a copy of the diagnostic and error messages available on your system. Study the listing and experiment with entering lines that generate diagnostic messages.

CHAPTER 3
SYSTEM COMMANDS

To fully utilize the resources of a computer, the reader must understand how to use system commands. System commands are special instructions directed to the computer that cause the machine to start running a program, that interrupt the execution of a program, or that direct the computer to list or store a program.

System commands are master control directions the computer uses to govern its overall operations. They differ from programming commands. Programming commands, discussed in detail in later chapters, are the specific directions of the program itself. But before a computer can execute program commands, it must be given its proper system commands.

This chapter describes how system commands are used to start the computer running, to store files, to input or erase programs, and so forth. The chapter concludes with a discussion of the more common system commands found on small computer systems. The reader should consult the reference manual for his/her own computer to determine specific forms of system commands used.

HOW A COMPUTER MEMORY WORKS

To appreciate system commands and their use in controlling the overall operation of the computer, let us review how computers store information and discuss cassette and diskette storage machines.

All computers have a primary memory system. The primary memory stores active programs and information being processed. Many computers have secondary storage systems such as magnetic tape and disk that store inactive information (Fig. 3.1).

PRIMARY MEMORY

Data or instructions stored in the central processing unit (CPU) of the computer are in *active storage*. These can be language programming instructions, data sets, operating systems, or any other control programs. These data are immediately accessible for process-

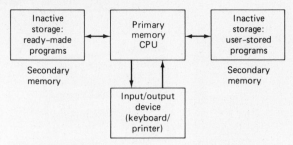

FIGURE 3.1 Active and inactive storage concepts.

ing and are moved in and out of active storage as needed. The primary memory capacity of small computers range from as little as 1,000 characters to 64,000.

SECONDARY MEMORY

Since the physical capacity of the primary memory to store data is limited to approximately 64,000 characters, computer systems have been designed to record on secondary storage devices data not immediately needed for processing. The devices include magnetic tape as well as disk and drum units and are often called *inactive storage.* Data in inactive storage may include programming instructions, data sets, and portions of control programs not needed by the CPU at that moment.

Data in inactive storage are usually readily accessible to the CPU but require a longer period of time to locate than if they were in primary memory. Secondary storage is relatively inexpensive and allows the user to store millions of characters of information on reels of magnetic tape, tape cassettes, or thin flexible disks.

Tape Cassette Storage

One of the most popular secondary storage devices available for use on home computers is the tape cassette unit (Fig. 3.2). Tape cassette units are similar to ordinary domestic tape recorders. In fact, many small computers use ordinary household tape recorders as secondary storage devices.

These tape recorders, costing under $100, store thousands of characters on an ordinary Phillips-type cassette. The programmer uses system commands to direct the computer to store information on a cassette or to transfer from a cassette back into the computer's primary memory. While tape cassette storage is inexpensive, it has some problems. The transfer rate of information between the cassette recorder and the microcomputer is relatively slow and cassette recorders are error-prone.

Some small computer systems use reel-to-reel recorders. These secondary storage systems, while more efficient than cassettes, still are relatively slow in transferring data.

Flexible Disk Storage

Another form of small computer system secondary storage memory is the flexible disk drive. These units use a flexible sheet of magnetically coated material to store thousands of characters. These thin disks are sometimes called *floppy* disks, or just *floppies* (Fig. 3.3). Floppy disks are removable and can be mailed and easily stored. They are inexpensive and can quickly transfer a large volume of data between the secondary storage drive and the CPU.

FIGURE 3.2 Tape cassette storage. (Radio Shack/Tandy Corp.)

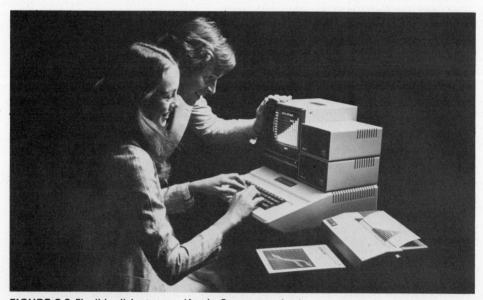

FIGURE 3.3 Flexible disk storage. (Apple Computers, Inc.)

Winchester Disks

The most recent addition to the small computer storage system is the Winchester disk (Fig. 3.4). The Winchester uses a $5\frac{1}{4}$- or 8-inch permanently mounted revolving disk. The Winchester drive is capable of storing millions of characters of information and can transfer data between the drive and the CPU at the rate of many thousands of characters per second. The disks are not removable, but their large volume of storage makes them very well suited to small computer applications.

Much of the small computer's power is based upon its ability to manipulate files or sets of information stored on secondary storage devices. The reader should understand how to use the proper system commands to read information onto a cassette or disk and back into memory.

MODES OF OPERATION

Computers perform their functions while operating in one of two modes: the interpreter mode or the system mode. There are many important differences between these two forms of operation and a different set of commands is used to direct the computer in each.

1. *System mode.* In the system mode, the computer operates under the control of a special program stored within the computer called the *operating system,* or *monitor.* In this mode, the computer calls in language translators, such as the BASIC interpreter,

FIGURE 3.4 Winchester disk storage. (Texas Instruments, Inc.)

executes programs, opens and closes files, stores programs, brings programs back from storage, and so on. This mode is sometimes called the *command mode.*

The programmer uses *system commands* to direct the computer in the system mode. System commands vary somewhat from one computer to another, but each system has a command to perform the different functions. Be sure to consult the manual provided by your computer manufacturer for the system commands for your computer.

2. *Interpreter mode.* In the interpreter mode of operation, the computer has loaded the language translator requested by the programmer and is ready to receive programming statements coded in that language. The interpreter translates the language statements into machine language ready for execution.

When you first turn on your computer, you will enter in the system mode. You remain in this mode until you request a given language translator, such as BASIC. You will operate under the interpreter mode until you direct control back to the system mode.

USING SYSTEM COMMANDS

On some computer systems, an extensive range of powerful system commands is available. They allow the programmer to edit files, merge files, automatically number statements, substitute words in a program, and so on. These commands add a great deal of power to the computing system and make the programmer's job much easier.

System commands are usually one or two words in length, not numbered, not part of the program proper, and usually different for each computer system.

For example, on one computer, the word DELETE is used to remove all lines from a file (by erasing them from storage); on another computer, CLEAR performs this function; whereas on still another, SCRATCH does the job.

Some of the more common tasks you will need system commands for are to

1. start up and shut down the computer
2. manipulate files; naming, storing files in inactive storage, loading files into active storage, deleting files, and so on.
3. enter input via the secondary storage devices such as cassette or diskette
4. list files and programs
5. correct programs and files, including entering new lines, deleting lines or single characters, and so on
6. call in language translators so that you can enter programming statements in BASIC
7. shift control from the language translator to the operating system and from the operating system back to the language translator
8. execute or run programs
9. interrupt execution of a program before normal program termination allowing you to stop the output and resume it later
10. trace or follow program flow for debugging and program analysis

COMMON SYSTEM COMMANDS

Since system commands are different on each computer, it would be impossible (and pointless) to list and discuss them all. Instead, this chapter covers the more common situations in which system commands are used and gives some examples. Nearly all systems have a command to perform these functions.

The situations have been grouped into classes. Each class lists the typical system commands used in the particular situation.

1. Entering BASIC

ENTER   Initiated by Programmer

Purpose: When the power on most small computers is turned on, a prompting signal or cursor is displayed on the cathode-ray tube or printer. This is often a right-pointing arrowhead. This signal, generated by the computer, is a system command that asks the operator what he or she wishes to do. On some systems, the programmer presses the ENTER key and this causes the computer to load the BASIC translator ready to receive programming commands. (Other systems require the programmer to type in the word BASIC.) Many computers respond with the word READY when the BASIC interpreter has been successfully loaded.

Example

```
Computer:     >
Programmer:   ENTER
Computer:     READY
```

The computer has asked the programmer what language he or she wants. The programmer replies, BASIC. The computer will then load the BASIC interpreter into active storage.

The exact usage of this command varies considerably from one computer to another. On some computers, the command is issued by the programmer to indicate that he or she wants to change to a different interpreter or system. On some systems, it can be issued only when the computer is in the operating mode. On others, it can be issued while in the interpreter mode.

2. Shifting Control from Interpreter to System Mode

SYSTEM   Initiated by Programmer

Purpose: This command directs the computer to leave the interpreter mode and return control to the system mode. The programmer may then issue more commands regarding his or her program (such as SAVE it in inactive storage or print it out on a line printer). Upon receiving this command, many systems print out an acknowledgment or symbol, such as a period or a hyphen, to indicate control has been returned to the system mode.

Example

```
RUN
. . . . . . .
. . . . . . .
SYSTEM
READY
```

The programmer has completed his program and wants to work on another program. He uses the SYSTEM command to return control to the system mode. The system responds with the word READY.

Note. Mode cues: Many computers will type out different cues or symbols when they are in the system mode and when they are in the interpreter mode. This makes it easier for the programmer to follow the action and respond with the proper command.

Note: On some systems, data in memory may be erased when control is returned to the system mode, unless it has been previously saved.

3. File Manipulation Commands

NEW   **Initiated by Programmer**
Purpose: This command clears the computer's memory and prepares it to receive a new program in BASIC.

Example

```
10. . . . . .
20. . . . . .
NEW
READY
```

In this example, the programmer has deleted any lines that are in primary memory and is now ready to enter a new program. On some computers, the command CLEAR performs this function.

SAVE   **Initiated by Programmer**
Purpose: This command causes the computer to save a program on magnetic tape or other storage device. Sometimes a file name is given after the word SAVE. The program is then stored on tape with this file name so it can later be reloaded by its particular name.

Example

```
SAVE "RANDY"
```

In this example, the programmer wishes to save a program that has been given the file name RANDY. The computer will then save the program, ready for retrieval later under this name. (The programmer must have ready the cassette tape recorder and have it turned on prior to issuing this command.) Some systems use the command CSAVE to perform this function.

LOAD   **Initiated by Programmer**
Purpose: This command lets the programmer load a stored program into primary memory. The secondary storage device must have had the program previously stored on it and it must be turned on and ready to operate when the LOAD command is issued.

Example

```
LOAD "RANDY"
```

In this example, the computer will search its secondary storage device for the program labeled RANDY and transfer it into primary memory. Since there may be several programs in memory, the computer will begin at the beginning and search each file in sequence until RANDY is encountered. Some systems will print out the list of file names encountered as it searches the secondary storage device. The CLOAD command is often used to perform this function on many computers.

CATALOG   Initiated by Programmer

Purpose: This command causes the computer to print out a listing of all files currently stored in inactive storage. The programmer issues this command when he or she wishes to determine what programs are in storage. (Sometimes DIR is used.)

Example

```
CATALOG
ACME SMITH DELTA
```

The computer lists three programs (ACME, SMITH, and DELTA) that are in storage, in response to the CATALOG command from the programmer.

4. Program Manipulation Commands

LIST   Initiated by Programmer

Purpose: This command is used to list the statements in a file. On some systems, it can be modified to list only selected lines of the program. It allows the programmer to direct the computer to print out the latest version of the programming lines he or she is working on, to print out statements of a program loaded into primary memory from inactive storage, or to print out only selected lines.

Example
(Program JODY in primary memory contains 10 lines)

```
LIST
```

The programmer has directed the computer to print out all the lines in the program named JODY.

```
LIST 50
```

The computer will print out only line 50 from memory.

```
LIST 30-50
```

The computer will print out all the lines between statements 30 and 50.

```
LIST 60, 80
```

The computer will print out only lines numbered 60 and 80.

The type of punctuation used in the LIST command varies from system to system. Some use commas and hyphens, while others use spaces.

RUN   Initiated by Programmer

Purpose: This command is universally used to instruct the computer to begin execution of a program. When the programmer keyboards the command RUN, the computer will begin executing the program instructions. If errors are present in the instructions, the computer will print out diagnostic messages referenced by line number.

Example
(Program TEXAS is in primary memory)

RUN

The programmer issues this command when he or she wants to execute the program TEXAS. The computer will attempt to follow the instructions in the program. If errors are detected, execution will stop and the system will print out diagnostic messages.

5. Commands That Terminate Execution

STOP   Initiated by Programmer

Purpose: This statement causes the computer to terminate execution of a program at any point during the run. The programmer uses the statement to stop a printout because the output contains errors, he or she must leave the computer, and so forth. On some systems, the character S, the CTRL-C character, the ALT MODE key, or the ATTN key performs this function. After the execution has been terminated, control returns to the beginning of the program. Typing the word CONT will cause the program to resume execution on many computers.

Example
(Program PLAN is printing out results)

STOP

TERMINATED

The programmer enters the STOP command on the keyboard. The computer interrupts execution of the program PLAN and prints out *TERMINATED* to signal the programmer. The programmer can now make corrections, change instructions, enter new data, clear the file, and so on.

6. Correcting or Altering Programs and Lines

LEFT ARROW   Initiated by Programmer

Purpose: This command is used to delete an error or unwanted character that has been keyboarded. Each time the left arrow ($\leftarrow$) is struck the last character transmitted is erased (if the carriage return has not yet been pressed). The left arrow may be struck several times in succession to erase several characters in a row.

Example

```
10  PRINT "OUTPUT RESS⌐ULTS"
20  LET A = B * D⌐C
30  IF A = 100 THEN 120⌐⌐⌐210
```

In statement 10, the computer will erase the second S and store the word RESULTS spelled correctly. In statement 20, it will store the statement as 20 LET A = B * C. In statement 30, three arrows have been struck to erase the last three characters (120). The correct number 210 will be stored in its place.

On some systems, this function is performed by pressing the backspace key, which physically moves the carrier one position to the left. The correct character is then struck over the incorrect one and is stored by the computer. More than one character may be corrected by backspacing the required number of spaces.

CTRL-X   **Initiated by Programmer**

Purpose: This command is used to delete a partially typed line. It is generated when the programmer presses CTRL-X. Striking this key will prevent the characters on the line from being stored by the computer, provided that the carriage return has not been pressed. On some systems, the ALT MODE or ESCAPE key is used to perform this function.

Examples

```
110  PRINT "CORRECT SPELLING (CTRL-X)
220  LET A = B(I) * (CTRL-X)
220  LET B = A(I) * C
```

Pressing CTRL-X at the end of the line has deleted the entire statement 110 from storage in the first example, and the incorrect statement 220 in the second example.

DELETE   **Initiated by Programmer**

Purpose: This command causes the computer to remove some or all of the lines from memory. (It is similar to the NEW command discussed earlier.) On some systems, the DELETE statement can be modified to erase only selected lines in a program.

Examples
(Program BETA in active memory)

```
DELETE 10, 20
```

The computer will erase the lines numbered 10 and 20 from the program named BETA.

```
DELETE 20-60
```

The computer will erase lines 20 through 60 from the program.

(Program ALPHA in memory)

DELETE ALPHA

The computer will erase all the lines of the program ALPHA.

Single lines can also be deleted from memory by typing in the line number and the carriage return. On some systems, the command NEW or CLEAR is used to perform this function.

7. Debugging System Commands

TRACE   Initiated by Programmer

Purpose: This is a debugging aid to help the programmer find errors in the program. It lists each line number as it is executed. Some systems use the word TRON to perform this function. When the programmer wishes to turn off the trace function, he or she enters the word NOTRACE or, on some systems, TROFF.

Example
(Program entered in memory containing errors)

TRACE
RUN

(Computer will print out each statement number it executes)

NOTRACE

In this example, the programmer has entered the TRACE command, which causes the computer to list each statement number as the program is executed. This will help him/her locate errors in the programming sequence. The programmer has entered NO-TRACE so the next time the program is run it will not list the statement numbers as they are executed.

8. Special System Commands

PEEK
POKE   Initiated by Programmer

Purpose: Many small computers allow the programmer to look at and change the contents of specific memory locations. The PEEK instruction displays the contents of a specified memory location. The instruction must refer to a valid memory address, usually in decimal form. The POKE instruction enables the programmer to correct or change the contents of any location.

Example

PEEK (8000)
064
POKE 8000,128

In this example, the programmer desires to know the value stored in memory location 8000. The computer returns the information 064. The programmer then uses the POKE instruction to change the contents of location 8000 to read 128. Commands such as these are useful because they enable the BASIC programmer to interrupt a program execution, look at the contents of specific memory locations, change them if necessary, and then resume execution.

9. Interpreting Commands from the Computer

READY   Initiated by Computer

Purpose: This command, typed by the computer, informs the programmer that the system has processed the last command and is now ready to receive further commands or programming statements. Some systems respond with a hyphen or other character printed out on the terminal to indicate that it is ready to proceed.

Example

```
LOAD KIWI
READY
```

The computer has loaded the program KIWI into active storage as directed. It prints out READY to indicate to the programmer that it is ready to receive additional commands or programming instructions.

WHAT?   Initiated by Computer

Purpose: This command, typed by the computer, informs the programmer that an unacceptable statement or command has been entered. It means that the computer does not recognize the command or characters entered by the programmer. The command must be reentered properly before the computer will proceed. The WHAT? command will usually be issued when a command has been misspelled or given in the wrong mode.

Example

```
RNN
WHAT?
RUN
```

The programmer has typed in the command incorrectly. The system responds with WHAT? indicating that it cannot interpret or recognize the command. The programmer enters the command with the correct spelling and the computer proceeds to run the program.

Other systems may print out a statement such as ILLEGAL COMMAND or PLEASE REENTER.

EXERCISES

1. Summarize the functions of system commands.
2. Study the list of the system commands related to your computer and determine how to perform the various functions described in this chapter.

3. Using the appropriate system command, call in the BASIC interpreter on your system. Enter one or two statements and then leave the interpreter and return to the system.
4. Name a file TEST1. Enter several program lines. Modify the file by adding several lines and rename it TEST2.
5. Name a file and enter several statements. Obtain a listing. Clear the file and again request a listing. Are lines present after you clear a file?
6. Generate a program containing several lines. Save the program. Then delete the file.
7. Enter a program with 10 lines. Instruct the computer to list the entire program. Obtain a listing of the fifth line only. Obtain a listing of the last three lines in the program.
8. Prepare a program with a simple loop that prints out your name 20 times. During the execution of the program, terminate the loop using the STOP, CTRL-C, or other "terminate execution" key before it has completed the loop.

PART
TWO
LANGUAGE
UNITS

HOW TO USE THE LANGUAGE UNITS

This section of the book contains a group of units that explain the elements of BASIC. The units are presented in the order in which they are encountered as the reader studies the sample programs in Part Three. Each sample program contains a list of the BASIC statements used in a given program. Study each statement in conjunction with the program and the language unit in this section.

Every language unit begins with a statement of purpose, which explains to the reader the nature of each command. Next, a general form is given that illustrates the command, together with sample data. Several additional examples are also presented to expand on the general form. A group of rules helps the reader prepare correctly written statements. These rules are not absolute, but serve as guidelines to help you write programs. You should consult your reference manual to see which rules specifically apply to your system. Each unit concludes with a group of exercises.

Upon completing the study of the language units, the reader has a valuable reference tool. It should be referred to frequently or whenever the reader is in doubt about the form, style, or rules pertaining to a given statement.

LIST OF LANGUAGE UNITS

1. REM   Program remarks
2. END   End of program
3. STOP   Terminating execution
4. PRINT   Print single or blank line
5. PRINT- Quotation marks   Print headings

6.	PRINT- Comma	Print standard columns
7.	PRINT- Semicolon	Print tightly spaced fields
8.	PRINT- Equations	Print computations and mixed data
9.	READ/DATA, RESTORE	Entering data via program
10.	GOTO	Branch unconditional
11.	INPUT	Entering data via keyboard
12.	LET	Entering data via program
13.	LET, Arithmetic operators	Performing mathematics
14.	LET	Counters
15.	IF/THEN, Relational operators	Branch conditional
16.	TAB	Tabbing to a column
17.	SQR, LOG, RND, etc.	Standard functions
18.	DEF	User-defined functions
19.	FOR/NEXT	Repeat a sequence
20.	DIM	Using subscripts to store data
21.	MAT†	Automatic read, print, and calculate
22.	GOSUB, RETURN	Subroutines

†Not available in Microsoft BASIC.

PROGRAM
REMARKS
(REM STATEMENT)

PURPOSE

The REM statement allows the programmer to add comments or explanatory lines throughout a program. REM statements have no effect upon program logic or execution. They aid the programmer by documenting the steps the computer follows in carrying out the program.

REM statements are inserted to indicate where branches, input/output sequences, and calculations are performed. They provide a convenient means of titling programs and inserting the name of the programmer, the date the program was written, or other details. REM statements should be included throughout a program to explain the major steps. Of necessity, REM statements must be kept to a minimum in programs run on computers which have limited memory.

The word REMARK is sometimes used for clarity instead of REM to perform this function. The interpreter reads only the first three letters of the command. Anything after that is considered part of the comment.

GENERAL FORM

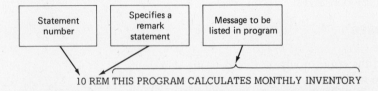

| Statement number | Specifies a remark statement | Message to be listed in program |

10 REM THIS PROGRAM CALCULATES MONTHLY INVENTORY

Statement 10 begins with the letters REM, which indicates it is a remark and not an executable statement. All characters following the REM will be printed out in the program listing. In this instance, they give the program description.

Examples

```
10 REM PROGRAM #37492, J. ORTIZ, ACCOUNTING DEPT.
```

In this example, the programmer has inserted a descriptive title line at the beginning of the program. The line gives the number of the program, the programmer's name, and the department. All characters following the REM will be listed as part of the message.

```
40 . . .
50 REM OUTPUTS DATA IN RANK ORDER
60 PRINT . . .
```

A REM statement is inserted before an output sequence. It explains that the information printed by statement 60 will be in rank order. It is included to document a feature of the program that might be easily forgotten later.

```
90 . . .
100 REM CALCULATE BALANCE (BALANCE = INVENTORY - SALES)
120 LET B = I - S
```

REM statement 100 documents the formula used in statement 120 to calculate the balance.

RULES

1. REM statements must begin with the word REM or REMARK. All characters following the letters REM will be listed as part of the message.

2. Statements, comments, or equations in a REM statement do not affect the execution or program flow.

3. All programs should begin with a REM statement to identify the name of the program.

4. More than one REM statement may be included in a single program to help document program flow.

5. REM statements should be included to document important steps in the program. They should be placed ahead of branches, input/output sequences, calculations, and so on.

6. Use several REM statements to show a title that extends onto more than one line:

```
10 REM THIS PROGRAM WILL PREPARE THE WEEKLY PAYROLL
20 REM FOR THE SALES, INVENTORY, AND MAINTENANCE
30 REM DEPARTMENTS
```

EXERCISES

1. Find the errors, if any, in the following statements:
   a. 10 REM LET A = 600
   b. 30 REMARK CREDIT-DEBIT PROGRAM
   c. 90 *** PROGRAM NO. 812-A ***
   d. 10 *REM* BASIC A6123-C
   e. 220 RMK SORT ROUTINE BEGINS HERE

2. Write a REM statement that lists your name.
3. Write a REM statement that titles an inventory maintenance program.
4. Write a REM statement that contains the title of a program, the programmer's name, and the date.
5. Write a REM statement that indicates a branching procedure is next.
6. Write a REM statement that indicates an output sequence is about to begin.
7. Write a REM statement that titles a program. Include asterisks before and after the name of the program.
8. Show how a program title that is too long for one line is handled.
9. Show a REM statement that titles a program for a statistical or mathematical calculation.

END OF
PROGRAM
(END STATEMENT)

PURPOSE

The END statement specifies that the end of the program has been reached and no more programming statements will be entered. It is used to direct the computer to begin executing the program. The END statement is the last statement in the program and must have the highest line number assigned in the program.

GENERAL FORM

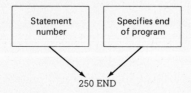

250 END

The END statement at line 250 tells the computer that there are no more instructions to be executed. When the computer reaches this statement while running the program, it will terminate execution.

Some systems do not require an END statement as part of the program. Execution is terminated when the computer can find no more programming instructions. Others allow subroutine statements to appear after an END statement.

Example

```
35 . . .
40 . . .
```

```
45 . . .
50 . . .
70 END
```

The END statement at line 70 tells the computer to stop executing the program.

RULES

1. On most systems, programs should conclude with an END statement as the last physical line in the program.

2. The END statement should be assigned the highest line number in the program.

EXERCISES

1. Find the errors, if any, in the following statements:
   a. END
   b. 10 . . .
      20 . . .
      1000 END
   c. 10 END
   d. 20 END OF PROGRAM
   e. 150 END
      160 PRINT "THE END"

2. How many END statements are in a program?
3. Where in a program is the END statement found?
4. What line number is assigned to the END statement?
5. What happens to any statements accidentally placed after the END statement?
6. Write an END statement for a program with five statements.
7. Write an END statement that terminates a program with 10 instructions.
8. Write an END statement that terminates a program with 20 instructions, numbered by 10s.
9. Write an END statement for the program in Exercise 8 if the lines are numbered by 100s.
10. Write an END statement for a program with 10 instructions, which leaves room for more statements to be added.

TERMINATING
EXECUTION
(STOP STATEMENT)

PURPOSE

The STOP statement is one of the methods used to terminate execution of a program. It directs the computer to go to the END statement from any point in the program where it has been encountered. It is a convenient means of terminating execution in programs with several branches. A STOP statement placed at the end of each branch assures that the program will terminate normally, regardless of which branch was taken.

Program execution may be terminated in several other ways as well. A GOTO statement can be used instead of the STOP statement to direct control to the END statement and, of course, reaching the END statement through normal program flow will also terminate execution.

GENERAL FORM

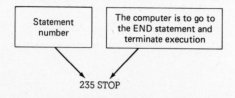

When the computer encounters statement 235, it will terminate execution. Any statement following 235 in the program will not be executed. STOP statements may be placed anywhere in the program except as the final statement. They are usually used as the last statement in a branch to assure normal program termination.

Example

```
110 . . .
120 PRINT A
130 IF A < 100 THEN 150
140 STOP
150 PRINT "SHORT SUPPLY"
160 . . .
170 . . .
180 END
```

For example, a STOP statement would be used in a program that branches to one of two sequences depending on whether the value A totaled more or less than 100. The STOP statement would be placed at the end of the first leg to terminate execution. The second leg would terminate normally at the END statement. The programmer must be careful to see that the program flow for other branches skips over STOP statements to avoid terminating execution at the wrong point.

Example

```
30 . . .
40 . . .
50 STOP
60 . . .
70 STOP
80 . . .
90 END
```

In this example, two STOP statements are used to terminate execution. When the computer encounters either statement 50 or 70, it will direct control to the END statement and execution will terminate. If normal program flow bypasses both STOP statements, execution will terminate when the END statement is encountered.

RULES

1. The computer will go to the END statement and terminate execution of a program when it encounters a STOP statement in a program.

2. The STOP statement consists of a line number and the command STOP.

3. One or more STOP statements may be used to terminate execution at different points in a single program.

4. STOP statements may not be used as the last statement in a program.

5. Care should be taken to route program flow around STOP statements when branches are not to terminate at that point.

EXERCISES

1. Find the errors, if any, in the following statements:
   a. 180 END
   b. 190 STOP
   c. 110 STOP GOTO END
   d. 10 . . .

```
      20 STOP
      30 . . .
      40 STOP
      50 . . .
      60 END
 e. 300 IF B = 300 THEN STOP
 f. 150 . . .
     160 STOP
     170 . . .
    3000 END
```

2. Can a STOP statement be used instead of an END statement to terminate execution?

3. Why are STOP statements used in a program?

4. Can more than one STOP statement be used in a program?

5. If a program has three branches, must each branch have a STOP statement? If so, why?

6. What logical error should a programmer be careful of when including STOP statements in a program?

7. Write a STOP statement that branches to END from line 50.

8. Show a program with two STOP statements in it.

9. Show the statements in a program which are necessary to branch to the END statement (line 300) from lines 40, 80, and 290.

10. Show how a program with three branches terminates execution after each branch.

PRINT SINGLE
OR
BLANK LINE
(PRINT STATEMENT)

PURPOSE

The PRINT statement is used to output information from the computer. It directs the computer to print out data beginning at the left margin and moving across the page to the right. The PRINT statement can be used in various ways to perform several different functions. One version prints out only one piece of data per line. Another uses punctuation marks, such as the comma or semicolon, to print two or more pieces of data on one line. Others print out text matter. The PRINT statement can also be used to double-space or skip lines when outputting data.

This unit explains the simplest form of PRINT statement: how to print out one piece of alphabetic or numeric data on a line and how to skip lines. The other functions of the PRINT statement will be explained in the following units.

The PRINT statement allows the programmer to print out a single piece of data, such as a name, word, or number, from computer storage. The data to be printed out must, of course, have been previously read into the computer, supplied to the program by an INPUT statement, or computed by the program.

GENERAL FORM

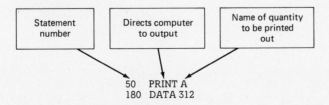

```
        Statement          Directs computer       Name of quantity
         number               to output            to be printed
                                                        out


                        50   PRINT A
                       180   DATA 312
```

OUTPUT

ƀ312			

Statement 180 supplies the data, a positive number, 312. Statement 50 directs the computer to print out this data, stored under the name A. Upon encountering statement 50, the computer will return the carrier to the left margin, leave one space for the sign, and print out the value beginning in the second space. Since the plus sign (+) is not normally printed out before a positive number, the space is left blank (ƀ represents a blank space). Negative numbers will be printed with a minus sign (−) in column 1, followed by the number. Any number without a sign is assumed to be positive.

Example

```
80 PRINT R
120 DATA −10.81
```

Output will begin in column 1:

−10.81			

The negative sign is printed out, followed by the decimal number in columns 2 through 6.

Example

```
30 PRINT A$
40 PRINT B
50 DATA "THOMAS", 10936
```

Output begins in column 1:

THOMAS			
ƀ10936			

Upon encountering statements 30 and 40, the computer will print out the alphabetic string THOMAS, beginning in column 1 of a new line. It will then skip to the next line and print the value of B, 10936. The digits start in column 2, since the first position is reserved for the sign—in this case, an implied plus sign. Alphabetic strings always begin in column 1, since no sign is needed.

Example

```
50 PRINT T$
60 PRINT
70 PRINT X
```

OUTPUT

PHOTO			
⊘3062			

In this example, a blank PRINT statement (60) has been inserted between statements 50 and 70 to double-space the printout. The computer will first print out the alphabetic string PHOTO, print a "blank" line, and then print the value of X on the third line. The programmer may insert one or more blank PRINT statements in the program to improve the appearance and spacing of the output. Several may be used in sequence to skip two or more lines.

RULES

1. The PRINT statement has an assigned line number, begins with the word PRINT, and is usually followed by the name of the quantity to be output.

2. Only quantities in storage can be output. These may be supplied to the program by having been previously read in or calculated in the program.

3. Alphabetic strings are printed out beginning in column 1.

4. The digits of a numeric variable will be printed out beginning in column 2. The first column is reserved for the sign. If a positive value is being printed out, a plus sign is assumed and column 1 is left blank. If the value is negative, a minus sign $(-)$ appears in column 1.

5. This form of the PRINT statement will print out one variable on a line. To print out a variable on a different line will require another PRINT statement.

6. Blank PRINT statements may be inserted anywhere in the program to skip lines and improve the spacing and appearance of the output.

EXERCISES

1. Find the errors, if any, in the following statements:

a. 50 PRINT C

312			

b. 40 PRINT S$

LOUISE			

c. 90 PRINT Z

Z			

d. 100 PRINT
   110 PRINT A

−100.16			

e. 120 PRINT T$
   130 PRINT
   140 PRINT N

ACRYLIC 650			

2. Write a PRINT statement that outputs the value 918. Show the printout.
3. Write a PRINT statement that outputs the value −67.312. Show the printout.
4. Write a PRINT statement that outputs your name. Show the output.
5. Show the statements used to print out a course name and number of students enrolled. Triple-space the output.
6. Show the statements used to print out your name, address, phone number, and age. Show the output.
7. Show the statements used to print out three numbers. The first and third are negative and the second positive. Show the output.
8. What kind of data can be output by a PRINT statement? How does the program get the data?
9. Where are positive numbers printed out on the page? Why?
10. Where are negative numbers printed out on the page? Why?

PRINT HEADINGS (PRINT-QUOTATION MARKS)

PURPOSE

The PRINT statement, containing text enclosed within quotation marks (" "), can be used to print out headings or descriptive lines for labeling output. These are called *literals,* or *literal statements.* Literal text, including spelling, form, punctuation, and spacing, is output exactly as it appears in the PRINT statement.

Literal text is used to head columns, identify quantities, or label the printout. It improves the form, appearance, and readability of output and should be used liberally.

GENERAL FORM

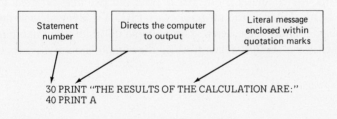

| Statement number | Directs the computer to output | Literal message enclosed within quotation marks |

```
30 PRINT "THE RESULTS OF THE CALCULATION ARE:"
40 PRINT A
```

OUTPUT

```
THE RESULTS OF THE CALCULATION ARE:
 212
```

This example illustrates the use of literal text to identify a number on a printout. Upon encountering statement 30, the computer will print out the text enclosed within quotation marks exactly as it appears. At statement 40, it prints the quantity "212", which was stored under the name A. Column 1, reserved for the sign, is left blank.

Example

```
10 PRINT "PROGRAM 4823                        BEN ORTIZ"
20 PRINT
30 PRINT "ACCOUNTING DEPARTMENT BILLING ROUTINE"
```

OUTPUT

PROGRAM 4823		BEN ORTIZ	

ACCOUNTING DEPARTMENT BILLING ROUTINE

This example illustrates the use of a literal statement to label a program by printing out a heading. At statement 10, the computer reproduces the line of literal text exactly as directed, skipping 16 spaces between the program number and programmer's name. Statement 20 prints a blank line. Statement 30 prints out a literal descriptive statement that further identifies the output.

Example

```
100 PRINT "COST              PERCENTAGE     SELL"
120 PRINT "                  MARKUP         PRICE"
```

OUTPUT

COST	PERCENTAGE MARKUP	SELL PRICE	
. . . . .	. . . . .	. . . . .	
. . . . .	. . . . .	. . . . .	

In these statements, the computer is directed to print out two lines of literal text to be used as column heads. Later in the program other PRINT statements will print out columns of data aligned under these heads. This example illustrates the importance of spacing carefully when using literal statements, since the computer always follows the text exactly.

RULES

1. The PRINT literal statement begins with the word PRINT followed by a message enclosed within quotation marks.

2. The text enclosed within the quotation marks will be printed out in the exact form, spelling, and spacing as in the PRINT statement.

3. Alphanumeric or numeric data may be used in a PRINT literal statement. But numeric data in a literal statement cannot be used for calculations or mathematical manipulation.

4. All literal statements must include both opening and closing quotation marks.

5. If a literal message is too long to fit on one line, it must be broken into two or more lines. Each line should be a separate PRINT literal statement, with its own opening and closing quotation marks.

6. PRINT literal statements should be used liberally throughout a program to improve readability and to label output.

7. A literal constant (the text enclosed within quotation marks) may contain any character in the standard character set except quotation marks.

EXERCISES

1. Find the errors, if any, in the following statements:

a. 10 PRINT "THIS IS A HEADING"

THIS IS A HEADING			

b. 20 PRINT "PRINT A"
 30 PRINT A

PRINT A			

c. 50 PRINT C
 60 PRINT
 70 PRINT "C IS THE ANSWER"

−21.91 IS THE ANSWER			

d. 150 PRINT "   COLUMN 1   COLUMN 2"

COLUMN 1	COLUMN 2		

e. 170 PRINT, HERE IS THE CALCULATION

HERE IS THE CALCULATION			

2. What kind of data can be included within the quotation marks of a PRINT statement?
3. What part of the text in a PRINT literal statement is printed out?
4. Write a PRINT literal statement that prints out your name. Show the output.

5. Write a PRINT literal statement that prints out headings for three columns. Show the output.

6. Write a PRINT literal statement that prints out the name of a program and the date. Show the output.

7. Write the statements that print out a heading too long for one line. Show the output.

8. Write the statements that will print out
```
        DECEMBER          DECEMBER
          1980              1985
```
Center the heads and show the output.

9. Show the statements that print out the following heading and show the output:
```
        MANUFACTURING CO., INC.
          INDUSTRIAL STREET
           BALTIMORE, MD.
```

10. Write the statements that identify a quantity and then print it out. Show the output.

PRINT
STANDARD
COLUMNS
(PRINT-COMMA)

PURPOSE

The standard column PRINT statement directs the computer to automatically print out a list of data evenly spaced across the line. The programmer can use this feature to print out alphanumerics, literal constants, or numerical items without having to specify the exact columns each is to occupy.

The programmer instructs the computer to follow the standard column spacing by inserting a comma between the data items listed in the PRINT statement. Standard column spacing consists of five fields 15 characters wide across one line, which allows a total of 75 characters per line.

Each item is aligned along the left margin of the field. In the case of numerics, the first column is reserved for the sign and the remaining 14 columns for data. Alphabetic variables or literal constants are printed out beginning in the first column of the field.

Note: Since some print units are only 72 characters wide, the last 3 characters will usually overprint. Some systems may use a standard field of 18 columns. Thus, only four columns of 18 characters will be available on one line.

FIELD 1	FIELD 2	FIELD 3	FIELD 4	FIELD 5
Columns 1–15	Columns 16–30	Columns 31–45	Columns 46–60	Columns 61–75

GENERAL FORM

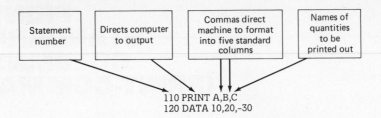

```
110 PRINT A,B,C
120 DATA 10,20,-30
```

OUTPUT

10	20	−30	

This example illustrates the use of the standard-spacing feature to print out three pieces of numeric data. When the program encounters statement 110, it will print out the data, 10, 20 and − 30, in the first three standard columns. Since the items being printed out are numerical, the first column of each field is reserved for the sign. The first and second items are positive values and the sign is not printed. The third item is negative, so the minus sign appears in column 1 of the third field.

Example

```
50 PRINT "GREEN", "HUSTON", "ROBERTS"
60 PRINT R,S,T
70 DATA 3, 12821,1021
```

OUTPUT

| GREEN | HUSTON | ROBERTS | |
| 3 | 12821 | 1021 | |

This example illustrates printing out literals and numeric data using standard column spacing. When the computer encounters statement 50, it prints out the three literal constants, spacing each flush left in the first three standard columns. Statement 60 directs the computer to print out three numeric pieces of data. The first, a one-digit number, will appear in column 2 (first space reserved for sign) of the first field. The second, a five-digit number, will appear in columns 2 through 6 of the second field; and the third, a four-digit number, in columns 2 through 5 of the third field.

Example

```
100 PRINT A$, B$, C$, D$
110 DATA "ST. PAUL", "CLEVELAND", "GARDEN GROVE RANCHO", "SAN DIEGO"
```

OUTPUT

| ST. PAUL | CLEVELAND | GARDEN GROVE RANCHO | SAN DIEGO |

In this example, four alphabetic strings are to be printed out. The third string, GARDEN GROVE RANCHO, exceeds the maximum width (15 characters) of the field.

Depending upon the system, the computer will handle this situation in one of several ways:

1. The third string will occupy more than one field. All succeeding strings will be repositioned.
2. Characters extending beyond the maximum number allowed for a field will be truncated (dropped).
3. An error message noting that the string is too long will be printed out.

Most systems will use the first option. The computer will use as many fields as necessary to print out the item. All subsequent items will be printed in the succeeding fields.

A whole field is reserved for each data item, regardless of whether it has 1 or 15 characters. Therefore, a string with 16 characters will require two fields, one with 31 characters three fields, and so on. Unused columns in a field are left blank.

Note: There are limitations on the number of characters that may be stored under one alphanumeric name or as a literal constant. While most systems allow a maximum of 255 characters, it varies from one system to another and should be checked in the reference manual.

Example

```
130 PRINT "ITEM", "QUANTITY", "COLOR", "PRICE"
140 PRINT A$,B,C$,D, "DEPARTMENT B"
150 DATA "SCARF", 100, "BLUE", 1.29
```

OUTPUT

ITEM	QUANTITY	COLOR	PRICE	
SCARF	100	BLUE	1.29	DEPARTMENT B

In this example, the programmer is printing out alphanumerics, numerics, and literal constants in the same PRINT statement. Since there are commas between the items, the computer will print them out following the standard column spacing. When it encounters line 130, it will print out the four literal constants in the first four fields across the line. Statement 140 directs it to print out five items of different types across one line. This feature gives the programmer great flexibility in the graphic arrangement of output.

Example

```
120 PRINT A,B,C,D,E,F,G
130 DATA 10,20,30,40,50,60,70
```

OUTPUT

10	20	30	40	50
60	70			

In this example, the PRINT statement has a data list with seven items to be printed out, using the standard column spacing. Since only five fields are available on each line, the computer will print the first five items in the standard fields across the page. Then it will automatically skip to the next line and print the last two numbers in the first two fields. A data list containing 13 items would extend onto three lines and one with 20 items onto four lines. By letting the computer handle the formatting technicalities, this feature allows the programmer to print out a data list with many items easily and conveniently.

RULES

1. Commas separating items in a PRINT statement direct the computer to follow standard column spacing. Each piece of data will occupy one of five standard fields (15 characters wide) across the page. (Note: Some systems use an 18-character-wide field, with four fields printed out across the page.)

2. Strings and literal constants are printed out aligned at the left margin of each field.

3. Numeric data are printed out beginning in the second column of each field. The first column is reserved for the sign. If a number is positive, no sign is printed and the first column is left blank. A negative value will have a minus sign printed out in column 1 of each field.

4. Each system handles overflow differently. If an item to be printed contains more characters than the maximum width a field allows (usually 15), the computer will print out an error message, truncate (ignore) the excess characters, or use more than one field to print out the item.

5. A whole field is used for each item regardless of whether it contains 1 or 15 characters. An item containing 16 characters will use two fields, and so on. Unused columns in a field are left blank.

6. Some print units are only 72 characters wide. The last 3 characters of the fifth standard field will usually overprint.

7. If a PRINT statement has more than five pieces of data, the computer will print the first five on one line, five more on the next line, and so on, until all items in the list have been printed out.

EXERCISES

1. Find the errors, if any, in the following statements:

a. 20 PRINT X,Y,Z

1,2,3			

b. 125 PRINT A,B,C,D,E,F,G

1 2 3 4 5 6 7			

c. 100 DATA "A", "B", "C"
140 PRINT A$,B$,C$

A	B	C	

d. 10 PRINT "ITEM", "PRICE", "QUANTITY"
20 PRINT I,P,Q

ITEM	PRICE	QUANTITY	
3406	38.95	4	

e. 20 PRINT "EMPLOYEE CLASSIFICATION", "PLANT",
"DEPARTMENT"
30 PRINT
40 PRINT E$,N,D$

EMPLOYEE CLASSIFICATION	PLANT	DEPARTMENT
PHYSICIST	820	RESEARCH

2. Write a PRINT statement that will output the numbers 100, 200, 300, 400, and 500 using standard column spacing.
3. Write the PRINT statement that will output the numbers 8016, 37218, 16, 409733 using standard column spacing. Show the output.
4. Write the PRINT statement that will output the following quantities using standard column spacing. Show the output. GEOGRAPHIC AREA, NW, 180, 368.29
5. Write the PRINT statement that will output six numbers and show the output.
6. Write the PRINT statement that will output 12 numbers and show the output.
7. Write the PRINT statement that will output the following:

YARN	380	BLUE	1.09	-.32

8. Write the PRINT statement that will produce the following output:

34C10-2	STOCKKEEPER'S ORDER NUMBER	PURCHASING NUMBER

9. Write the PRINT statement that will output five alphabetic quantities on one line.
10. Write the PRINT statements that will label five columns across the top of the page and four rows down the left margin.

PRINT TIGHTLY SPACED FIELDS (PRINT-SEMICOLON)

PURPOSE

The PRINT-semicolon statement directs the computer to print alphabetic and numeric data tightly spaced across a line. The programmer uses this feature when he or she wants the data items to be spaced more closely together than they would be using the standard column spacing. This timesaving feature allows the programmer to conveniently have the computer print out lists of data, alphabetic words or phrases, and literal constants and to produce many forms of graphic output.

The programmer instructs the computer to follow a close spacing format by separating the items in a PRINT statement with a semicolon. The spacing conventions differ for alphabetic data and numeric data as follows.

Alphabetic data will always be *concatenated,* or tightly packed. That is, alphabetic items will be printed with no extra spaces inserted either before or after the item. Alphabetic items separated by semicolons in a PRINT statement can be linked together to form phrases or sentences.

Numeric data items separated by semicolons in a PRINT statement are printed out according to a variable spacing pattern. The amount of space reserved for each piece of numeric data depends on the amount of digits each number has and the computer system used.

One commonly used packed-zone arrangement is shown in the table below.

NUMBER OF CHARACTERS IN FIELD	LENGTH OF PACKED ZONE
1–4	6
5–7	9
8–10	12
11–13	15

As the table illustrates, a number composed of 1 to 4 digits (including the sign) will occupy a packed zone that is 6 characters wide. Numbers with 8 to 10 digits (including the sign) will occupy packed zones of 12 spaces.

The number of zones (or fields) that can be printed across one line will vary, of course, depending on the length of the zones. Thus, 12 zones containing 4 characters each can fit on one line, but only 6 zones of 12 character fields will fit the same area.

The example below illustrates the relationship of field width to number of packed zones that will fit on one line. Lines can also contain zones of mixed sizes. This somewhat complicates aligning data into neat vertical columns when using the packed spacing arrangement.

One to four character fields:

| −1ƀƀƀ | 12ƀƀƀ | −123ƀƀ | 123ƀƀ | −123ƀƀ | 123ƀƀ | −123ƀƀ | 123ƀƀ | −123ƀƀ | 123ƀƀ | −123ƀƀ | 123ƀƀ |

Five to seven character fields:

| −1234ƀƀƀ | 12345ƀƀƀ | −123456ƀƀ | 123456ƀƀ | −123456ƀƀ | 123456ƀƀ | −123456ƀƀ | 123456ƀƀ |

Eight to ten character fields:

| −1234567ƀƀƀƀ | 12345678ƀƀƀ | −123456789ƀƀ | 123456789ƀƀ | −123456789ƀƀ | 123456789ƀƀ |

Eleven to thirteen character fields:

| −1234567890ƀƀƀ | 12345678901ƀƀƀ | −123456789012ƀƀ | 123456789012ƀƀ | −123456789012ƀƀ |

Each piece of numeric data is left justified in the zone, with a space reserved for the sign. The first column is left blank if the number is positive. A minus sign appears in the first position if the number is negative.

GENERAL FORM

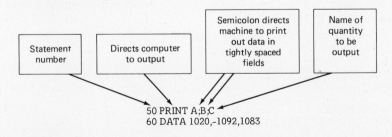

OUTPUT

In this example, three pieces of data, each five columns wide (including the sign), are to be printed out tightly spaced. When the computer encounters statement 50, it prints out the values of A, B, and C, left justified, in three fields, each nine characters wide. Since A and C are positive numbers, the first column in each field is left blank. B is a negative number, and a minus sign appears in column 1.

Example

```
20 PRINT E;F;G
30 DATA — 12096,105,1939483
```

OUTPUT

−12096	105	1939483	

This example illustrates how several numbers of different sizes are printed out in the close spacing mode. The first number has five digits and a sign and occupies a field nine columns wide. The second number has three digits and a sign and occupies a field six columns wide. The last number occupies 8 columns and will be printed in a 12-column field.

On many computer systems, numbers containing more than nine digits will be printed out using the E or exponent format.

Example

```
60 PRINT A$;B$;C$;D$
70 DATA "I AM", " THE", " KIN", "G"
```

OUTPUT

I AM THE KING			

Four alphabetic strings, each four characters wide, are separated by semicolons in a PRINT statement. This instructs the computer to concatenate them—that is, to link them together—when printing them out. This type of statement allows the programmer to print out and reconstruct text lines. Spaces between words and punctuation must be explicitly shown in the PRINT statement.

Note: Computer systems vary in the number of characters allowed in an alphabetic string.

Example

```
130 PRINT A$;X
140 DATA "YEARS",1985
```

OUTPUT

YEARS	1985			

In this example, an alphabetic string and a numeric variable are to be printed on one line. The computer will output the alphabetic string beginning in column 1. The numeric data requires five columns and will be assigned a nine-column field. Since a semicolon separates the items in the PRINT statement, the number is printed out next to the alphabetic string without intervening spaces.

Example

```
80 PRINT A$;B$;
90 PRINT X
100 DATA "LUG ", "NUTS",60192
```

OUTPUT

LUG NUTS	60192		

In this instance, two alphabetic strings and one numeric piece of data are to be printed out. The fourth character of A$ is a blank space, since all spaces between words must be explicitly indicated. A semicolon following the last data item in the PRINT statement (B$;) acts as a carriage inhibitor. It instructs the computer to remain on the same print line and not to automatically skip to a new line for the next PRINT statement. When the computer reaches statement 90, variable X will be printed in the next field on the same line with A$ and B$.

Example

```
90 PRINT A;B;C;D;E;F;G;H;I;J;K;L;M;N;O;P;Q;R;S;T
100 DATA 1,2,3,4,5,6,7,8,9,10,11,12,13,14,15,16,17,18,19,20
```

OUTPUT

1	2	3	4	5	6	7	8	9	10	11	12
13	14	15	16	17	18	19	20				

In this example, the data listed in a PRINT statement contain more items than can fit on one line. The computer will automatically print items on the first line, skip to the next line, and finish printing out the values.

The spacing and number of lines required will vary, of course, depending on the number of digits in each number and the number of values in the data list.

Example

```
50 PRINT A$; ", THE BOOK YOU REQUESTED, ";B$;", IS READY."
60 DATA "MRS. ONO", "FRENCH FOLK SONGS"
```

OUTPUT

MRS. ONO, THE BOOK YOU REQUESTED, FRENCH FOLK SONGS, IS READY.

In this example, the computer will print out a text line containing both literal constants and alphanumeric variables in the tight spacing mode. Punctuation and spaces have been included to improve readability.

RULES

1. Items in a PRINT statement separated by semicolons appear closely spaced (concatenated) on the print line. Alphabetic variables and literal constants are printed with no space between them. Numeric quantities are printed in fields that vary in size from 6 to over 15 characters, depending upon the number of digits in the value and the computer system used.

2. The arrangement and size of the printing fields in the packed-zone format vary according to the computer system. The student should consult the language implementation manual for details on his/her system.

3. The printing fields for numeric data printed out using the semicolon vary according to the number of digits in a value. They may not line up in neat, vertical columns. If data must be aligned, the programmer should use standard column spacing, indicated by a comma.

4. Numeric data will be printed out beginning in the second column of a field, with the first column reserved for the sign. Alphanumeric data and literal constants begin in the first column of a field.

5. Alphabetic strings should be separated by a semicolon whenever the programmer wants to reconstruct text lines with normal print-page readability.

6. When a semicolon appears at the end of the PRINT statement, the first piece of data in the next PRINT statement will be printed on the same line in close-packed format.

7. If a PRINT statement contains more items in its data list than can fit on one print line, the computer will automatically skip to another line and continue printing.

8. Most computers limit the number of digits that will be printed out for each numeric value. Any value containing more digits than the limit will be printed out using the E format.

EXERCISES

1. Find the errors, if any, in the following statements:

a. `20 PRINT X;Y;Z`

−20.3	69.1	100.182	

b. `40 PRINT;A;B;C`
c. `60 PRINT A$;B;C$`

NAME	−12.82CITY		

    d. 55 PRINT L;M;";";N;O
    e. 66 PRINT "NAME";A$;";";B$

2. Write the PRINT statement that will output the quantities 68.4 and 39.10 in tight spacing. Show the output.
3. Write the PRINT statement that will output the following quantities in tight spacing: 12, 19, 14, 25, 66, 78. Show the output.
4. Write the PRINT statement that will produce the following output:

ALICE- 21	SUE- 19	GLORIA- 20	

5. Write the PRINT statement that will produce the following output:

⌀68⌀⌀⌀⌀3221⌀⌀⌀⌀TEST   21

6. Write the PRINT statement that will produce the following output:

RATE-B21	1680⌀⌀⌀⌀2190		

7. Write the PRINT statement that will produce the following output:

******** 300 ********		

8. Write the PRINT statement that will produce the following output:

ALPHA 10.16	BETA 11.82		

9. Write the PRINT statement that will produce the following output:

100⌀⌀⌀⌀⌀⌀	31		

10. Write the PRINT statement that will print out 20 two-digit numbers.

PRINT COMPUTATIONS AND MIXED DATA (PRINT-EQUATIONS)

PURPOSE

The PRINT statement can be used not only to print out numeric variables, alphabetic character strings, and literal constants, but to perform mathematical calculations as well. All these functions can be combined in one PRINT statement to save programming time and effort.

The programmer can perform one or more mathematical calculations, label the results with several words or phrases, and indicate varied spacing arrangements for the output using just one PRINT statement. This unit introduces the concepts of combining the various functions of the PRINT statement in one instruction.

The techniques of performing mathematical calculations are covered in Unit 13. The student may want to study that section in conjunction with this one to learn the rules for coding simple and complex mathematical operations.

GENERAL FORM

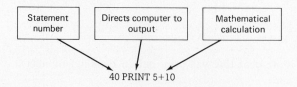

| Statement number | Directs computer to output | Mathematical calculation |

40 PRINT 5+10

OUTPUT

| 15 | | | | |

This statement directs the computer to sum two numbers and print out the results. It is the same as

```
30 LET A=5+10
40 PRINT A
```

Example

```
10 LET A=20
20 PRINT A*10+2
```

OUTPUT

202			

In this example, one PRINT statement is used to perform multiplication and addition operations (using both constants and variables) and to print out the results (202).

Example

```
20 LET A=20
30 LET B=5
40 LET C=2
50 PRINT A/(B*C)
```

OUTPUT

2			

In this example, a PRINT statement is used to perform a more complex mathematical equation, involving division, clearing parentheses, and so on, and to print out results.

Example

```
40 PRINT "THE SUM IS", 50+25
```

OUTPUT

THE SUM IS	75		

In statement 40, the computer will perform an addition operation and print out a literal constant. Since the two elements are separated by a comma, the computer will follow the standard column spacing rules, aligning the literal constant in the first print field and the results of the calculation in the second print field.

Below is the same text, showing the output when a semicolon is used in the PRINT statement:

```
40 PRINT "THE SUM IS";50+25
```

OUTPUT

THE SUM IS 75			

Example

```
10 LET A$="WHEEL"
20 LET B=100
30 LET C=25
40 PRINT A$;" $";B/C
```

OUTPUT

WHEEL ¦ $ ¦ 4			

In this instance, an alphabetic variable, a literal constant, and a mathematical equation have been combined in one PRINT statement. When the computer reaches statement 40, it will print the alphabetic variable beginning in column 1, and then print the literal constant (" $") concatenated, perform the calculation, and print out the result, with no intervening spaces between fields. The blank space between the dollar sign and the numeral 4 is the column reserved for the sign. Since any spaces needed for readability must be included in the alphanumeric string or literal constant, a space has been inserted before the dollar sign.

Example

```
10 LET A=300
20 LET B=64
30 PRINT "THE ELEVATION IS";A+B; "FEET"
```

OUTPUT

THE ELEVATION IS¦ 364 ¦FEET			

This example illustrates the combining of literal text with a calculation. Semicolons separate the elements so that the output will be concatenated. The computer will print out the first literal element followed by the results of the calculation. No ending space is inserted following the word *is,* since the first column of the numeric field is reserved for the sign and will be left blank. The computer next prints out the last literal constant. The programmer does not know the size of field that A+B will occupy, but since all numeric fields contain at least two blank trailing spaces, he or she does not insert any spaces before the literal constant FEET.

Example

```
40 LET I=990
50 LET A=3.01
60 LET B$="AXLES"
```

```
70 LET C=291
80 PRINT "COST $";A,"ITEM - ";B$,"COUNT:";I-C
```

OUTPUT

COST $ 3.01	ITEM − AXLES	COUNT: 699	

Several elements have been combined in a single PRINT statement in this example to print out current price and inventory of an item. When the computer encounters statement 80, it prints the first literal constant (COST $) aligned left in the first field. The numeric variable A is printed without any intervening spaces. (The first column of the number field is reserved for the sign.) Since the variable A is followed by a comma, the machine skips to the next standard print zone and prints out the second literal constant, (ITEM—) followed closely by the alphabetic variable B$ (AXLES). Extra spaces and punctuation have been inserted in the literal constant to improve readability. The machine moves to the next standard column print zone and prints out the last literal constant (COUNT:). The results of the calculations $I-C$ (which computes the current inventory) are printed next.

RULES

1. Numeric and alphanumeric variables, literal and numeric constants, and mathematical calculations may be combined in a single PRINT statement.

2. Both standard column spacing (commas) and packed-zone spacing (semicolons) may be used in a single PRINT statement. Each item in the output will be spaced out according to the format indicated by the preceding punctuation.

3. The rules of coding mathematical calculations in BASIC are discussed in the next unit. These rules also apply to coding mathematical operations within a PRINT statement.

EXERCISES

1. Find the errors, if any, in the following statements:
   a. PRINT 20/4
   b. PRINT;20/4
   c. PRINT "20/4"
   d. PRINT "20/4";20/4
   e. PRINT A$/B

2. Write a PRINT statement that will multiply two numbers and label the output RESULT.
3. Write a PRINT statement that will add four variables and label the output TOTAL.
4. Write the statements that will label two columns TEST 1 and TEST 2 and place the result of a calculation under each.
5. Print out the result of a calculation beginning in the third field.
6. Write the PRINT statement that will output the following: TRANSMISSION RATE IS 2400 BPS, where 2400 is the result of a calculation.

7. Write a PRINT statement that will add two whole numbers and divide by a third.
8. Write a PRINT statement that will multiply 10 inches by 3.14 and label the output.
9. Write a PRINT statement that will intermix three literal constants and three variables. Show the output.
10. Write a PRINT statement that will intermix two literal constants and two calculations. Show the output.

ENTERING DATA VIA PROGRAM (READ/DATA AND RESTORE STATEMENTS)

PURPOSE

The READ, DATA, and RESTORE statements enable the programmer to enter data from the program. The READ and DATA statements are a convenient means of placing tables, lists, and data into storage for use during a program run. Since DATA statements are often grouped at the beginning or end of a program, they can be changed easily to enter new data for processing. They are a more flexible means of data entry than the LET statement.

Each READ statement is coupled to a DATA statement. Each name listed in a READ statement is assigned to the next item listed in sequence in the DATA statement. More than one DATA statement may be used to satisfy a READ statement, and a DATA statement may contain sufficient items to satisfy more than one READ statement.

The items in a DATA statement may be used over again by including a RESTORE statement in the program. This causes the computer to go back to the beginning of the list of items in the DATA statement and assign them to the names in the next READ statement. This is used to test different loops in a program with the same data, to assign the same values to another set of variable names, or to perform several procedures on the same set of data.

Data entered into storage via the READ/DATA statements in a program can be referenced at any point in the program by their assigned names. They can be manipulated, processed, or output by reference to these names.

GENERAL FORM

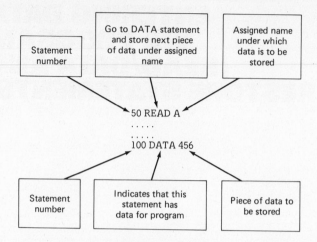

In this example, the programmer wants to enter a piece of data (the numeric quantity 456) into the program. At statement 50, he or she directs the computer to READ in a value and store it in the location named A. The related DATA statement at line 100 lists the item (456) to be read in and stored. When the computer encounters the READ statement at line 50, it will scan the programming instructions and locate a DATA statement. It will assign the first piece of data in the DATA statement to the storage location named in the READ statement. Thus, the number 456 will be assigned to storage location A.

In this instance, only one name appears in the READ statement and only one item in the DATA statement. The programmer could have used a LET statement to perform this same function: 50 LET A = 456. However, the READ/DATA statements are more flexible, since the data can be easily changed by entering a new DATA statement.

Example

```
20 READ A,B,C,D
 . . . .
 . . . .
150 DATA 1,2,3,4
```

In this example, the programmer instructs the computer to read in and store four pieces of data. The computer will store the first piece of data (1) under the name A, the second (2) under B, the third (3) under C, and the fourth (4) under D.

Example

```
10 READ A,B,C,D
 . . . .
 . . . .
200 DATA 1,2
210 DATA 3,4
```

In this example, two DATA statements are used to satisfy one READ statement. The computer will assign the items, in sequence, to the storage locations. The first item (1) will be stored under the name A and the second (2) under the name B. Then the computer will search through the program for another DATA statement and assign the next two items to the locations named C and D.

Using two or more DATA statements in a program facilitates entering new data for processing. It also makes keyboarding easier, since one small error in a long list of data items could mean that the entire line must be rekeyboarded.

Example

```
10 DATA "NAME", 201, "6ATS9F"
 . . .
 . . .
80 READ A$
 . . .
100 READ B
 . . .
140 READ C$
```

In this example, one DATA statement contains sufficient items to satisfy three READ statements. The computer will read in and store the first data item, an alphabetic word (NAME), under the name A$. When it reaches statement 100 it will store the next item, a numeric quantity (201), under the name B. Later, when it encounters statement 140, it will store the alphanumeric quantity (6ATS9F) under the name C$.

The programmer selects the variable names used in the READ statement. Assigned names must follow certain rules, depending upon whether they are referencing numeric or alphanumeric data. Names assigned to numerical data must consist of one alphabetic letter or one alphabetic letter and one digit. Thus, there are 260 possible names that can be assigned in one program (A to Z, A1 to Z9).

Examples of acceptable numeric names are

A	A1	D	H6
K	L9	Z	X4

Names assigned to alphabetic data follow a different rule. On most systems, they consist of one alphabetic character followed by a dollar sign ($). Thus, there are 26 possible names that can be assigned to alphabetic variables in one program.

Examples of acceptable alphabetic names are

A$	D$	G$	V$

Some systems use a double alphabetic letter instead to name their alphabetic variables. Check your system manual to determine which is the correct form on your computer.

Examples of acceptable alphabetic names for these systems are

AA	GG	HH	QQ

Each variable (representing a storage location) in a program must have a unique name, although the value of the variable may change.

Some systems also require that alphabetic variables entered from READ/DATA statements be enclosed in quotation marks. Nearly all systems require that variables being read in under alphabetic names that begin with a numeric digit or special character be enclosed in quotes.

Data read in under alphabetic names can be manipulated and processed by other statements in the program, but they cannot be operated upon arithmetically.

A program must have as many data items in the DATA statements as there are assigned names in the READ statements. If it does not, the computer will print out an error message and terminate execution. If there are more data items than names present, the excess data is ignored.

Example

```
10 READ A
20 READ B
30 RESTORE
40 READ C
50 READ D
60 DATA 2,6
```

In this example, four READ statements are present. Each will need a piece of data, but only one DATA statement, containing two items, is included in the program. The RESTORE statement at line 30 directs the computer to go back to the beginning of the DATA statement and read in and store the data items under different names.

The computer will load the numbers 2 and 6 into storage under the names A and B as directed in statements 10 and 20. It will then restore the data set read in and store the numbers 2 and 6 under the names C and D.

RULES

1. A program containing a READ statement must also have at least one DATA statement.

2. A program must have enough data items to meet the needs of the READ statements or an error condition will be present. Excess data items will be ignored by the computer.

3. More than one DATA statement may be used to satisfy one READ statement and more than one READ statement may be satisfied from one DATA statement.

4. A RESTORE statement may be used to cycle the computer back to the beginning of the DATA statement to reuse the same data items for other READ statements.

5. DATA statements may be placed anywhere in the program ahead of the END statement. Items are assigned to storage locations in the sequence in which they appear in the program.

6. Each item in the READ list must be separated by a comma.

7. Each item in the DATA list must be separated by a comma.

8. Names assigned to numeric data must consist of one alphabetic letter or one alphabetic letter and one digit: A, B, G5, T8.

9 Names assigned to alphanumeric data must consist of one alphabetic letter followed by a dollar sign ($). In some systems a double alphabetic letter is used to name alphabetic strings.

10. Data items stored under alphabetic names must be enclosed in quotation marks on some systems.

11. Data items stored under alphabetic names, and beginning with a number or special character (such as 3OT4), must be enclosed in quotes on most systems.

12. Data read in under READ/DATA statements may be used for manipulation or processing by reference to their assigned names.

13. Data read in under alphabetic names cannot be used for arithmetic calculations.

EXERCISES

1. Find the errors, if any, in the following statements:
   a. 20 READ 5
      50 DATA A,B
   b. 30 READ A,B,C
      150 DATA 1
      160 DATA 2
      170 DATA 3
   c. 20 DATA 5,6
      50 READ A
   d. 30 READ A,
      40 READ B,
      50 READ C,
      60 DATA 150, 2.10, 60012
   e. 40 READ N,A,M,E, B$
      150 DATA "SARA", "TOM", "JOSE", "MARY", FOUR

2. Write READ and DATA statements that input three numeric values.
3. Write READ and DATA statements that input two numeric values and two names.
4. Show a program in which one DATA statement has sufficient items for three READ statements.
5. Show a program in which one READ statement inputs data items from three DATA statements.
6. Show a program with three sets of READ/DATA statements. The first set reads in one numeric value, the second two alphabetic strings, and the third three numeric values and an alphabetic string.
7. Show the READ/DATA statements that would read in a part name, part number, amount in stock, and price.
8. Show the READ/DATA statements that would read in 10 test values ranging from 90 to 110.
9. Using the data items from Exercise 8, show the statements that would direct the computer to store the same data under different names.
10. Describe which numbers input by READ/DATA statements can be used in mathematical calculations in the program, and which cannot.

BRANCH UNCONDITIONAL (GOTO STATEMENT)

PURPOSE

Unless directed to do otherwise, the computer will always execute a program by moving from the first instruction (statement with the lowest number) down to the last (END statement, with the highest number). Many programming algorithms and techniques require program flow to move in a different sequence. The programmer may want to branch back to the beginning of a sequence, go to another point in the program, or skip certain statements.

The sequence that the computer follows when executing instructions is altered and controlled with a GOTO statement (written GO TO in some systems). This statement tells the computer to stop line-by-line execution and process a specific statement next, which is located at another point in the program.

The GOTO statement is a useful tool, but should be used judiciously. GOTO statements can create confusing "spaghettilike" code which is hard to follow. Many programmers prefer to use the FOR/NEXT statement, described elsewhere, in place of the GOTO. GOTO statements allow programmers to repeat procedures without having to recode each repetition or restart program execution. It allows them to build in many alternate paths to increase the flexibility and variety of ways in which data can be manipulated.

A GOTO statement is an unconditional branch because program flow will always be altered in the same way each time the statement is encountered.

GENERAL FORM

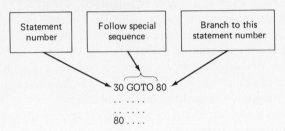

In this example, statement 30 directs the computer to go directly to statement 80 next, skipping all instructions in between. Program flow resumes with normal line-by-line execution at statement 80. The GOTO statement includes the word GOTO and the line number of the statement the program is to branch to. The program will always branch to statement 80 upon reaching statement 30, in this example.

Example

```
20 . . . .
 .  .  . . .
 .  .  . . .
90 GOTO 20
```

A GOTO statement can direct control to any other executable statement in the program, regardless of whether it has a lower or a higher line number. In this example, the programmer is using a GOTO statement to set up a loop. He or she is directing control back to statement 20 from line 90. All instructions between 20 and 90 will be executed again each time the computer repeats the loop.

Example

```
40 GOTO 250
 .  .  . . .
 .  .  . . .
250 END
```

This example illustrates using a GOTO statement to branch control to the END statement from the middle of the program. Statements such as these are often placed at the end of parallel branches to stop execution when an end-of-file has been read or a sequence has been performed a predetermined number of times.

RULES

1. A GOTO statement directs the computer to stop sequential execution and transfer control to the statement number indicated.

2. The GOTO statement is composed of a line number, the word GOTO, and the number of the statement to be executed next. Some systems use the form GO TO with a space in between. Check your manual for details.

3. The GOTO statement is unconditional. The program will always branch as directed when the statement is executed.

4. A GOTO statement can direct control to any executable statement in the program, regardless of whether it has a lower or a higher line number.

5. When control is directed to a statement with a higher line number, the instructions that are skipped will not be executed. Instructions must be included in the program to execute these statements at the proper point in the program.

6. When control is directed to a statement with a lower line number, all the instructions in between will be executed again. The programmer should include some means of ending such a loop after it has been executed the proper number of times.

7. A GOTO statement can direct the computer to the END statement from any point in the program to terminate execution.

8. Use GOTO statements with care and avoid jumping in and out of sequences illogically.

EXERCISES

1. Find the errors, if any, in the following statements:
   a. 40 GOTO 999
   b. 50 GO TO 999
   c. 69 GOTO "999"
   d. 70 GOTO A9
   e. 85 GOTO 3/2

2. Write a statement that will branch control of the program to statement 100.
3. Write a statement that will branch control of the program to statement number 73.
4. Write a statement that will branch control of the program to statement 60.
5. Write a statement that will branch control of the program to statement 10.
6. Write a statement that will branch control of the program to the END statement.
7. Write a statement that will branch control to an earlier sequence in the program.
8. What would be the result of branching to a nonexistent statement?
9. Give an example of where GOTO statements are useful in a program.
10. Why is the GOTO instruction considered an unconditional branch?

ENTERING DATA VIA KEYBOARD (INPUT STATEMENT)

PURPOSE

The INPUT statement allows the programmer to enter data from the keyboard while the program is executing. Each time the computer encounters an INPUT statement in the program, it prints a question mark (?) and waits for data to be keyed in.

The INPUT statement differs from the LET and READ/DATA statements in that data is supplied to the program during execution and not as part of the program proper. Data can be changed easily by inputting different data each time a program is run. INPUT statements are a convenient means of allowing the programmer to select optional branches or to direct the computer to repeat part, or all, of the program while it is executing.

GENERAL FORM

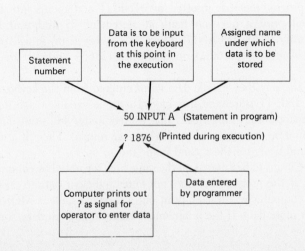

| Statement number | Data is to be input from the keyboard at this point in the execution | Assigned name under which data is to be stored |

50 INPUT A   (Statement in program)

? 1876   (Printed during execution)

| Computer prints out ? as signal for operator to enter data | Data entered by programmer |

In this example, the computer executes the program down to statement 50. At that point it encounters an INPUT statement, prints out a question mark, and waits for data to be entered. The programmer enters a value (1876) from the keyboard. The machine stores this value under the assigned name A. The programmer may use this value later in the program for computations, output, or other processing.

INPUT statements may be placed anywhere in the program before the END statement. Names assigned to the data read in must follow the rules for naming quantities.

Each computer system has its own limits on the size of numbers and alphabetic strings which can be read in under one assigned name. Some systems will read in as little as 6 characters, while others can handle strings of up to 255 characters. Some systems require alphabetic data to be enclosed in quotes. Be sure to check your language manual for details.

Example

```
200 INPUT A, B$, R, T$
```
                                           (Statement in program)

```
? 21, ROBERT, 19, GLENN
```
                                           (Printed during execution)

This example illustrates how several types of variables are read in using one INPUT statement. When the computer encounters statement 200, it prints out a question mark and waits for data to be keyboarded. The programmer must enter the data items in the order and form prescribed in the INPUT statement. The quantities 21, ROBERT, 19, and GLENN, separated by commas, are keyed in by the programmer.

Example

```
75 INPUT A$
80 INPUT A,B
```
```
? CLEVELAND
? 25674, 10
```

In this example, the programmer has inserted two INPUT statements into the program. The computer will print a question mark at statement 75 and wait for input of an alphabetic quantity (CLEVELAND). Once this is keyed in, it will proceed to statement 80 and wait for two numeric quantities (25674 and 10) to be keyed in.

Note: Systems vary in the way they handle data items entered from the keyboard. Some require that when an INPUT statement lists more than one variable, each item must be keyboarded on a separate line. This means that the computer will print out a question mark and wait for an item to be entered (with a carriage return). Then, it prints out another question mark and waits for the second item, and so on.

Other systems allow the items to be entered on the same line, separated by commas, as shown in these examples. If the programmer does not enter sufficient data to satisfy the INPUT statement, the computer will usually print out a message such as MORE? on the next line and wait for more data. If the programmer enters too much data, some systems will ignore the excess, some will print out a message and ignore the excess, and others will consider it an error condition and terminate execution.

Example

```
200 PRINT "REPEAT PROCESS? ENTER 1 FOR YES, 0 FOR NO"
220 INPUT A
```

This example illustrates the use of an INPUT statement to control branching. At line 200, a PRINT statement asks the programmer to enter a 1 or 0. Statement 220 inputs the programmer's answer. In succeeding statements, the program will test the input value and branch accordingly. This is a convenient way to allow a user to process several sets of data during one program run and then to direct the computer to terminate execution when he or she is finished. The program can, of course, be written to branch to other points in the program. In this way, it allows the programmer to select additional processes to be performed on the same data, or to enter a new data set and repeat part or all of the program.

RULES

1. INPUT statements may be placed anywhere in the program before the END statement. The computer will stop each time it encounters an INPUT statement, print out a question mark (?), and wait for data to be keyed in.

2. More than one INPUT statement may be used in a program.

3. Quantities entered from the keyboard in response to an INPUT statement must be in the same order and type as requested in the INPUT statement.

4. One item must be entered from the keyboard for each assigned name listed in the INPUT statement. If insufficient items are entered, the computer will print a message requesting more data, wait for more data without a request, or consider it an error condition and terminate execution.

5. If too much data is entered from the keyboard in response to an INPUT statement, the computer may ignore the excess or terminate execution due to an error condition.

6. If more than one variable is entered on one line following a question mark, they must be separated by commas.

7. The names assigned to quantities read into storage with an INPUT statement must agree with the rules for naming quantities.

8. Both alphabetic and numeric quantities can be read in and stored under an alphabetic name, using an INPUT statement. This data cannot be used for mathematical calculations in the program. Only numeric quantities can be read in under a numeric name; and this data can be used for further processing, including mathematical calculations.

9. The length of the alphabetic character strings, or the size of numbers that may be read in, varies with the computer system. On some systems alphabetic data must be enclosed in quotes when entered from the keyboard. Check your language manual to determine how your system handles these conditions.

EXERCISES

1. Find the errors, if any, in the following statements:

   a. `20 INPUT A1,A2`
   `? 1,2`
   b. `30 INPUT A,B,C`
   `40 DATA 10,20,30`
   c. `80 INPUT S$`
   `? "THIS IS WRONG"`
   d. `150 INPUT Z$`
   `? "THIS", "IS", "CORRECT"`
   e. `60 INPUT X`
   `70 INPUT Y`
   `80 INPUT Z`
   `? 49,62, 81`

2. What happens if insufficient data for an INPUT statement has been entered from the keyboard?
3. What happens if too much data is entered from the keyboard?
4. Write an INPUT statement that inputs three numeric variables and show the data entered from the keyboard.
5. Write an INPUT statement that inputs an alphabetic string and show the data entered from the keyboard.
6. Write three INPUT statements. The first reads in your name, the second your age, and the third your color of eyes.
7. Use one INPUT statement to input a file containing five records. Show the data being entered.
8. Use five INPUT statements to read in the same file. Show the data being entered.
9. Show the INPUT statement a programmer would use to ask the user if he or she wishes to repeat a program. Show the data being entered.
10. Write the statements that input an account name, previous balance, charges, and payments. Use two INPUT statements and show the data being entered.

ENTERING DATA VIA PROGRAM (LET STATEMENT)

PURPOSE

LET statements can be used by the programmer to enter data for processing from the program. Such data are an integral part of the program and are interpreted with the programming instructions. They can be operated upon, manipulated, printed out, or used for further calculations. (LET statements can also be used for other functions in BASIC programming. These are explained later.)

The LET statement is the simplest and most direct means of entering data into a program. It can be used to place both numeric data and strings of alphanumeric characters in storage. The LET statement tells the computer to assign the name the programmer has selected to a specific location in computer storage. Any data assigned to that name is placed in that location.

GENERAL FORM

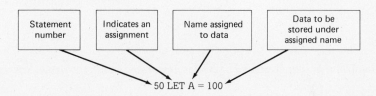

| Statement number | Indicates an assignment | Name assigned to data | Data to be stored under assigned name |

50 LET A = 100

In this example, the programmer wishes to enter numeric data (the number 100) as part of the program. The LET statement directs the computer to place the data (100) in a storage location named A. Whenever the name A appears in the program, the computer will substitute the value 100. The programmer can have the value of A (100) printed out, using a PRINT statement, or use the quantity for calculations.

The value assigned to A at statement 50 is a constant quantity. The variable A is always equal to 100 when the computer reaches this statement. The value of A can be changed by assigning it different quantities at other points in the program or by entering a new statement 50.

The conventions for naming numeric or alphabetic variables, previously discussed, must be followed when preparing a LET statement. Names assigned to alphabetic quantities are composed of one alphabetic letter followed by a dollar sign ($). This allows 26 alphabetic variables to be assigned in one program. Some systems allow double letters, such as AA, SS, or YY, to be used. Numeric data names must consist of one alphabetic letter or one alphabetic letter and one digit. There are 260 possible combinations from A to Z and A1 to Z9.

Examples

```
60 LET F8 = 6595
```

In this example, the programmer has assigned the name F8 to the data 6595. The computer will store this data under the assigned name F8. At any time in the program, the programmer can use the data in a calculation, print it out, or manipulate it in other ways by including its name F8 in a programming instruction.

```
200 LET A$ = "BENNY"
```

In this example, the programmer has assigned the name A$ to the alphabetic character string BENNY. The computer will store this string under the name A$. Once read in, it may be manipulated or printed out by reference to the name A$. (It cannot be used in arithmetic calculations.) Most systems require that alphanumeric data assigned with a LET statement be enclosed in quotation marks.

Data stored under one name can be moved to another storage location and also saved under another name. The LET statement is used to name the second storage location and indicate which data is to be moved or "copied." The data will then be stored in two locations under two different names. (Data is not erased or changed until new data is read into that storage location.)

Examples

```
20 LET T = 200
 . .
50 LET A=T
```

In this example, the value stored in T (200) is now stored under the name A as well.

```
30 LET C$ = "COST"
 . .
90 LET D$ = C$
```

In this example, an alpha string has been copied into a second storage location under a different name. The same data is now stored under both C$ and D$.

RULES

1. LET statements are composed of the word LET, followed by an assigned name, an equals sign ($=$), and the data to be stored under that name.

Example

70 LET G3 = 500

2. Many systems require alphanumeric strings in a LET statement to be enclosed in quotation marks.
3. Each system has a limit on the number of alphabetic characters that may be read in and assigned under one name, or the number of digits that can be assigned under one name. Be sure to consult your language implementation manual to determine these limits. If you exceed the allowed number, the computer may disregard the excess or print out an error message. Some systems are limited to 6 alphabetic characters or 18 numeric digits per name.
4. Once read in, numeric data can be used for calculating, manipulating, or printing out.
5. Data read in under alphanumeric names cannot be used in arithmetic calculations. They can be printed out, assigned to different storage locations, and so on.
6. A name can be assigned to represent only one variable in a given program, although the value of the variable may change.
7. Data read in by the LET statement becomes an integral part of the program and is interpreted with the programming instructions.

EXERCISES

1. Find the errors, if any, in the following statements:
   a. 10 LET A=4169.28
   b. 50 LET Z$="Z$"
   c. 50 LET X1=1
   d. 70 LET ID=312
   e. 195 LET N="J.S.LIU"

2. Write a LET statement that assigns the value of 325 to X.
3. Write a LET statement that assigns the value 614.3926 to N1.
4. Write a LET statement that assigns the course name BUSINESS 1 to C$.
5. Write a LET statement that assigns the value 10 to a variable.
6. Show how a programmer could change the value of N1 in Exercise 3 to 100 later in the program.
7. Show how a programmer would enter the values 10, 15, and 20 into storage.
8. Show how a programmer would enter a name, street address, and city into storage.
9. How might a programmer enter three numeric values into storage and have each variable name begin with T?
10. Show two ways in which an ID number might be entered into storage.

PERFORMING MATHEMATICS (LET STATEMENT, ARITHMETIC OPERATORS)

PURPOSE

One of the computer's most valuable attributes is its ability to perform sophisticated mathematical calculations quickly and accurately. The programmer can direct the machine to add, subtract, multiply, divide, raise a number to a power (exponentiation), and so forth.

Mathematical instructions must be given to the computer in a specialized form. It cannot understand mathematical formulas written in conventional algebraic notation. The programmer must convert the steps in an algebraic or statistical formula into a form recognized by the computer.

A group of symbols, called *mathematical operators*, are used in a LET statement (or PRINT statement) to direct the computer to perform mathematical computations. The mathematical operators used on most BASIC systems are

SYMBOL	FUNCTION
↑	Exponentiation. On some systems, two asterisks (**) or an upward pointing caret (^) are used instead
*	Multiplication
/	Division
−	Subtraction
+	Addition

GENERAL FORM

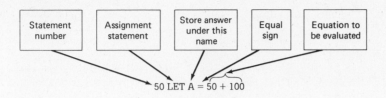

Statement number | Assignment statement | Store answer under this name | Equal sign | Equation to be evaluated

50 LET A = 50 + 100

RESULT

A = 150

The LET statement is composed of two parts. On the left of the equals sign is an assigned name under which the answer will be stored. On the right of the equals sign is the mathematical expression to be evaluated. When the computer encounters this type of statement, it performs the mathematical operations indicated on the right side of the equals sign and places the results in storage under the assigned name on the left. These results can be used later in the program for further calculations or printed out.

In the example above, when the computer encounters statement 50, it adds 50 and 100 and places the results (150) in the storage location named A. By referencing the name A, the programmer can print out these results later or use them in other calculations.

Mathematical operations in a LET (or PRINT) statement are always carried out in a certain specified order. The rules governing this order are called the *hierarchy of operations.* The computer will

1. clear parentheses
2. perform exponentiation
3. perform multiplication and division
4. perform addition and subtraction

The computer always moves from left to right when evaluating an expression. It performs any operations enclosed within parentheses first. Then, it performs any exponentiation that is indicated. Next, multiplication and division are performed moving from left to right; and finally, addition and subtraction operations are completed.

Examples

Each example below will show the algebraic form of the problem and how it has been converted into a BASIC instruction. It may often require more than one BASIC instruction to convert an equation.

The numeric variables used in the examples will have the following values:

```
LET A = 10
LET B = 20
LET C = 15
LET D = 6
LET E = 2
```

Algebraic notation:

$$F = A + B + C - \frac{D}{E}$$

BASIC instruction:

40 LET F=A+B+C−D/E

RESULT

F=42

The computer will scan the equation moving from left to right. First, D (6) will be divided by E (2). Then, the machine will again scan from left to right, adding A (10), B (20), and C (15). Finally D/E will be subtracted.

Example
Algebraic notation:

$$F = A + B + \frac{C - D}{E}$$

BASIC instruction:

40 LET F = A+B+(C−D)/E

RESULT

F = 34.5

This is the same example as above, except that parentheses have been added. This has the effect of changing the order in which the mathematical steps are performed; and as a result, the answer will be different. Following the hierarchy of operations, the machine will scan from left to right and clear the parentheses first (C−D=9). Next, this intermediate answer will be divided by E (9/2=4.5). The machine again scans the equation from left to right and adds this value to A (10) and B (20) to reach the final answer, 34.5.

Example
Algebraic notation:

$$F = 40 + A^2$$

BASIC instruction:

140 LET F = 40 + A↑2

RESULT

F = 140

This example illustrates exponentiation. The computer is instructed to raise a number (A) to a power (2) with the operator, an upward arrow, followed by the value of the power. On some systems, a double asterisk or upward pointing caret would be used instead of an arrow:

$$A^2 = A\uparrow 2 = A^{**}2 = A\char`\^2$$

Following the rules of the hierarchy, the computer will first perform exponentiation and then addition. The results will be stored under the assigned name F.

Example
Algebraic notation:

$$F = \frac{D^2 - C}{3.14 \times E}$$

BASIC instruction:

```
50 LET F=(D**2−C)/(3.14*E)
```

RESULT

```
F = 3.34
```

This example illustrates a complex statement that includes exponentiation, two sets of parentheses, subtraction, multiplication, and division. The computer will clear the first parentheses, performing exponentiation and subtraction; and then clear the second set of parentheses and finally perform the division.

When coding a complex algebraic equation in BASIC, it will be easier for the novice programmer to use many small steps to solve for each intermediate value. These intermediate values are then combined to solve for the final answer. After the programmer gains more experience, he or she can combine steps together by using more complex BASIC instructions and hence solve the problem in fewer statements.

Example
Algebraic notation:

$$A + \frac{10}{15} = 16 - C + \frac{3}{5}$$

BASIC instructions:

```
30 LET X = 10/15
40 LET Y = 3/5
50 LET A = 16−C+Y−X
```

The BASIC instruction could also have been written

```
50 LET A=16−C+3/5−10/15
```

Example
Algebraic notation:

$$\frac{B^2}{6} + X = (A + B)(A - C) + \frac{4 + AB}{\sqrt{C}}$$

BASIC Instructions:

```
20 LET T1=A+B
30 LET T2=A-C
40 LET A1=T1*T2
50 LET T3=SQR(C)
60 LET T4=A*B+4
70 LET A2=T4/T3
80 LET T5=B↑2
90 LET A3=T5/6
100 LET X=A1+A2-A3
```

The steps in this problem could be combined to use only four or six statements, or even only two statements as shown below:

```
20 LET C1=SQR(C)
30 LET X=(A+B)*(A-C)+(4+(A*B))/C1-(B↑2)/6
```

Note: See the unit on functions for details on how to find the square root of a number.

Example
Statistical formula—analysis of variance:

$$s^2 = \frac{\Sigma(X - \overline{X})^2}{n}$$

BASIC instructions:

```
40 LET I = (X-M)↑2
50 LET S = S+I
60 LET V = S/N
```

Statistical symbols have been assigned names in accordance with BASIC conventions.

S and I are intermediate values
Σ means sum of
$\quad V = s^2 =$ variance
$\quad X = X =$ score
$\quad N = n =$ number of scores
$\quad M = \overline{X} =$ mean

In this example, the statistical formula for the *analysis of variance* is coded in BASIC. It has been broken down into three statements for simplicity, although steps 40 and 50 could have been combined into one:

40 LET S=S+(X−M)↑2

RULES

1. The LET statement is composed of two parts: an assigned name (representing the answer) to the left of the equals sign and a mathematical expression on the right. Only one value, representing the answer, may appear on the left.

2. Mathematical expressions are always evaluated from left to right, following the hierarchy of operations.

3. The order in which statements are evaluated follows the hierarchy of operations. The computer will

   a. clear parentheses
   b. perform exponentiation
   c. perform multiplication and division
   d. perform addition and subtraction

4. The programmer must assign a name to the result of the expression to be evaluated. The assigned name must agree with the rules for naming numbers.

5. No subscript or superscript numbers may be used in coding mathematical formulas in BASIC. All characters must be aligned on the typing line.

Thus, the equation

$$X = \frac{A^2 - C_1 + C_2}{D^4}$$

must be converted to

$$X = (A{\uparrow}2 - C1 + C2)/D{\uparrow}4$$

6. More than one BASIC instruction may be used when converting an equation from conventional algebraic notation.

7. Only mathematical operators that are part of the standard character set may be used in coding mathematical expressions in BASIC. These are

   ↑ Exponentiation (** or ^)
   * Multiplication
   / Division
   − Subtraction
   + Addition

8. Two mathematical operators cannot appear next to each other in an expression. They must be separated by a value or parentheses. For example, A*−8+C should be written as A*(−8)+C.

9. Data read in as literals or alphabetic variables cannot be used for mathematical computations.

10. Both numeric variables and constants can be used in the LET statement.

EXERCISES

1. Find the errors, if any, in the following statements:
   a. 1 LET "A"=B/C
   b. 5 LET R=S*V/D
   c. 15 LET R="S*V/D"
   d. 20 "LET" L=F*21+R
   e. LET Q = "S"+21 × 10
2. Write a statement that will add the following values and place the answer under T: A, 6, 3, 98.
3. Write a statement that will raise Z to the third power.
4. Write a statement that will add A to B, divide by C, and square the result.
5. Write a statement that will convert the following algebraic equation to BASIC instructions:

$$P = \frac{10}{4} \times 9$$

6. Write a statement that will abstract the square root of A+B.
7. Convert the following algebraic equation to BASIC instructions:

$$X = \frac{A + D}{6 - M}$$

8. Convert the following algebraic equation to BASIC instructions:

$$E = (2 + I) \frac{(D - A)}{2}$$

9. Convert the following algebraic equation to BASIC instructions:

$$T = \frac{3 + A}{Q + 12^3}$$

10. Write the statements that will add 12 numbers and find their average.

COUNTERS
(LET STATEMENT)

PURPOSE

Counting pieces of data read in or the number of times a process is performed is a very useful programming technique. The final tally can be used in other calculations in the program as a limit on the number of times a procedure is performed, as an index, or it can be printed out.

Counting in BASIC is done by setting up *counters* in a program. Counters are composed of two or more LET statements. The first LET statement assigns the name and sets the initial value of the counter. The second, usually placed within a loop, increments the counter each time the computer goes through the loop.

Counters in a program can index positively or negatively, which means that the value in a counter can increase or decrease each pass. The increment value of a counter can be any value the programmer needs—1, 2, 10, .6, and so on.

GENERAL FORM

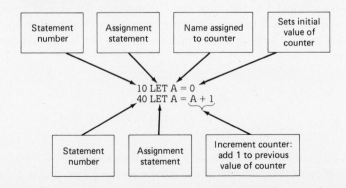

In this example, two LET statements set up and increment a counter. The first LET statement (10) sets up and initializes the counter, named A, to 0. (Names for counters are assigned by the programmer in accordance with the rules for naming numeric variables.)

A second LET statement (40) increments the counter. Each time the computer passes statement 40, it will increase the value of A by 1. Assume that the incrementing statement is included within a loop. The value of the counter after initialization is 0. The first time the computer passes statement 40, the value will index to 1. On the second pass, the computer indexes to 2, on the third pass, to 3, and so on. At the end of the program, the programmer can print out the tally, use it in a calculation, and so forth.

The programmer must indicate the initial value for a counter. Otherwise, data in that storage location from a previous program could be used by a program and such a circumstance would lead to erroneous results. Counters may be initialized to any value desired, the most common being 0. The statement that initializes a counter is most often placed at the beginning of a program. However, some algorithms require it to be included in a loop, placed just after a loop, and so on. Care should be taken when inserting initializing statements, since wrong placement is a common logical error in programming.

Example

```
20 LET B=10
50 LET B=B−1
```

This example illustrates the use of a negative counter. Statement 20 sets up a counter B and initializes it to 10. Each time the computer passes statement 50, it will reduce the value of B by 1. The first pass B will be equal to 9, the next to 8, and so on.

Example

```
40 LET C=0
50 LET C=C+5
```

This example illustrates the use of a positive counter, which increments by 5 each pass. Statement 40 names and initializes the counter to 0. Each time statement 50 is encountered, the computer will add 5 to the value of C. If statement 50 were in a loop, the value of C would increase from 0 to 5 on the first pass; on the second pass, it would become equal to 10; and so on. The programmer may use any amount he or she wishes to increment a counter.

Example

```
10 LET K=0
80 LET K=K+.2
```

In this example, the counter K will increase by .2 each time statement 80 is passed. This type of counter may be used to add fractions of a dollar, parts of a set, and so forth.

RULES

1. Counters are written into a program by inserting two LET statements. The first LET statement names and initializes the counter. The second LET statement, usually placed within a loop, indicates the incrementing value.

2. The incrementing value of a counter may be any number or fraction of a number.

3. Counters must be initialized to prevent erroneous results from data left in storage by other programs.

4. The placement in a program of the initializing statement must be carefully chosen to prevent logical errors from occurring during a program run.

5.Counters may run in a negative or positive direction, adding or subtracting each pass. The mathematical operator in the second LET statement indicates the direction of the counter.

6. The tally of a counter may be used in calculations, in the control of looping, or in other processes; or it may be printed out.

7. The rules for naming counters are the same as those for naming numeric variables.

EXERCISES

1. Find the errors, if any, in the following counters:
   a. 40 LET COUNTER=0
   b. 50 LET C=0.0
   c. 75 LET T=T+2
      90 LET T=0.0
   d. 20 LET K=0
      40 LET K=A−1
   e. 69 LET B=0
      74 PRINT "B=B+1"

2. Set up a counter named C and increase it by 1 each pass.
3. Set up a counter named V and initialize it to 10. Increase it by 1 each pass.
4. Set up a counter named Z. Initialize it to 5 and increase it by 5 each pass.
5. Set up a counter named N and initialize it to 100. Decrease it by 1 each pass.
6. Set up two counters. Initialize each to 0. Increase the first by 1 and the second by 5 each pass.
7. Write the statements that will set up a counter, initialize it, increase it, and print out the tally.
8. Set up a counter, initialize it, and increase it by the variable Q.
9. Set up a counter, initialize it, and increase it by a fraction.
10. Set up a counter, initialize it, and decrease it by V.

BRANCH CONDITIONAL (IF/THEN STATEMENT, RELATIONAL OPERATORS)

PURPOSE

One of the most powerful statements in BASIC is the IF/THEN command, which tests the relationship between two values. The computer can test for three conditions: if a value is equal to, greater than, or less than another value. If the relationship being tested in the statement is true, the computer branches to another point in the program. If the relationship is not true, the computer drops down to execute the next statement in the program.

This invaluable instruction enables the programmer to make conditional branches, that is, to take an alternate path only when certain conditions are true. He or she can compare numeric or alphanumeric literals and variables and mathematical expressions. This gives the programmer the ability to write programs that will sort, merge, alphabetize, or perform different procedures on data depending on its relationship to other data or to a standard.

Most systems allow the programmer to test for two of the three conditions in one IF/THEN statement. The conditions are specified by relational operators. The symbols used as relational operators are

OPERATOR	MEANING
=	Equal to
>	Greater than
<	Less than
> =	Greater than or equal to
< =	Less than or equal to
< >	Not equal to

GENERAL FORM

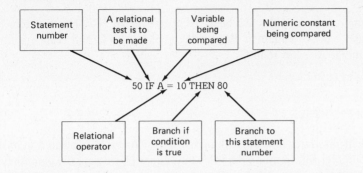

When the computer reaches statement 50, it will make a relational comparison and test the equality of the values of A and 10. If the relationship is true (A = 10), the computer branches control to statement 80. If it is not true (A is less than or greater than 10), the computer drops down to the next statement in the program.

Suppose that a different relational operator had been used:

50 IF A>10 THEN 80

The computer would branch to statement 80 only if the value of A were greater than 10. If A were 10 or less, the computer would drop down to the next statement.

If statement 50 had been written

50 IF A<10 THEN 80

the computer would branch to statement 80 only if the value of A were less than 10.

The IF/THEN statement is a conditional branch. The line-by-line sequence of execution is altered only when the conditions in the statement are met.

Example

90 IF A >=60.5 THEN 150

The IF/THEN statement in this example is testing for two conditions and two relational operators are shown. When statement 90 is encountered, the computer will compare the value of A to 60.5. If A is greater than or equal to 60.5, the computer will branch control to statement 150. If the value is less than 60.5, the next statement in sequence will be executed.

Example

90 IF A<>60.5 THEN 150

In this instance, the computer will determine whether or not the value of A is equal to 60.5. The branch to statement 150 will occur in all instances unless A is equal to 60.5.

Example

```
30 IF A < C THEN 70
```

In this example, two variables are being compared in an IF/THEN statement. When the computer reaches statement 30, it will compare A to C and branch control to statement 70 only if A is less than C.

Example

```
50 IF A = (C*D) THEN 100
```

This statement illustrates how an arithmetic expression can be evaluated in an IF statement. The computer will compute the value of C times D, clearing the parentheses. Then, it will compare the value of A to the product. Control will branch to statement 100 only if they are equal.

Alphabetic strings may be compared in an IF/THEN statement. The computer does this by assigning a numeric equivalent to each symbol in the standard character set. Thus, each alphanumeric character also has a numeric "code" number. The computer compares these code numbers to test an alphabetic string.

Figure 2.5 shows the numeric equivalent of each alphanumeric character in the column labeled "code." Alphabetic codes will differ among computer systems, but all are based on alphabetic order. Thus, "fox" will have a higher numeric equivalent than "company" and "except" will have a lower value than "expect."

Example

```
60 IF A$ = "ZZZZ" THEN 85
```

In this case, the computer is comparing an alphabetic variable (A$) to an alphabetic constant (ZZZZ). The computer converts both alphabetic strings to their numeric codes and compares the resulting values as though numeric quantities were involved. These values may be found by reference to Fig. 2.5. Alphabetic constants in an IF/THEN statement must be enclosed within quotation marks.

Example

```
80 IF A$>B$ THEN 165
```

This statement compares two alphabetic strings, using the relational operator greater than. The computer tests the numeric codes of A$ against B$ and transfers control to statement 165 only if the value of A$ is greater.

IF/THEN statements may be used in conjunction with trailer records to terminate program input from the keyboard or a DATA statement. In such a case, a test for last record is placed immediately after the INPUT or READ statement. Each time a record is input, the computer will test the specified variable. When the test value is equal to the trailer value, the computer will branch to the next procedure.

Example

```
50 READ A$, B
60 IF A$ = "ZZZZ" THEN 85
. . . . .
. . . . .
80 GO TO 50
85 . . . (continue processing)
```

If more than one variable is listed in a READ or INPUT statement, the trailer record must have a value for each. If there are not enough data to satisfy the number of variables in a READ or INPUT statement, an out-of-data error message will be generated before the computer can move to the next statement and test the trailer value. Therefore, in the example above, the trailer record should look like this:

```
150 DATA "ZZZZ",9
```

If the test value were numeric, the last record test might be written like this:

```
60 IF B = 999 THEN 85
```

The trailer record should have two values to satisfy the requirements of the READ statement.

```
150 DATA "Z",999
```

Example

```
IF (A/10) <= (B+C*3.14) THEN 200
```

Two numeric expressions will be evaluated and compared in this example. The computer will compute each expression and then compare the results. If the first expression is equal to or less than the second, the branch will take place. If the conditions are not true, the computer will continue line-by-line execution.

IF/THEN statements are often included in a BASIC program to give the programmer a means of directing program flow during interactive sessions.

Example

```
. . . . . .
100 PRINT "DO YOU WISH TO REPEAT THE CALCULATION?"
110 PRINT "ANSWER 1 FOR YES, 0 FOR NO."
120 INPUT A
130 IF A = 1 THEN 10
140 END
```

In this example, the program will print out a question to the programmer. Then it will test the answer (A) to see if he or she has input a 1, at which point it will branch back to the beginning of the program and continue processing. If the programmer has answered with a 0 (or any other character), control will drop to the next statement and, in this case, terminate execution.

This technique is also used to offer the programmer a selection of optional procedures during a program run.

RULES

1. IF/THEN statements are composed of the word IF followed by a quantity to be tested, a relational operator, the second quantity to be tested, the word THEN, and a statement number.

2. Only the relational operators shown may be used in the IF/THEN statement. (Systems may vary slightly in the symbols used to represent these operators.)

OPERATOR	MEANING
=	Equal to
>	Greater than
<	Less than
> =	Equal to or greater than
< =	Equal to or less than
< >	Not equal to

3. The IF/THEN statement is a conditional branch. The computer takes the alternate path only when the conditions specified by the relational operators are true. If they are not true, control passes to the next statement.

4. Numeric literals and variables may be compared in an IF/THEN statement. The comparison is exact: .9999 is not considered equal to 1.

5. Mathematical expressions, enclosed within parentheses, may be evaluated and compared in an IF/THEN statement.

6. Alphabetic strings and variables can be compared in an IF/THEN statement. The computer uses the numeric equivalents for the comparison. (See Fig. 2.5 for the numeric codes.) *Note:* Codes vary from one system to another.

7. Comparisons cannot be made between alphabetic and numeric values.

8. Alphabetic strings in an IF/THEN statement must be enclosed in quotation marks.

9. A trailer record must have a variable for each field listed in the READ or INPUT statements, even if only one field is tested.

EXERCISES

1. Find the errors, if any, in the following statements:
   a. 30 IF Y=Z THEN 100
   b. 50 IF Y=Y THEN 100
   c. 80 IF F IS EQUAL TO 5 THEN 20
   d. 90 IF A = 10 THEN 350
   e. 40 IF V "=" 8.3 THEN 29

2. Write a statement that tests an alphabetic string of three characters and branches to statement 90.

3. Write a statement that tests to see if one alphabetic string is greater than another.

4. Write a statement that tests the value of A against $3+D$ and branches to statement 140.
5. Write a statement that branches if X is not equal to 10.
6. Write a statement that tests whether C$ is equal to or greater than a literal constant.
7. Write a statement that evaluates two equations and compares the results.
8. Write a statement that adds three numbers and branches if the sum is greater than 100.
9. Give several examples of where conditional branches are used in a program.
10. List the common relational operators.

PURPOSE

Many BASIC interpreters have extensions—modifications or additional features added to the original Dartmouth BASIC. These extensions include tabbing to a column, PAUSE and PRINT USING statements, advanced matrix arithmetic statements, and so on. Your language implementation manual should be checked to see which are available on your system.

This unit discusses a very useful extension found on many BASIC interpreters—the TAB statement. The TAB statement directs the computer to move the carrier on the print unit to a given column before printing out data. It is much like the function of the TAB key on an ordinary typewriter.

The TAB command is used in a PRINT statement. The word TAB followed by a column number is inserted before the name of the data item to be output. It directs the computer to tab to the column specified and then print the item. A single PRINT statement may have one or more TAB statements within it.

GENERAL FORM

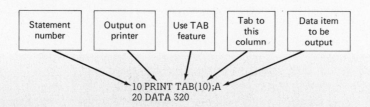

| Statement number | Output on printer | Use TAB feature | Tab to this column | Data item to be output |

```
10 PRINT TAB(10);A
20 DATA 320
```

OUTPUT
Column 10
  ↓

```
    320
```

When the computer encounters statement 10, it will tab to column 10 before print-ing out the value of A. The TAB instruction precedes the name of the variable, or data item being output. The column number after the word TAB is always enclosed within parentheses and followed by a semicolon. The first space of the field is left blank for the sign.

Example

```
10 LET X=8
20 PRINT TAB(X);A
30 DATA 500
```

OUTPUT
Column 8
  ↓

```
    500
```

In this example, a variable, X, is used in place of the column number. When the computer reaches statement 20, it will substitute the value of X (8) and tab over to column 8 before printing out A. Mathematical expressions can also be used as the column indica-tor.

Statements such as these are used when printing out charts, graphs, histograms, and so on. The value of the column indicator can be computed elsewhere in the program and substituted at the time the PRINT statement is executed.

Example

```
10 LET A=30
20 LET B=40
30 PRINT TAB(5);A;TAB(10);B
```

OUTPUT
Column Column
  5   10
  ↓   ↓

```
    30     40
```

In this instance, two TAB commands have been used in one PRINT statement. The computer will tab to column 5, print out the value of A (leaving the first space blank for the sign), tab to column 10, and then print out the value of B. A semicolon is inserted between the variable A and the next TAB command. If a comma had been used, the computer would have ignored the TAB command and printed out B at the next standard column spacing position.

Example

```
10 LET A=5
20 LET B=15
30 LET R=3089
40 LET N$="SMITH"
50 PRINT TAB (A+B);R;TAB(30);N$
```

OUTPUT

```
        Column    Column
        20        30
        ↓         ↓
```

```
        3089      SMITH
```

A mathematical expression has been used in statement 50 in conjunction with the TAB command. When the computer reaches statement 50, it will evaluate the expression (add A to B) and place the result within the parentheses. The computer will use this value as the column indicator, tabbing to column 20 to print out R and then to column 30 to print out N$ (SMITH).

RULES

1. The TAB command is a language extension and is not available on all systems. Check your language manual to learn which extensions are available on your system.

2. To tab to a given column before printing a data item, insert the word TAB in a PRINT statement followed by the column number enclosed within parentheses and a semicolon.

3. A numeric constant, variable, or mathematical expression may be placed within the parentheses of a TAB statement as the column indicator.

4. The TAB command must be set off from other elements in the PRINT statement by semicolons.

5. More than one TAB instruction may be used in a PRINT statement. Packed-zone spacing must be used in a PRINT statement with more than one TAB instruction.

6. The tabbing positions must move from left to right across the page. The carrier cannot backspace.

EXERCISES

1. Find the errors, if any, in the following statements:

    a. `5 PRINT TAB(5);A5`
    b. `20 PRINT TAB4;A`
    c. `50 PRINT TAB(L);10`

       d. `70 PRINT TAB(5)A,TAB(20)B`
       e. `65 PRINT TAB(2,5);X`

2. Write a statement that prints out an alphabetic quantity beginning in column 51.
3. Write a statement that prints out two numeric quantities in columns 20 and 30.
4. Write a statement that prints out six numeric quantities tabbed 10 spaces apart.
5. Write a statement that prints out two alphabetic and two numeric quantities, alternately, spaced 10 spaces apart and beginning in column 5.
6. Write a statement in which the column number of the TAB command is the result of a calculation in a previous statement.
7. Write a PRINT statement in which the column number of the TAB command is the result of summing R and L.
8. Write a PRINT statement in which the column number of the TAB command is the difference between A and B.
9. How does the TAB command save programming effort?
10. What is meant by a language extension?

STANDARD FUNCTIONS (SQR, LOG, RND...)

PURPOSE

An important feature of BASIC is the standard, or built-in, functions written into the interpreter. A function is a subroutine, or program, that performs a specific mathematical operation, such as generating random numbers and finding absolute value, square roots, cosines, and so on. A programmer can use a standard function in his or her program by including a statement giving the name of the function and the value it is to operate on.

The commonly available functions are given in the following table:

FUNCTION	PURPOSE
ABS(X)	Absolute value of X
ATN(X)	Angle (in radians) whose tangent is X
COS(X)	Cosine of X radians
EXP(X)	Natural exponent of X (e to the power X)
INT(X)	Integral part of X
LOG(X)	Logarithm of X to the base e (In x)
RND(X)	A random number between 0 and 1

SGN(X)	Sign of X, defined as:
	    If $X < 0$ SGN(X) $= -1$
	    If $X = 0$ SGN(X) $= 0$
	    If $X > 0$ SGN(X) $= +1$

SIN(X)	Sine of X radians
SQR(X)	Positive square root of X
TAN(X)	Tangent of X radians

Some computing systems have additional standard functions available. The programmer should consult his or her language manual for details on available functions.

Each function has a name consisting of three letters followed by an X in parentheses. The quantity within the parentheses is called the *argument*. The argument represents the quantity to be operated upon. The programmer replaces the dummy argument (X) with the value he or she wants the function to manipulate. When the statement is executed, the computer will call the standard function from storage and execute it on the argument. The resulting value will be stored under the assigned name to the left of the equals sign. This value may be printed out or used for further calculations during the program run.

GENERAL FORM

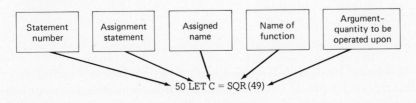

| Statement number | Assignment statement | Assigned name | Name of function | Argument–quantity to be operated upon |

50 LET C = SQR (49)

RESULT

7

Statement 50 calls out the standard function SQR, which computes the square root of the argument, 49. When the computer reaches this statement, it will call the standard function for square root from the interpreter, compute the square root (7), and place the result under the name C. All standard functions must be followed by an argument (the value to be operated upon). The argument may be either a constant, a variable, or an arithmetic expression.

Example

```
50 LET A = 68
60 LET B=SQR (A+32)
```

RESULT

10

In this example, the computer is to calculate the square root of an arithmetic expression. The computer will first evaluate the expression ($68+32=100$). Then it will compute the square root from 100 (10) and place it in storage under the name B.

Example

```
10 LET A = (−10.2)
20 PRINT ABS(A)
```

OUTPUT

10.2

This example calls in the standard function ABS, which computes the absolute value of an argument. The absolute value is a number without any sign. When the computer reaches statement 20, it will substitute the value −10.2 for the variable name A, drop the sign, and print out the resulting number. (Note that parentheses are placed around −10.2 so that the minus sign and the equals sign will not be adjacent. This would generate an error message.)

Example

```
60 LET R = 19.30
70 PRINT INT(R)
```

OUTPUT

```
19
```

The standard function INT is called into use in this example. The INT function will retain the integer part of a number and discard the remaining fractional portion. When the computer reaches statement 70, it will determine the integer portion of the 19.30 and print it out (19).

The INT function can be used as a convenient way of rounding off numbers. First, add one-half the base of the numbering system to the value, then drop the fractional part of the result. In the following example, the programmer wants to round off the value of T (a decimal number, base 10):

Example

```
100 LET T = 29.70
110 PRINT INT(T+.5)
```

OUTPUT

```
30
```

When the computer reaches statement 110, it will add .5 to the value of T (29.70 + .5 = 30.20), save the integer part of the sum (30), and print it out. If the fractional part of a value is less than 5, it will still be fractional after .5 has been added to it and will be dropped by the INT function. 29.40 + .5 = 29.9, INT value = 29.

Another very useful standard function in BASIC is the RND function, which computes a pseudo random number. Random numbers are numbers that occur by chance—that is, each number in a set has the same possibility of appearing each time. For example, a die contains symbols representing the numbers from 1 to 6. Each time the die is tossed, each of the six numbers has the same chance of landing on top.

Random numbers are frequently used in programs such as games, where the programmer wants to introduce the element of chance.

The random-number generator in the BASIC interpreter is designed to produce six-digit numbers ranging from 0 to 1. A 0 used as the argument will produce a different random number each time the statement is executed, but the program will always start with the same number each time it is run. If a negative number is used as the argument, a different starting number will be produced each time the program is run. If a positive number is used as the argument, the same number will be generated each time the statement is executed.

Random numbers can be manipulated to produce whole numbers and to limit their range. For example, on some systems the statement

```
100 PRINT RND(0)
```

will produce the following output:

```
.936719
```

If we multiply this value by 10, as follows,

```
100 PRINT (10*RND(0))
```

we will get

```
9.36719
```

Using the INT function to drop the fractional part,

```
100 PRINT INT (10*RND(0))
```

would produce

```
9
```

This gives us a whole number equal to or greater than 0. Since the highest possible fractional value would be .999999, which converts to 9, this technique also sets the upper limit of the range of random numbers (in this case, 9). If the random value were multiplied by 100, the upper limit would be 90 (100 × .9); if it were 31, the limit would be 27 (31 × .9), and so on.

Placing this statement in a loop would produce the following five random numbers:

```
10 FOR I=1 TO 5
20 PRINT INT(10*RND(0))
30 NEXT I

OUTPUT

9
3
0
6
7
```

Since the argument is a 0, the program will generate 9 as the first random number each time it is executed on that system.

Example

```
10 PRINT INT (1+(10*RND(0)))
```

This statement illustrates another way to manipulate the range in which the random numbers will fall. A 1 will be added to the random numbers generated, and all numbers generated will be between 1 and 10 (9 + 1). If a 5 had been used instead of a 1, all numbers would be between 5 and 14 (9 + 5).

Example

```
10 PRINT INT(1+(13*RND(-1)))
```

This statement will produce random numbers ranging from 1 to 13. The numbers will be different each time the program is run. These numbers might represent a pair of dice being used in a game.

Placing this statement in a loop would represent five dice being tossed.

OUTPUT

```
11
2
4
7
9
```

The RND function can be used in a game to branch to different paths depending on the score on the dice:

```
. . . . .
40 LET A = INT(1 + (13*RND(-1)))
50 IF A > 10 THEN 100
60 IF A < 10 THEN 150
. . . . .
```

RULES

1. Only the standard functions available on a system may be used in a BASIC program. The language manual should be consulted for a list of functions available.

2. A function is called in by its three-letter name and an argument.

3. The argument represents the quantity to be operated on and is always placed within parentheses.

4. Arguments may consist of numeric constants, variables, or arithmetic expressions. The computer will perform the function on the argument and either output results or place them in storage under an assigned name.

5. A function may be used in a LET statement or a PRINT statement. In a LET statement, the results are stored under the assigned name to the left of the equals sign. In a PRINT statement, the results are output.

6. The RND function calls in a random-number generator, which outputs six-digit numbers between 0 and 1. If the argument is a negative value, the computer will output different numbers each time the program is executed. A 0 as the argument directs the computer to generate the same starting number each time the program is executed. A positive number will result in the same number being generated each time that number is used as the argument.

7. Only one value, or answer, is returned to the main program by a function.

EXERCISES

1. Find the errors, if any, in the following statements:
   a. 55 LET S=SQR(S1)
   b. 89 LET B=INT(X)
   c. 30 PRINT "LOG";X'LOG(X)
   d. 60 LET T=SQR
   e. 80 READ ABS(A)

2. Write the statement that calculates the absolute value of X and places it under Z.
3. Write a statement that prints out the cosine of X radians.
4. Write a statement that will generate a random number between 0 and 1.
5. Write a statement that will generate a random number between 1 and 10.
6. Write a statement that will generate a random number between 3 and 33.
7. Write a statement that will generate the same sequence of random numbers each time the program is run.
8. Write a statement that will generate a different random number each time the program is run.
9. Write a statement that will round off the value of Y.
10. Write a statement that will print out and round off the result of the calculation A*6.

USER-DEFINED FUNCTIONS (DEF STATEMENTS)

PURPOSE

BASIC allows a user to write his or her own functions and call them into use in a program as needed. Up to 26 user-defined functions may be placed in a single program.

User-defined functions are used where a mathematical sequence is to be repeated several times in one program. If these instructions are written as a user-defined function, they need only be coded once and can then be called out as often as desired.

A user-defined function is named, described, and coded in a DEF statement. The function is called in elsewhere in the program by the name assigned in the DEF statement. It will operate on an argument as though it were a standard function, outputting results or placing them in storage under an assigned name.

GENERAL FORM

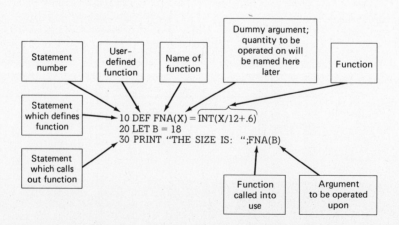

OUTPUT

THE SIZE IS: 2			

The function is first defined using the DEF statement, which names and describes the function. Names of user-defined functions have three alphabetic letters. The first two must be F and N. The last is an assigned alphabetic letter. For example, FNA, FNB, and FNY are acceptable names. Twenty-six functions can be named in one program.

Statement 10 in the example above is a DEF statement that assigns the name FNA to a user-defined function. The variable X in parentheses next to the name is a dummy argument and will later be replaced by the value to be operated upon. The mathematical expression on the right of the equals sign is the user-defined function. In this example, it is a formula that converts inches into feet, rounding off the answer to the nearest foot.

Statement 20 assigns a value to the variable B. Statement 30 calls in the user-defined function FNA and directs it to operate upon the argument named B. The computer will substitute the value of B (18) for the dummy argument X in the DEF statement and proceed to process B following the steps indicated in the function.

First, it divides 18 by 12, giving 1.5. Next, it adds .6, giving 2.1. Then, it retains the integer part of the number and drops the fraction. The answer, 2, is printed out as directed. FNA will probably be used several times during the program, operating on different variables each time.

Example

```
10 DEF FNR(X) = INT(1+(31*RND(-1)))
20 PRINT "YOUR ENROLLMENT DATE IS JULY";FNR(X)
30 PRINT "YOUR REGISTRATION DATE IS AUGUST";FNR(X)
40 END
```

OUTPUT

```
YOUR ENROLLMENT DATE IS JULY 30
YOUR REGISTRATION DATE IS AUGUST 4
```

In this example, a user-defined function is used to assign enrollment and registration dates on a random basis. (The use of the random number generator was described in the unit on standard functions.) At statement 10, the computer will set up a function called FNR, which generates a random number between 1 and 31. Statement 20 prints out a literal line of text and the first random number. Statement 30 calls in the user-defined function again and prints the next random number. (Since a random-number generator is being used, the dummy argument does not have to be replaced.)

Example

```
10 DEF FNP(X) = X+(X*.4+2)
20 READ A,B,C
30 PRINT "SALE PRICE, CUFFLINKS $";FNP(A)
40 PRINT "SALE PRICE, LOCKETS $";FNP(B)
50 PRINT "SALE PRICE, EARRINGS $";FNP(C)
60 DATA 6.20, 9.18, 7.98
```

OUTPUT

```
SALE PRICE, CUFFLINKS $ 10.68
SALE PRICE, LOCKETS $ 14.852
SALE PRICE, EARRINGS $ 13.172
```

In this example, a user-defined function that calculates the sale price of an item, based upon its wholesale cost, is called in to operate upon three different categories. Statement 10 names and defines the function, FNP. First, it calculates 40 percent of the wholesale cost. Then, it adds $2 for handling and the 40 percent markup to the wholesale cost. When statement 30 is reached, the computer will call in the function FNP and calculate the selling price of the first variable, A. At statement 40, it calculates the sale price for item B and at statement 50 that for item C.

User-defined functions can be written to round off and truncate a number that has several places past the decimal. The user-defined function below will print out a number with only the number of decimal places that the programmer has indicated. This allows the programmer to conveniently print out dollars and cents amounts, for example.

Example

```
DEF FNT(X)=INT(X*1E2+.5)*1E2
```

If X = 10.69452
then the output will be 10.69
If X = 213.999
then the output will be 214.00
The number of places output past the decimal can be controlled by varying the number in the term 1E2. If it is 1E2, then two places will be output. If it is 1E4, then four places will appear. If it is 1E5, then five places are output.

RULES

1. User-defined functions are named and described in a DEF statement. The DEF statement must appear ahead of any statement that calls out the function.

2. The name assigned to the function must begin with the letters F and N and end with one of the 26 letters of the alphabet. Examples: FNE, FNY, FNZ.

3. When the user-defined function is called into the program, the dummy argument shown in the DEF statement must be replaced with the argument on which it is to operate.

4. The mathematical equation in a user-defined function may include other user-defined functions or standard functions.

5. The results of the user-defined function will be printed out or stored under the name assigned by the programmer; they can be used for other calculations later in the program.

6. Only one value is returned to the main program from the user-defined function.

7. A user-defined function may be called out by a LET statement or a PRINT statement.

8. A separate DEF statement must be inserted for each user-defined function in a program.

9. A user-defined function in one program cannot be called in by another program. Each program must have its own DEF statements.

10. Some systems allow user-defined functions to extend onto two or more lines. Check your language manual for details.

11. The mathematical equation defined in the user-defined function may contain numeric variables and constants, other user-defined functions, and standard functions.

EXERCISES

1. Find the errors, if any, in the following statements:
   a. `100 DEF FNZ(X)=A*B/C`
   b. `32 DEF FNB=A*B`
   c. `10 FNA(X)=INT (X/12+.6)`
   d. `20 DEF FNA$(X)=(C$;S$)`
   e. `PRINT "OUTPUT";FNA(L)`

2. Write a user-defined function that adds two variables and divides the sum by 3.
3. Write a user-defined function that calculates simple interest. (Interest= principal * rate * time.)
4. Write a user-defined function that contains a random-number generator.
5. Write a user-defined function that adds 100 and squares a number.
6. Write a user-defined function that adds 40 percent to the cost of goods and prints out the selling price.
7. What are the naming conventions regarding user-defined functions?
8. How many user-defined functions can be placed in a single program?
9. In what situations are user-defined functions useful?
10. What is the "dummy argument" in the user-defined function?

REPEAT A SEQUENCE (FOR/NEXT STATEMENTS)

PURPOSE

The ability to repeat a sequence, or group of instructions, is an important technique available to the programmer. It becomes an even more valuable tool when the number of repetitions made can be determined and limited with ease and convenience. FOR/NEXT statements serve this purpose in BASIC programming. They direct the computer to repeat a particular group of instructions a specified number of times and then to move to the next statement in the program and continue processing.

The FOR/NEXT loop consists of two control statements: (1) the FOR statement, which tells the computer which instructions to repeat and the number of times to do so and (2) the NEXT statement, which marks the end of the range of the loop.

The statements to be repeated will be inserted between the FOR and NEXT commands. The computer repeats the sequence within the loop, automatically keeping track of the number of times the sequence is executed, until the limit set by the programmer is reached. After it has reached the limit, the computer drops down to the next statement in the program.

Looping can also be set up and controlled by using GOTO statements and counters. In some instances, this is the only way it can be done. But this method tends to be more inefficient than using FOR/NEXT loops.

GENERAL FORM

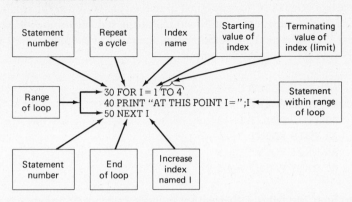

In this example, a PRINT statement is placed within the range of a FOR/NEXT loop. Statements 30 and 50 contain the necessary instructions to perform the looping sequence. When the computer reaches statement 30, it will set up an index I (name assigned by the programmer) to keep tally of the number of times the loop is executed. The starting value of I is set at 1 and the limiting value at 4. The computer will execute the instructions down to the NEXT statement (50). Then, it will increase the index by 1 and test it against the limit. If it does not exceed the limit, the computer will repeat the statements within the range of the FOR/NEXT loop. In the example above, the sequence will be repeated four times. When the index exceeds the limit, the computer will drop down to the next statement in the program and continue processing.

A PRINT statement that prints out a literal message and the value of its index, I, has been placed within the range of a FOR/NEXT loop. It will be repeated four times, printing out a different value of I each pass:

```
First Pass:    AT THIS POINT I = 1
Second Pass:   AT THIS POINT I = 2
Third Pass     AT THIS POINT I = 3
Fourth Pass    AT THIS POINT I = 4
```

At the end of the first pass, the index will equal 1; the second pass, 2; the third, 3; and the fourth, 4. The computer will increase the index to 5 and test it against the limit. Since it exceeds the limit, looping will stop.

On some systems, I will now be equal to 5. On others, its value will be returned to 4. Since the value of I is sometimes used in a program to control repetitions of other procedures or in calculations, and so on, care must be taken to learn how your system handles this particular point.

Example

```
50 LET N=6
60 FOR I=1 TO N
70  PRINT "AT THIS POINT I=";I
80 NEXT I
```

In this example, the limit of the loop is set to N. The computer will execute the loop N times. The actual value of N (6) is assigned in statement 50. When the computer reaches statement 60, it will substitute 6 for N and repeat the statements down to statement 80 six times. A PRINT statement, placed within the range of the loop, will be executed six times and produce the following output:

```
First Pass:     AT THIS POINT I= 1
Second Pass:    AT THIS POINT I= 2
Third Pass:     AT THIS POINT I= 3
Fourth Pass:    AT THIS POINT I= 4
Fifth Pass:     AT THIS POINT I= 5
Sixth Pass:     AT THIS POINT I= 6
```

The ability to limit the index, either with a numeric constant or a dummy value (such as N, X, etc.), gives the programmer more flexibility in programming. The value of the dummy variable can be assigned elsewhere in the program by substituting the results of a calculation, by using a counter, from the keyboard (with an INPUT statement), and so forth.

In the examples above, the statements within the range of the FOR/NEXT loops are indented one or more spaces. This is done only for clarity to help the programmer locate the loops in his program easily. They may be keyboarded flush left if the programmer prefers.

In the previous examples, all the indexes began at 1 and increased by 1 each pass. If the programmer requires, he or she can use other values to initialize and increment the index.

Example

```
40 FOR I=5 TO 25 STEP 5
50  PRINT "AT THIS POINT I=";I
60 NEXT I
```

In this example, the index starts at 5 and will stop at 25. The increment, or "step," is 5. To indicate an increment other than 1, the programmer inserts the word STEP followed by the incremental value at the end of the FOR statement. The output from this example will look like the following:

```
First Pass:     AT THIS POINT I= 5
Second Pass:    AT THIS POINT I= 10
Third Pass:     AT THIS POINT I= 15
Fourth Pass:    AT THIS POINT I= 20
Fifth Pass:     AT THIS POINT I= 25
```

If the increment, or step, clause is omitted from the FOR statement, the step value is assumed to be 1. If the step value is any number other than 1, the STEP clause must be included in the statement.

Mathematical expressions may also be used to set the initial value of the index and the increment and its limit.

Example

```
10 LET B=10
20 LET L=27-2
30 LET S=4
40 FOR I=(B-5) TO L STEP (S+1)
50  PRINT "I=";I, "L=";L, "S=";(S+1)
60 NEXT I
70 END
```

In this example, simple mathematical expressions are used to set the initial value of the index and the step. The limit has been assigned in statement 20. Index I is derived by taking the value of B established in line 10 and subtracting 5. Output will be

```
I= 5      L= 25     S= 5
I= 10     L= 25     S= 5
I= 15     L= 25     S= 5
I= 20     L= 25     S= 5
I= 25     L= 25     S= 5
```

Example

```
10 FOR I=0 TO 1 STEP .2
20  PRINT "AT THIS POINT I=";I
30 NEXT I
40 END
```

This example illustrates the use of a fractional value as the step. The computer will execute the loop six times, and the output will be as follows:

First Pass: AT THIS POINT I= 0
Second Pass: AT THIS POINT I= .2
Third Pass: AT THIS POINT I= .4
Fourth Pass: AT THIS POINT I= .6
Fifth Pass: AT THIS POINT I= .8
Sixth Pass: AT THIS POINT I= 1

It is also possible to run an index in a negative direction, decreasing each pass.

Example

```
70 FOR K=9 TO 0 STEP -3
80  PRINT "AT THIS POINT K=";K
90 NEXT K
```

The resulting output is

First Pass: AT THIS POINT K= 9
Second Pass: AT THIS POINT K= 6
Third Pass: AT THIS POINT K= 3
Fourth Pass: AT THIS POINT K= 0

The initial value of the index K is set at 9 in this example, and its limit is set at 0. The computer will deduct 3 each pass, as instructed by the STEP −3 clause, until the limit has been reached. This is a useful technique in cases where the values of the limit and increment are assigned elsewhere in the program.

NESTED FOR/NEXT LOOPS

A FOR/NEXT loop may be placed within the range of another FOR/NEXT loop. This is called *nesting*. It allows the programmer to easily execute one or more procedures several times and then go back and repeat all the procedures again. The technique is used in sorting, calculating, printing out groups of data or tables, and so on. Nested loops are also used to process subscripted data, a technique that is explained in the next unit.

Example

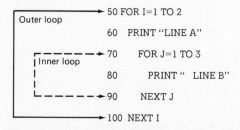

```
Outer loop ──────→ 50 FOR I=1 TO 2
                   60    PRINT "LINE A"
   ┌ ─ ─ ─ ─ →     70    FOR J=1 TO 3
   │ Inner loop
   │               80      PRINT "  LINE B"
   │
   └ ─ ─ ─ ─ →     90    NEXT J
           ──────→ 100 NEXT I
```

The output from the nested loops will be

```
LINE A
  LINE B
  LINE B
  LINE B
LINE A
  LINE B
  LINE B
  LINE B
```

Statement 50 directs the computer to execute the outer loop two times. It will first print the literal text LINE A and then move to statement 70, which marks the beginning of the inner loop. It will process the inner loop, printing out LINE B three times. Then it reaches line 100, which directs it back to line 50 to repeat the entire cycle again. Everytime the outer loop is executed, the inner loop will be repeated three times. Since there are two passes through the outer loop, there will be six repetitions of the inner loop. Note that the indexes of nested FOR/NEXT loops must have different names.

More than one loop can be nested within an outer loop. The following example shows one version and its output.

Example

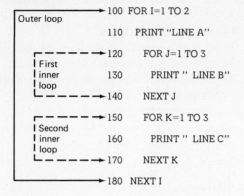

```
             ┌──────────→ 100  FOR I=1 TO 2
 Outer loop  │
             │            110    PRINT "LINE A"
             │
             │ ┌─ ─ ─ ─ ─→ 120    FOR J=1 TO 3
             │ │First
             │ │inner      130      PRINT " LINE B"
             │ │loop
             │ └─ ─ ─ ─ ─→ 140    NEXT J
             │
             │ ┌─ ─ ─ ─ ─→ 150    FOR K=1 TO 3
             │ │Second
             │ │inner      160      PRINT " LINE C"
             │ │loop
             │ └─ ─ ─ ─ ─→ 170    NEXT K
             │
             └──────────→ 180  NEXT I
```

OUTPUT

```
LINE A
   LINE B
   LINE B
   LINE B
      LINE C
      LINE C
      LINE C
LINE A
   LINE B
   LINE B
   LINE B
      LINE C
      LINE C
      LINE C
```

Each time the computer executes the outer loop, it will repeat the first inner loop three times and then the second inner loop three times. Afterwards it will branch back to repeat the entire cycle again.

RULES

1. The FOR/NEXT loop has two control statements. The FOR statement gives the assigned name of the index and its initial and terminating values and the increment. The NEXT statement contains the name of the index and marks the end of the range of the FOR/NEXT loop.

2. All statements within the range of the FOR/NEXT loop will be executed the number of times indicated in the FOR statement.

3. The index, limit, and increment of a FOR/NEXT loop can be mathematical expressions, numeric variables, or constants.

4. The values of the index, limit, and increment can be set or assigned elsewhere in the program.

5. Loops may be incremented by any value. The increment is indicated by including a STEP clause in the FOR statement. If no STEP clause is present, the increment is assumed to be 1.

6. Loops may increment in a positive or negative direction.

7. On some systems, the value of the index will be equal to the limit (or the closest step value) when the loop terminates. On others, it will be greater than the limit.

8. Loops may be nested. However, the range of one loop may not cross over another.

Permitted   Not permitted

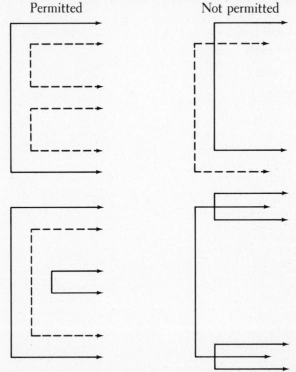

9. The index for each set of nested loops should have its own unique name.

10. The program can branch out of a FOR/NEXT loop at any point with an IF statement.

11. The programmer should branch to a FOR/NEXT loop only at the FOR statement. Branching into the range at any other point in the loop may give erroneous results and is not permitted on many systems.

12. For better program readability, lines within a FOR/NEXT loop should be indented.

EXERCISES

1. Find the errors, if any, in the following statements:
   a. 20 NEXT I
      30 . . .
      40 . . .
      50 FOR I=1 TO 4

b. 20 FOR K=1 TO 100
  . . .
  60 NEXT K
c. 33 FOR I=1 TO 33
  . . .
  39 NEXT K
d. 50 FOR A$=1 TO 40
  . . .
  90 NEXT A$
e. 100 FOR I=1 TO 2
  110 PRINT "REPEAT THIS LINE 20 TIMES"
  120 NEXT I

2. Write a FOR/NEXT loop that will repeat a PRINT statement 10 times.
3. Write a FOR/NEXT loop that will repeat a mathematical calculation four times.
4. Write a FOR/NEXT loop that will repeat a mathematical calculation 10 times and print out the result of each loop.
5. Write a FOR/NEXT loop that will repeat a PRINT statement 10 times with a step of 2.
6. Write the statements that will cause the computer to execute two FOR/NEXT loops in sequence.
7. Write the statements that will cause the computer to execute an outer FOR/NEXT loop 5 times and an inner loop 10 times.
8. Write the statements that will cause the computer to execute an outer FOR/NEXT loop three times, one inner loop two times, and a second inner loop four times.
9. Write a FOR/NEXT loop in which the limit and counter are set by calculations elsewhere in the program.
10. Write a FOR/NEXT loop that will print out the value of its index.

USING SUBSCRIPTS TO STORE DATA (DIM STATEMENT, SUBSCRIPTS)

PURPOSE

It is the programmer's responsibility to assign storage locations to hold data being read in via the READ and INPUT statements. He or she does this by giving each storage location a unique name (sometimes called an address). The computer will automatically load the data into the proper storage locations as they are read in. The programmer can reference each piece of data later by using the name (or address) of the location in which it is stored.

When only a few pieces of data are to be read into storage, it is practical for the programmer to assign the names. However, if many pieces of data are involved, it is more convenient to direct the computer to assign the names automatically. In BASIC, this is done by telling the computer to reserve a sufficient number of adjacent storage locations to hold all the data. This block of locations, called an *array*, is assigned one name by the programmer. The computer will automatically assign a number, called a *subscript*, to each location in the array, depending on its position. In this way, each location has a unique name—the array name and a subscript. The data stored in that location can be referenced by using its unique name.

In BASIC, a DIM statement is used to reserve the storage slots for the data to be read in. READ or INPUT statements are inserted within a FOR/NEXT loop to read in the data and assign it to the proper locations in the array.

Arrays can also be loaded with loops composed of counters and GOTO statements. As a rule, though, the FOR/NEXT loops will be more efficient and convenient for the programmer to use.

GENERAL FORM

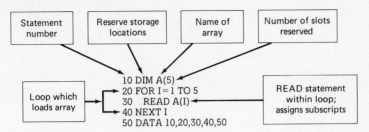

Statement 10 names an array A and reserves five adjacent storage locations. The FOR/NEXT loop directs the computer to read in five pieces of data and assign each to a unique storage location. In the first pass, I=1, and the computer reads in the first piece of data (10). It substitutes the value of I in statement 30 and assigns the data to the storage location, A(1). In the second pass, I=2, and data item 20 is stored in A(2). When execution of the FOR/NEXT loop is terminated, the data in storage will look like this:

ARRAY A

STORAGE LOCATION (ARRAY NAME AND SUBSCRIPT)	DATA IN STORAGE
A(1)	10
A(2)	20
A(3)	30
A(4)	40
A(5)	50

The DIM statement must always appear in the program before the arrays listed in it are loaded. DIM statements are often placed first in the program.

Any single element in the array may be printed out or used elsewhere in the program by reference to its name and subscript. For example,

```
LET C = A(2)
```

would assign the value of A(2), or 20, to C.

In the example

```
LET D = A(1) + A(5) + 40
```

the result would be D=100.

The value of the subscript can be substituted from another instruction. A dummy subscript is used to do this:

```
LET I = 4
. . .
. . .
LET D = A(I)
```

In this example, D would be equal to 40.

If I were a counter in a loop, its value would change each pass, and in this way the programmer could easily perform a series of mathematical calculations on each item in the array:

```
50 LET I = I + 1
60 LET D = A(I)
· · · · ·
· · · · ·
100 GOTO 50
```

In this example, each time the computer executes the loop, the value of I increases by 1. The new value of I is substituted in statement 60 and calls out the next element in the array.

Calculations can also be performed within a FOR/NEXT loop:

```
50 FOR I = 1 TO 5
60  LET D = A(I)
· · · ·
· · · ·
100 NEXT I
```

A single item in an array can be printed out by using its unique name:

```
120 PRINT A(4)
```

The output would be.

40			

An entire array can be printed out using a FOR/NEXT loop. Since the PRINT statement is not followed by punctuation, each element in the array will be printed out on a separate line as follows:

```
60 FOR I = 1 TO 5
70  PRINT A(I)
80 NEXT I
```

```
1
2
3
4
5
```

A comma in statement 70 would result in standard column spacing:

```
70 PRINT A(I),
```

1	2	3	4	5

A semicolon in statement 70 would result in packed-zone spacing:

```
70 PRINT A(I);
```

1	2	3	4	5			

The programmer may, in some cases, want the subscripting to start with a number other than 1. To do this, he or she uses these numbers as the initializing and terminating values of the index:

```
10 DIM A(5)
20 FOR I = 6 TO 10
30  READ A(I)
40 NEXT I
50 DATA 1,2,3,4,5
```

The computer will assign the first item (1) to storage location A(6), the second (2) to A(7), and so on.

Example

A program may contain several arrays. Each one must have its own array name and sufficient storage spaces. One DIM statement may be used to set up several arrays.

There are several ways to load arrays when more than one is present. They can all be loaded by one READ statement, or each loaded individually. The contents of the loaded arrays will differ, depending on the method used.

For example, to load two arrays with one FOR/NEXT loop,

```
10 DIM A(5), B(5)
20 FOR I = 1 TO 5
30  READ A(I), B(I)
40 NEXT I
50 DATA 10,20,30,40,50,60,70,80,90,100
```

This program sets up and loads two arrays, A and B. In each pass through the FOR/NEXT loop, the computer will load one item into each array. Both dummy subscripts must have the same name as the index in the FOR statement.

This is how the arrays look in storage:

LOCATION (ROW)	ARRAY A	ARRAY B
1	10	20
2	30	40
3	50	60
4	70	80
5	90	100

In the first pass, the index I is equal to 1. The first piece of data will be loaded into array A. The computer will substitute the value of I and assign it to location 1. The second piece of data (20) will be loaded into location 1 of array B. In the second pass,

I is equal to 2. The third piece of data (30) will be loaded into location 2 of array A, and the fourth piece of data into location 2 of array B. This will continue until both arrays are loaded. Under this arrangement, the arrays are loaded alternately. If three arrays were being loaded, the first location of each would load first, then the second, and so on.

Example
In this example, the programmer wants to load each array separately:

```
10 DIM A(5), B(5)
20 FOR I=1 TO 5
30  READ A(I)
40 NEXT I
50 FOR I=1 TO 5
60  READ B(I)
70 NEXT I
80 DATA 10,20,30,40,50,60,70,80,90,100
```

The computer will set up two arrays, A and B, as before. However, array A will load first and then array B. The computer executes the first FOR/NEXT loop five times, loading the first five pieces of data into array A. Then, it drops to the second FOR/NEXT loop and loads the remaining five pieces of data into array B. The data in storage looks like this:

LOCATION (ROW)	ARRAY A	ARRAY B
1	10	60
2	20	70
3	30	80
4	40	90
5	50	100

Alphabetic as well as numeric data can also be loaded into arrays. A DIM statement must reserve a sufficient number of slots to hold the data.

Example

```
10 DIM A$(4)
20 FOR I=1 TO 4
30  READ A$(I)
40 NEXT I
50 DATA "GLENN", "JIM", "SUE", "KAREN"
```

When the computer encounters statement 10, it will set aside four adjacent storage locations and name them A$. The FOR/NEXT loop will load the alphabetic data listed in statement 50 into the array. The data in storage will look like this:

LOCATION (ROW)	ARRAY A$
1	GLENN
2	JIM
3	SUE
4	KAREN

The contents of the array may be printed out by placing a PRINT statement in a FOR/NEXT loop:

```
70 FOR I=1 TO 4
80  PRINT A$ (I)
90 NEXT I
```

Since no punctuation has been used in statement 80, the output will appear this way:

```
GLENN
JIM
SUE
KAREN
```

Punctuation can be used to modify the output as follows:

```
80 PRINT A$(I),
```

OUTPUT:

GLENN	JIM	SUE	KAREN

Up to this point, all the examples of arrays we have discussed are *one-dimensional arrays,* which means that they are one column wide. The elements are loaded into the array from the top row down to the bottom row of one column. This kind of manipulation is suitable for many kinds of data but not adequate for loading large amounts of tabular data into the computer.

Two-dimensional arrays, which store data in two or more columns, are used to process tabular data. The DIM statement, which reserves storage spaces for a two-dimensional array, must tell the computer how many columns are needed and how many rows will be in each column.

For example,

```
10 DIM A(8,4),B(3,6)
```

Array A will have eight rows and four columns. Array B will have three rows and six columns. Note that the row dimension is listed first, followed by the columns. If no column dimension is listed, it is assumed to be 1.

Nested FOR/NEXT loops are used to manipulate data in a two-dimensional array.

Below is an example illustrating how 20 numbers are loaded into an array with four rows and five columns.

Example

```
10 DIM A(4,5)
20 FOR I=1 TO 4
30  FOR J=1 TO 5
40   READ (I,J)
50  NEXT J
60 NEXT I
70 DATA 10,20,30,40,50,60,70,80,90,100
80 DATA 110,120,130,140,150,160,170,180,190,200
```

Statement 10 reserves a two-dimensional array, A, with five columns and four rows. Statements 20 to 60 are nested FOR/NEXT loops, which will load the data into the array as follows:

ARRAY A

ROW	COLUMNS				
	$J=1$	$J=2$	$J=3$	$J=4$	$J=5$
$I=1$	10	20	30	40	50
$I=2$	60	70	80	90	100
$I=3$	110	120	130	140	150
$I=4$	160	170	180	190	200

The first pass through the outer loop, the I index, which loads the rows, is set at 1. The J index of the inner loop will load the columns. The first pass through the outer loop, $J=1$ and data item (10), is stored in location A(1,1)—the first row of the first column. The inner loop is repeated: $J=2$ and the next data item (20) is placed in location A(1,2)—the first row of the second column. Then, J becomes equal to 3 and the next data item is loaded into A(1,3). This continues for two more repetitions of the inner loop. After the fifth pass through the inner loop, control will return to statement 20 and I will be set to 2. Index J will be reset to 1 and the second row of the columns will be loaded. This process continues until all rows have been loaded.

Once an array is loaded, the programmer can direct the computer to print out its contents by placing a PRINT statement in nested FOR/NEXT loops:

Example

```
80 FOR I=1 TO 4
90  FOR J=1 TO 5
100   PRINT (I,J),
110  NEXT J
120 NEXT I
```

Since a comma has been used as punctuation in statement 100, the standard column spacing will be used in the output:

10	20	30	40	50
60	70	80	90	100
110	120	130	140	150
160	170	180	190	200

The rules that the computer follows when printing out arrays are slightly different from those used in printing single items. A comma used as punctuation will direct the computer to print out all items in the array in standard column spacing. The items will be printed out, five to a line, across the page, regardless of the number of columns in the array.

If a semicolon is used as punctuation, all items will be printed out in packed-zone format, six or more to a line, depending on the number of digits in each value. The number of columns in the arrays will have no effect on how many values are printed out on one line.

For example, if line 100 appeared as

```
100 PRINT (I,J);
```

the output would be

10	20	30	40	50	60	70	80	90	100	110	120
130	140	150	160	170	180	190	200				

If no punctuation is used, each piece of data is output on a separate line.

If the programmer wants to print out an array using less than five columns across the page, he or she must explicitly direct the computer to do so, by calling out each column by name.

For example, these statements will print out columns 1, 2, and 3 of array A in standard column spacing:

```
80 FOR I=1 TO 4
100  PRINT (I,1),(I,2),(I,3)
120 NEXT I
```

OUTPUT

10	20	30	
60	70	80	
110	120	130	
160	170	180	

This example will print out all five columns in packed-zone spacing:

```
80 FOR I=1 TO 4
100  PRINT (I,1);(I,2);(I,3);(I,4);(I,5)
110 NEXT I
```

OUTPUT

10	20	30	40	50
60	70	80	90	100
110	120	130	140	150
160	170	180	190	200

In the examples above, the arrays were loaded horizontally. Arrays can be loaded vertically by reversing the indexes in the nested FOR/NEXT loops. Since the index in the inner loop is satisfied first, it controls which dimension is filled first. In this example, the I index loads the rows and the J index the columns.

Example

```
10 DIM B(4,5)
20 FOR J=1 TO 5
30   FOR I=1 TO 4
40     READ B(I,J)
50   NEXT I
60 NEXT J
70 DATA 10,20,30,40,50,60,70,80,90,100
80 DATA 110,120,130,140,150,160,170,180,190,200
```

Data in storage:

ARRAY B

ROW	COLUMNS				
	J=1	J=2	J=3	J=4	J=5
I=1	10	50	90	130	170
I=2	20	60	100	140	180
I=3	30	70	110	150	190
I=4	40	80	120	160	200

Single elements in a two-dimensional array can be used in other processes in the program by referencing their unique names. For example, LET C = B(3,4) will assign the value of the element stored in the third row, fourth column, of array B to C. C will be equal to 150.

Alphabetic data can also be loaded into two-dimensional arrays on some systems. The length of the character string permitted will vary with the system; the student should check his language manual for details.

RULES

1. Storage locations for an array must be reserved by a DIM statement. It must show the number of rows and columns in the array. If the number of columns is omitted, it is assumed to be one. Examples:

        DIM A(8,6) DIM B(10)

2. More than one array may be dimensioned in a single DIM statement.

3. The DIM statement must appear in the program before its arrays are loaded.

4. All storage spaces reserved for an array do not have to be filled by the program. But if the program attempts to load more data than there are reserved locations, an error condition may be present.

5. If an array is being loaded by one or more FOR/NEXT loops, there must be a sufficient number of data items to satisfy the indexes.

6. An element in an array may be referenced by the array name and the subscripts assigned to its storage location. An element may be used elsewhere in the program—in calculations, print statements, and so on.

7. Arrays can be manipulated by placing the processing statements within the range of a FOR/NEXT loop or a loop controlled by a counter and GOTO statement. Nested loops are used to manipulate two-dimensional arrays.

8. The dummy subscript names in the arrays must be the same as the index names in the FOR/NEXT loops or counters in order to come under their control.

9. More than one array can be manipulated in one statement. If more than one array is in a READ statement, they will be loaded alternately. The arrays must have the same number of elements.

10. Arrays may hold either numeric or alphanumeric data. The name of the array must agree with the rules for naming variables.

11. Two-dimensional alphabetic arrays are not permitted on some systems. Check language manual for details.

12. The number of characters in an alphabetic string read in under one name in an array varies with the system. Check language manuals for details.

13. Two-dimensional arrays may be manipulated either horizontally or vertically depending on the order of the indexes in the controlling loops. The index in the inner loop will be satisfied first.

14. Subscripts do not have to begin at 1. The programmer may direct the computer to assign subscripts starting with another number by using this value to initialize the index in the statement that loads the array.

15. The computer can be directed to print out elements in an array in standard column spacing, packed-zone spacing, or single lines by using the appropriate punctuation in a PRINT statement.

16. The computer will print out elements in an array five on a line in standard column spacing, or six or more on a line using packed-zone spacing, regardless of the number of columns in the array.

17. If the programmer wishes to print out the array in a nonstandard format, he or she must call out the columns by name:

        PRINT A(I,1),A(I,2),A(I,3)

EXERCISES

   1. Find the errors, if any, in the following statements:
      a. ARRAY A(12)
      b. DIM DIM(6)

    c. DIM A(2), B(2), C(6)
    d. DIM T(2,4), Z(4,2)
    e. DIM X(I)

2. Write the statement that will direct the computer to set aside five storage locations for an array named L.
3. Write the statements that will set aside 33 storage locations for the array named Q$.
4. Write the statement that will set aside storage locations for four arrays.
5. Write the statement that will set aside storage locations for an array named E that is 5×10 in size and one named G that is 10×10.
6. Write a statement to set aside storage locations for array A, which is 5×2 in size; array A$, which is 10×1; array Z, which is 10×1; and array Z$, which is 3×1.
7. Write the statements that dimension and load the array A(5).
8. Write the statements that dimension and load the arrays M(10) and N(10) alternately.
9. Write the statements that dimension and load the arrays S(5) and T(20).
10. Write the statements that dimension and load the array P(4,5).

AUTOMATIC READ, PRINT, AND CALCULATE (MAT READ, MAT PRINT, AND MAT ARITHMETIC STATEMENTS)

PURPOSE

The matrix processing capability of BASIC offers great flexibility and convenience to the programmer for manipulating large amounts of data. In mathematics, a matrix is a two-dimensional rectangular array of quantities. Matrices are manipulated in accordance with the rules of matrix algebra.

In BASIC, matrix (MAT)† statements are used to perform this manipulation. MAT statements will direct the computer to read in, store, print out, or perform several mathematical processes on all the data items in an array. These statements tell the computer to automatically handle all subscripts, counters, increments, tests of limits, and so on, when manipulating the data. They eliminate the need to perform these functions under the control of FOR/NEXT loops.

All elements in an array are processed in matrix arithmetic. MAT statements cannot be used to process single elements.

GENERAL FORM

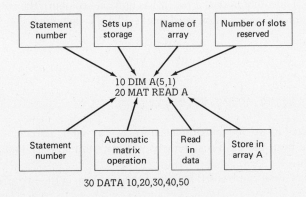

†The MAT statement is not available in Microsoft BASIC.

Statement 10 is a dimension statement that sets up storage for an array named A, with five rows and one column. The MAT READ statement (20) directs the computer to automatically read in and subscript five pieces of data from the DATA statement. The data in storage will look like this:

ARRAY A

ROW	COLUMN 1
1	10
2	20
3	30
4	40
5	50

Once the data is in storage, a MAT PRINT statement can be used to output the elements in the array. The computer will automatically print out each item on a separate line or will follow standard column or packed-zone spacing, depending on the punctuation used in the statement.

The statement

```
40 MAT PRINT A
```

in the program will produce the following output:

```
10
20
30
40
50
```

The computer will print out each element in the array in the exact position it occupies in storage. Since this is a one-dimensional array (it has only one column), the output will be the same regardless of the punctuation used in the PRINT statement.

Example

```
10 DIM A(5,1), B(5,1)
20 MAT READ A,B
30 DATA 10,20,30,40,50,60,70,80,90,100
```

In this example, storage for two one-dimensional arrays is reserved by statement 10. The first five pieces of data from the DATA statement will load into array A, and the last five into array B.

One MAT PRINT statement can be used to output the elements in the two arrays:

```
40 MAT PRINT A,B
```

Since both arrays are one-dimensional, items appear on separate lines.

OUTPUT

```
10
20
30
40
50
60
70
80
90
100
```

In the example below, two two-dimensional arrays are being read in and printed out by MAT statements.

Example
```
10 DIM A(2,3), B(3,4)
20 MAT READ A,B
30 DATA 10,20,30,40,50,60,1,2,3,4,5,6,7,8,9,10,11,12
40 MAT PRINT A;B;
```

The first six items will be loaded into array A, which has two rows and three columns. The last twelve items will fill the three rows and four columns of array B. The arrays are loaded horizontally, with the rows filling first. The computer will automatically assign subscripts to the storage locations. The data in storage will look like this:

ARRAY A

ROW	COLUMN 1	COLUMN 2	COLUMN 3
1	10	20	30
2	40	50	60

ARRAY B

ROW	COLUMN 1	COLUMN 2	COLUMN 3	COLUMN 4
1	1	2	3	4
2	5	6	7	8
3	9	10	11	12

The MAT PRINT statement (40) directs the computer to output both arrays. Semicolons have been used to indicate packed-zone spacing. Items will appear exactly as they are in storage.

OUTPUT

ARRAY A

```
10   20   30
40   50   60
```

ARRAY B

```
1    2    3    4
5    6    7    8
9   10   11   12
```

Three numbers were printed across each line in array A, and four in array B. This corresponds to the number of columns in the arrays. When a MAT PRINT statement is used, the computer does not fill all the spaces on a print line before moving to the next line as it does in a regular PRINT statement.

MAT arithmetic statements can be used by the programmer to manipulate numeric data stored in arrays. Addition, subtraction, scalar multiplication, matrix multiplication, transposition, inversion, and initialization can be performed.

For example, the following program will add the elements of arrays A and B together. Both arrays must have the same number of elements and the same configuration (number of rows and columns). A third array, C, with the same configuration, has been set up to hold the sums of the additions.

```
10 DIM A(3,3), B(3,3), C(3,3)
20 MAT READ A,B
30 MAT C=A+B
40 MAT PRINT A,B,C,
50 DATA 5,10,15,20,25,30,35,40,45,1,2,3,4,5,6,7,8,9
```

Statement 10 will set up three two-dimensional arrays. Each array has three rows and three columns. The first two arrays, A and B, hold the data being read in. The third array, C, is the answer array and will hold the results of the mathematical process.

Statement 30 tells the computer to perform a matrix arithmetic operation—in this case, addition. The computer will add corresponding elements in both arrays and place the answer in the corresponding storage location of array C. Thus, the item stored in A(1,1) will be added to B(1,1) and the sum placed in C(1,1). Then A(1,2) will be added to B(1,2) and the result placed in C(1,2), and so on.

Here is how the three arrays will look in storage:

MATRIX A

ROW	COLUMN 1	COLUMN 2	COLUMN 3
1	5	10	15
2	20	25	30
3	35	40	45

MATRIX B

ROW	COLUMN 1	COLUMN 2	COLUMN 3
1	1	2	3
2	4	5	6
3	7	8	9

MATRIX C

ROW	COLUMN 1	COLUMN 2	COLUMN 3
1	6	12	18
2	24	30	36
3	42	48	54

The sums could have been placed in either array A or B rather than in a separate array. But in this case, the sums would have been read in over the old data, thereby erasing it.

Subtraction may also be performed on matrices. Again, the two data arrays and the answer array must have the same configuration.

Had statement 30 in the above program read

    30 MAT C=A−B

each element in array B would be subtracted from the element in the corresponding position in array A and the answer placed in array C. The item in $B(1,1)$ would be subtracted from $A(1,1)$, $B(1,2)$ subtracted from $A(1,2)$, and so on.

In this case, the answer, array C, would look like this:

MATRIX C

ROW	COLUMN 1	COLUMN 2	COLUMN 3
1	4	8	12
2	16	20	24
3	28	32	36

Several forms of matrix multiplication are possible, depending upon the language implementation available. One common method is scalar multiplication. Each element in an array is multiplied by a constant and the quotient is placed in the answer array. The answer array must, in this case, have the same configuration as the data array.

If statement 30 in the above program had been written

`30 MAT C= (2)*A`

the following output would result:

MATRIX C

ROW	COLUMN 1	COLUMN 2	COLUMN 3
1	10	20	30
2	40	50	60
3	70	80	90

Each element in array A has been multiplied by 2.

Several other processes can also be performed on matrices. These include multiplication of one array by another: MAT C=A*B; and matrix inversion: MAT C = INV(A). These operations follow the rules of matrix algebra. The student should check language manual and texts on matrix arithmetic for more details.

Another matrix operation that can be performed is matrix transposition. This involves rearranging the elements in an array so that they are loaded vertically instead of horizontally. If statement 30 had been written

`30 MAT C = TRN(A)`

the following output would result:

MATRIX C

ROW	COLUMN 1	COLUMN 2	COLUMN 3
1	5	20	35
2	10	25	40
3	15	30	45

In order to properly transpose a matrix, the rows and columns of the answer array must be the reverse of those in the original array. (Matrices C and A in the example above have the same number of rows as columns, and the reversal is not apparent.)

Example

```
10 DIM F(5,3), E(3,5)
· · · · ·
· · · · ·
60 MAT E = TRN(F)
```

In the example above, matrix F is being transposed. It has five rows and three columns and the answer, matrix E, has five columns and three rows. The output will be:

MATRIX F (BEFORE TRANSPOSITION)

ROW	COLUMN 1	COLUMN 2	COLUMN 3
1	1	2	3
2	4	5	6
3	7	8	9
4	10	11	12
5	13	14	15

MATRIX E (AFTER TRANSPOSITION)

ROW	COLUMN 1	COLUMN 2	COLUMN 3	COLUMN 4	COLUMN 5
1	1	4	7	10	13
2	2	5	8	11	14
3	3	6	9	12	15

Most systems also have three other MAT statements:

```
10 DIM A(2,3), B(3,2), C(3,3)
20 MAT A = ZER
30 MAT B = CON
40 MAT C = IDN
```

Statement 20 will load matrix A with all 0s, which is an efficient way to set up and initialize an array and load it with various values calculated during a program.

Matrix A in storage will look like this:

ROW	COLUMN 1	COLUMN 2	COLUMN 3
1	0	0	0
2	0	0	0

Statement 30 will load matrix B with 1s. This is also a form of initialization.

Matrix B in storage will look like this:

ROW	COLUMN 1	COLUMN 2
1	1	1
2	1	1
3	1	1

Statement 40 loads an identity matrix, used in matrix arithmetic. The matrix will contain all 0s except for 1s in a diagonal line.

Matrix C will look like this in storage:

ROW	COLUMN 1	COLUMN 2	COLUMN 3
1	1	0	0
2	0	1	0
3	0	0	1

RULES

1. A matrix must have a unique name consisting of a single alphabetic character.

2. Matrices may be named and dimensioned in a DIM statement or in the MAT READ statement.

3. Matrices must be two-dimensional. On some systems, if a dimension is not specified, the computer will assume it to be one-dimensional.

4. A program must contain sufficient data to fill a matrix. Every storage location reserved must be loaded or an error condition will be present.

5. The MAT PRINT statement will output elements exactly as they are stored in the matrix. If no punctuation or only a comma is used, the computer will follow standard column spacing. One to five elements will be printed out across the line, depending on the number of columns in the matrix. If a semicolon is used, the computer will follow packed-zone spacing, printing out 1 to 12 elements across a line, depending on the number of columns in the matrix.

6. More than one matrix can be printed out or loaded in a MAT READ or PRINT statement.

7. Matrix arithmetic follows the rules of matrix algebra. All elements in an array are processed.

8. A matrix statement cannot be used to process single elements in a matrix. Single elements in a matrix can be referenced by name and subscript and manipulated by other arithmetic statements in the language.

9. Arrays to be manipulated by matrix addition or subtraction must have the same dimensions.

10. In matrix addition, corresponding elements in two arrays are added together.

11. In matrix subtraction, an element from one array is subtracted from the corresponding element in the other array.

12. In matrix addition and subtraction, the results may be placed in one of the original arrays. In such a case, the original data will be lost.

13. An answer array can be set up to receive the results of matrix addition and subtraction. It must have the same dimensions as the contributing arrays.

14. In scalar multiplication, each element in a matrix is multiplied by a constant. The constant must be enclosed within parentheses: MAT B = (2)*A. The answer array must have the same configuration as the data array.

15. MAT multiplication and inversion and manipulation of identity matrices follow

the rules of matrix algebra. Dimensioning and manipulation must be exact. Check the language manual and arithmetic texts for details.

16. In matrix transposition, the elements of one array are loaded vertically into a second array. The rows and columns of the second array must be the reverse of the original.

17. MAT ZER and CON statements may be used to fill an array with all 0s or all 1s.

18. Only numeric data can be manipulated by the MAT statements.

EXERCISES

1. Find the errors, if any, in the following statements:
   a. 10 DIM X(2,2)
      30 MAT READ X
   b. 10 DIM A(6,9)
      20 PRINT MAT A
   c. 10 DIM M(10,10)
      40 MAT READ N
   d. 10 MAT Q=L+T
   e. 30 MAT B=A+B/C

2. Write the statements that read in a 12 × 8 matrix.
3. Write the statements that print out a 4 × 6 matrix.
4. Write the statements that load in two matrices, A(4,5) and B(6,3).
5. Write the dimension and math statements that will add two 6 × 9 arrays and place the result in array R.
6. Write the statements that will print out the elements in matrix E in tight zone spacing.
7. Write the dimension and math statements that will subtract the matrix D(3,6) from F(3,6) and place the answer in T.
8. Show the statements that will transpose the elements in matrix A(6,3).
9. Write the dimension and math statements that will multiply each element in a matrix by 2.
10. Write the statements that will initialize each element in a matrix to 0.

SUBROUTINES (GOSUB, RETURN STATEMENTS)

PURPOSE

A programmer often wants to repeat a sequence of instructions or a process at different points in a program. He or she can recode each sequence in the proper place, but this is time-consuming, introduces additional chances for errors, and uses more interpreter time. Loops using GOTO statements are inefficient because control must return to a different point in the program each time the sequence is executed. The best way to handle the situation is to write the sequence of instructions as a subroutine, sometimes referred to as a subprogram, and call it into the main program as often as needed.

Subroutines are procedures or routines written as an independent block or module. They are often used to perform sorts, merges, arithmetic calculations, heading routines, and so on. Often a previously written, functioning program may be included as a subroutine in another program.

In BASIC, the GOSUB instruction is used to direct control to a subroutine and the RETURN statement directs control back to the statement following the GOSUB.

Suppose that a situation arises where a programmer wants to perform a given operation, say a sort routine, at four different points in a main program. The programmer could, of course, write four sets of sort instructions and place them at the appropriate places in the main program. But this would require a duplication of programming and keyboarding effort.

Instead, the programmer writes a sort routine as a block of instructions and places a RETURN statement as the last instruction. He or she inserts this module into the main program, usually just before the END statement. Each time the main program requires the sort routine, a GOSUB statement directs the computer to the subroutine. At the end of each execution of the subroutine, the RETURN statement tells the computer to return to the statement following the last GOSUB executed.

The following diagram illustrates this sequence:

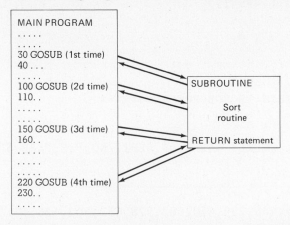

When the computer encounters the first GOSUB statement (30), it will branch control to the subroutine. After the subroutine is executed, control is transferred back to statement 40. When the computer reaches the second GOSUB (statement 100), control is again transferred to the subroutine. After the second execution, control returns to the main program at statement 110. This continues until the main program has executed the subroutine four times.

A subroutine differs from a user-defined function in one major aspect: in the user-defined function only one value (answer) is transferred back to the main program. The subroutine may, on the other hand, contain several arguments. This allows several quantities to be transferred from the subroutine back to the main program.

In addition, many systems limit a user-defined function to a mathematical instruction. A subroutine may be many lines of instructions directing the computer to perform any procedure.

Example
```
10 REM GOSUB EXAMPLE
20 LET T=0
30 LET C=0
40 PRINT "DAILY SALES ARE:"
50 FOR I=1 TO 5
60    READ S(I)
70    LET A=S(I)+(.2*S(I))
80    LET T=T+A
90    PRINT "      "; A
100 NEXT I
110 GOSUB 230
120 LET T=0
```

```
130 PRINT "DAILY SALES ARE:"
140 FOR I=1 TO 7
150    READ S(I)
160    LET A=S(I)+(.4*S(I))
170    LET T=T+A
180    PRINT "        "; A
190 NEXT I
200 GOSUB 230
210 GOTO 300
220 REM *******NEXT IS SUBPROGRAM*******
230 PRINT
240 LET C=C+1
250 PRINT "TOTAL WEEKLY SALES OF DEPT. NO.";C;"ARE $";T
260 PRINT
270 PRINT
280 RETURN
290 DATA 300,330,406,299,450,602,578,612,502,426,521,638
300 END
```

OUTPUT

```
DAILY SALES ARE:
     360
     396
     487.2
     358.8
     540


TOTAL WEEKLY SALES OF DEPT. NO. 1 ARE $ 2142


DAILY SALES ARE:
     842.8
     809.2
     856.8
     702.8
     596.4
     729.4
     893.2


TOTAL WEEKLY SALES OF DEPT. NO. 2 ARE $ 5430.6
```

This program totals the weekly wholesale prices for each department in a company and then multiplies the total for each department by a different markup percentage. A subroutine prints out the total sales by department.

The sequence of steps followed by the main program is outlined below.

T (total weekly sales) and C (the counter for department number) are initialized to 0 in statements 20 and 30. Statement 40 prints out a heading. Statements 50 through 100 is a FOR/NEXT loop that reads in and prints out five values (daily sales), multiplies each by 2 percent, and adds them together. Statement 110 calls in the subroutine, which begins at statement 230. The subroutine skips a line, increases the department number counter by 1, and prints out a literal line showing department number and total weekly sales.

Control returns to statement 120, where T is again initialized to 0. Statements 130 to 190 read in and print out seven values (daily sales for the next department), multiply each by 40 percent, and add them together. Statement 200 calls in the subroutine at statement 230 to print out the department number and total.

Control returns to statement 210 and is directed to the END statement at line 300 to terminate program execution.

Example

```
10 REM GOSUB GRAPH EXAMPLE
20 LET D=0
30 READ A,B,C
40 LET D=A+B+C
50 LET A$="QUALITY 1"
60 GOSUB 150
70 LET D=A+B-C
80 LET A$="QUALITY 2"
90 GOSUB 150
100 LET D=B+C
110 LET A$="QUALITY 3"
120 GOSUB 150
130 GOTO 300
140 REM ****** SUBPROGRAM ******
150 LET E=0
160 LET F=0
170 LET E=D/1000
180 LET F=INT(E+.5)
190 IF F<=5 THEN 220
200 LET S$="*"
210 GOTO 230
220 LET S$="+"
230 PRINT A$; "-";
240 FOR I=1 TO F
250   PRINT S$;
260 NEXT I
270 PRINT
280 RETURN
290 DATA 3360,4100,1986
300 END
```

OUTPUT

```
QUALITY 1-*********
QUALITY 2-+++++
QUALITY 3-******
```

This program reads in three values and manipulates them mathematically in various ways to measure three different qualities. A subroutine is used to process each quality so that it can be illustrated graphically.

The sequence of steps followed in the program is outlined below.

Statement 20 initializes D (the total) to 0. Statement 30 reads in variables A, B, and C. Statement 40 adds them together and places the answer in D. Statement 50 assigns the alphabetic string QUALITY 1 to A$. Statement 60 calls in the subroutine at statement 150.

The subroutine first initializes two intermediate storage slots to 0 (E and F). Then it converts D into F by dividing it by 1,000, rounding off, and dropping the fractional portion. F is compared with 5. If it is less than or equal to 5, control branches to statement 220, which assigns the symbol + to S$. If F is greater than 5, * is assigned to S$. Statements 230 to 270 print out A$ (quality name) and S$ (symbol) F times.

Control returns to statement 70, where QUALITY 2 is determined. The subroutine is again called in to convert D into F, assign the appropriate symbol, and print it out F times. Control now returns to statement 100, which computes QUALITY 3. The subroutine again determines the value of F and prints out the graphic illustration of QUALITY 3. Control returns to statement 130, which directs it to the END statement to terminate execution.

RULES

1. A subroutine is called in by a GOSUB statement, which must list the line number containing the first instruction in the subroutine.

2. After a subroutine is executed, the RETURN statement directs control back to the statement following the GOSUB command in the main program.

3. A main program may contain one or more subroutines.

4. The statement numbers in a subroutine may not conflict with those in the main program.

5. A subroutine may direct the computer to perform any process.

6. A subroutine can be called in only by a GOSUB statement and cannot be entered at any other point.

7. Control may not be branched out of a subroutine at any point, except from the RETURN statement.

EXERCISES

1. Answer the following true and false questions:
   a. GOSUB statements must be labeled GOSUB and can be used only once in a program.　　T　F
   b. Each subroutine must terminate in a RETURN statement.　　　T　F

    c. REM statements may not appear in subroutines.   T F

    d. The statement numbers in a subroutine must be different from those in the main program.   T F

    e. A subroutine is called in by the RETURN statement.   T F

2. Write a subroutine that prints out a group of column headings.

3. Write a subroutine that performs a mathematical calculation.

4. Write a subroutine that will round off a number.

5. Write a subroutine that includes a counter to count the number of times the subroutine is called in.

6. Trace the flow through a main program that calls in a subroutine three times.

PART THREE

SAMPLE PROGRAMS FOR STUDY

HOW TO USE THIS SECTION

Part Three of this book contains several dozen complete working programs that have been thoroughly documented. The programs range in difficulty from simple to complex. This section is designed to be used in conjunction with Part Two, which contained a detailed discussion of each language statement used in the various sample programs.

Each sample program begins with a listing of the BASIC statements used in the program. The abstract that precedes the program describes the logic and sequence of steps used in each sample program.

Each program gives a list of variable names that represent data to be read in or manipulated. The program listing explains in ordinary English what each programming statement does. This information is keyed to the program by statement number.

The program flowchart illustrates in a visual way the logic used in the program. You may wish to refer to Appendix A before proceeding further, to gain an understanding of how flowcharts are used and the meaning of the symbols. Each sample program contains a program listing. This is an actual computer listing showing each line of the program as it was entered in the computer. The program run illustrates the output as it was generated by the computer. Finally, each sample program includes a series of exercises that allow the reader to expand or modify the programs in this section.

The reader should systematically study each of the programs in this section and understand the computer logic and statements that are used. Upon completing study of the sample programs, the reader will have a useful set of programs that can be referred to later as his or her programming knowledge expands.

BASIC STATEMENTS USED

```
REM
PRINT
END
```

ABSTRACT

This program demonstrates the computer's ability to print out words and phrases. It introduces the reader to the PRINT statement and to the REM and END statements, which are an integral part of virtually all BASIC programs. The computer proceeds through the program in sequence and merely prints out the information incorporated in each PRINT statement. Upon reaching the END statement, the computer terminates execution.

VARIABLE NAMES

(No variables are used in this program)

PROGRAM LISTING

```
10      REM statement identifies program and should be used as the first state-
        ment at the beginning of every program.
20      PRINT statement prints out a blank line, a convenient way of skipping
        a line.
30      PRINT statement prints out the words enclosed in the quotation marks.
40      PRINT statement prints out words in quotation marks.
50      PRINT statement prints out words in quotation marks.
```

60   PRINT statement prints out a blank line.
70   END statement terminates execution and should be the last statement in every BASIC program.

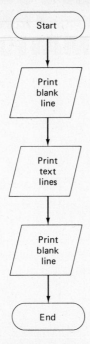

PROGRAM

```
10 REM DEMONSTRATES USE OF PRINT STATEMENT (DEMOPR)
20 PRINT
30 PRINT "THE COMPUTER CAN PRINT OUT"
40 PRINT "WORDS, PHRASES, OR OTHER"
50 PRINT "INFORMATION AS DESIRED."
60 PRINT
70 END
```

PROGRAM RUN

```
THE COMPUTER CAN PRINT OUT
WORDS, PHRASES, OR OTHER
INFORMATION AS DESIRED.
```

EXERCISES

1. Write a program that will use a PRINT statement and print out your name, address, and telephone number. Be sure to include a REM and END statement.
2. Write a program that will print out a paragraph of text. You may use any copy as long as there are over 10 lines of output.

PROGRAM 2
PRINTING OUT RESULTS OF CALCULATIONS

BASIC STATEMENTS USED

```
REM
PRINT
END
```

ABSTRACT

This program demonstrates the computer's ability to print out the result of simple arithmetic calculations as well as words and phrases. It introduces the reader to how the PRINT statement can be used to perform simple mathematical calculations. The computer proceeds through the program, printing out the results of each calculation as the statement is encountered. Upon reaching the END statement, the computer terminates execution.

VARIABLE NAMES

(No variables are used in this program)

PROGRAM LISTING

10	REM statement identifies program.
20	PRINT statement prints out results of addition calculation.

30	PRINT statement prints out results of subtraction calculation.
40	PRINT statement prints out results of multiplication calculation.
50	PRINT statement prints out results of division calculation.
60	PRINT statement skips a line.
70	PRINT statement prints out a descriptive header on same line as results of the calculation.
80	PRINT statement prints out header and results of calculation.
90	PRINT statement prints out header and results of calculation.
100	PRINT statement prints out header and results of calculation.
110	END statement terminates execution.

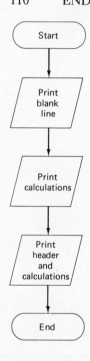

PROGRAM

```
10 REM DEMONSTRATES PRINT STATEMENT CALCULATIONS (DEMCAL)
20 PRINT 10+30
30 PRINT 50-20
40 PRINT 6*5
50 PRINT 100/5
60 PRINT
70 PRINT "ADD",10+30
80 PRINT "SUBTRACT",50-20
90 PRINT "MULTIPLY",6*5
100 PRINT "DIVIDE",100/5
110 END
```

PROGRAM RUN

```
40
30
30
20

ADD             40
SUBTRACT        30
MULTIPLY        30
DIVIDE          20
```

EXERCISES

1. Write a program that contains at least two arithmetic calculations. Output the results using PRINT statements.
2. Write a program that performs at least three arithmetic calculations. Include PRINT statements (headers) that identify the output.

BASIC STATEMENTS USED

```
REM
PRINT
READ/DATA
END
```

ABSTRACT

This program illustrates the use of the READ/DATA statement and how information contained within a program is printed out. The previous two programs described the
PRINT statement as a means of outputting text lines or the results of calculations. This
program illustrates another means of outputting information. The data printed out in this
program is contained within the program itself. Later the reader will learn how to read
information stored on disk or other means, manipulate it, and output it. The computer
proceeds through this program in sequence. Upon reaching the READ statement, it loads
values contained in the DATA statement into the variables A, B, and C. A PRINT statement is then used to print out the value of the variables.

VARIABLE NAMES

A = First element in DATA statement
B = Second element in DATA statement
C = Third element in DATA statement

PROGRAM LISTING

10	REM statement identifies program.
20	READ statement contains list of variables that will be loaded from DATA statement number 60.
30	PRINT statement prints out header line.
40	PRINT statement skips a line.
50	PRINT statement prints out quantities stored under A, B, and C.
60	DATA statement contains quantities that will be loaded into READ statement.
70	END statement terminates execution.

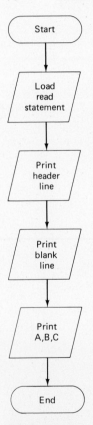

PROGRAM

```
10 REM DEMONSTRATES USE OF READ/DATA (DEMREA)
20 READ A,B,C
30 PRINT "THE FOLLOWING VALUES WERE READ IN"
40 PRINT
50 PRINT A,B,C
60 DATA 10,20,30
70 END
```

PROGRAM RUN

THE FOLLOWING VALUES WERE READ IN

10   20   30

EXERCISES

1. Write a program that reads in and prints out three quantities, using the READ/DATA statement.
2. Write a program that reads in four quantities, using the READ/DATA statement. Label the output with a header, using appropriate PRINT statements.

BASIC STATEMENTS USED

```
REM
PRINT
READ/DATA
GOTO
END
```

ABSTRACT

This program prepares a simple enrollment report from information read in from DATA statements. First, the program prints a row of stars and the report title. Then, it prints column heads, which are positioned over the columns by spacing them carefully within the PRINT statements. Next, the program encounters a simple loop that reads in and prints out five variables each pass. READ/DATA and PRINT statements are contained within the loop to perform these processes. The looping continues until the computer runs out of data. Control shifts back to the monitor, an "out-of-data" message appears, and execution terminates.

VARIABLE NAMES

A = Year
B = Nonstudents
C = Elementary students
D = High school students
E = College students

PROGRAM LISTING

10	REM statement identifies program.
20	PRINT statement prints out row of stars.
30	PRINT statement skips a line.
40	PRINT statement outputs title.
50,60	PRINT statements each skip one line.
70–90	PRINT statements output column heads.
100	PRINT statement skips a line.
110	Tells computer to read in five variables from DATA statement.
120	Tells computer to print out five variables (read in at statement 110) across one line, following standard column spacing.
130	Tells computer to loop back to statement 100 to process five more variables.
140–180	DATA statements, each containing five quantities, corresponding to variable names. Data items are read in at READ statement 110.
190	END statement terminates execution.

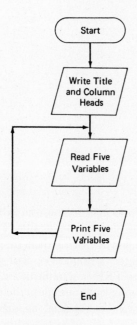

PROGRAM

```
10 REM ENROLLMENT REPORT (ENROLL)
20 PRINT "          *************************************************"
30 PRINT
40 PRINT "                           ENROLLMENT REPORT"
50 PRINT
60 PRINT
70 PRINT "          NON-STUDENTS              STUDENTS BY SCHOOL"
```

```
80 PRINT " YEAR          TOTAL       ELEMENTARY    HIGH SCHOOL";
90 PRINT "    COLLEGE"
100 PRINT
110 READ A,B,C,D,E
120 PRINT A,B,C,D,E
130 GOTO 100
140 DATA 1960, 10821, 1902, 1800, 400
150 DATA 1965, 18938, 2620, 2291, 605
160 DATA 1970, 26809, 3201, 3809, 709
170 DATA 1975, 33111, 4189, 3970, 905
180 DATA 1980, 39701, 4372, 41200, 1093
190 END
```

PROGRAM RUN

```
****************************************************
```

ENROLLMENT REPORT

YEAR	NON-STUDENTS TOTAL	STUDENTS BY SCHOOL		
		ELEMENTARY	HIGH SCHOOL	COLLEGE
1960	10821	1902	1800	400
1965	18938	2620	2291	605
1970	26809	3201	3809	709
1975	33111	4189	3970	905
1980	39701	4372	41200	1093

Out of DATA in 110

EXERCISES

1. Write a program that will read in several pieces of data and print out the form below. Include literal headings, as shown.

```
    WORK STATION ASSIGNMENT

EMPLOYEE NUMBER STATION      SHIFT

    1032            32         1
    1621            31         3
    . . . .          . .        .
```

2. Write a program that will read in several pieces of data and print out the form below. Include literal headings, as shown.

INVENTORY CONTROL SHEET
VEHICLES IN STOCK

MODEL NO.	HORSE POWER	COLOR CODE	TRIM CODE
661872	100	301	43
. .	. . .	. . .	. .

PROGRAM 5
REPRO REPORT

BASIC STATEMENTS USED

```
REM
PRINT
INPUT
END
```

ABSTRACT

This program prepares a business form for the reproduction department. It also illustrates interactive programming on the computer. Programs such as these prepare job tickets, order forms, job specifications, and so on.

The program is designed to execute the sequence of instructions only once. To prepare more than one form, the program would either have to be rerun for each set of data or modified to include a loop. INPUT statements ask the programmer to enter job specifications. After all data has been input, the program executes a series of PRINT statements that print out the order confirmation. Both alphanumeric and numeric data are processed by the INPUT and PRINT statements. Variables and literal text are intermixed in the same PRINT statements. The text is spaced out in the literal PRINT statements to produce a graphically pleasing output.

VARIABLE NAMES

C$ = Color of ink
D$ = Delivery date
J$ = Job name

Q = Quantity
R$ = Date order received
S1 = Size of job
S2 = Size of job

PROGRAM LISTING

10	REM statement identifies program.
20	Requests user to enter information on keyboard.
30	Reads in date from keyboard (R$).
40	Requests user to enter information on keyboard.
50	Reads in name of job (J$) from keyboard.
60	Requests information from keyboard.
70	Reads in quantity (Q) from keyboard.
80	Requests information from keyboard.
90	Reads in color of ink (C$) from keyboard.
100	Requests information from keyboard.
110	Reads in size of job (S1, S2).
120	Requests information from keyboard.
130	Reads in delivery date from keyboard (D$).
140	Skips a line.
150	Prints out a row of stars.
160	Skips a line.
170, 180	Print out heading.
190, 200	Skip lines.
210	Prints out literal text and variable J$.
220–240	Print out text.
250	Prints out variable R$ and literal symbol.
260–390	Print out text intermixed with variables.
400–420	Print three closing lines.
430, 440	Skip two lines.
450	Prints out row of stars.
460	END statement terminates execution.

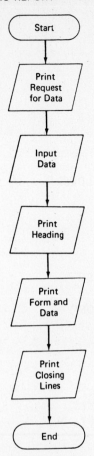

PROGRAM

```
10 REM REPRO REPORT (REPREP)
20 PRINT "ENTER DATE ORDER RECEIVED"
30 INPUT R$
40 PRINT "ENTER NAME OF JOB"
50 INPUT J$
60 PRINT "ENTER QUANTITY"
70 INPUT Q
80 PRINT "ENTER COLOR INK"
90 INPUT C$
100 PRINT "ENTER SIZE OF JOB"
110 INPUT S1,S2
120 PRINT "ENTER DELIVERY DATE"
130 INPUT D$
140 PRINT
150 PRINT "................................................."
160 PRINT
```

```
170 PRINT "            REPRODUCTION DEPARTMENT"
180 PRINT "             ORDER CONFIRMATION"
190 PRINT
200 PRINT
210 PRINT "        YOUR ORDER FOR: "; J$
220 PRINT
230 PRINT "WAS RECEIVED IN THIS DEPARTMENT ON:"
240 PRINT
250 PRINT R$;"."
260 PRINT
270 PRINT "        SPECIFICATIONS ARE AS FOLLOWS:"
280 PRINT
290 PRINT "            QUANTITY:  "; Q
300 PRINT
310 PRINT "            COLOR INK:  ";C$
320 PRINT
330 PRINT "            SIZE:  ";S1; "X"; S2
340 PRINT
350 PRINT "        YOUR ORDER WILL BE READY ON"
360 PRINT
370 PRINT D$;"."
380 PRINT
390 PRINT
400 PRINT "               THANK YOU,"
410 PRINT "               B. MARTINEZ"
420 PRINT "               REPRO. DEPT. MGR."
430 PRINT
440 PRINT
450 PRINT ".................................................."
460 END
```

PROGRAM RUN

```
ENTER DATE ORDER RECEIVED
? 9/23
ENTER NAME OF JOB
? CARDS
ENTER QUANTITY
? 1000
ENTER COLOR INK
? BLUE
ENTER SIZE OF JOB
? 2,4
ENTER DELIVERY DATE
? 9/28
```

• •

REPRODUCTION DEPARTMENT
ORDER CONFIRMATION

YOUR ORDER FOR: CARDS

WAS RECEIVED IN THIS DEPARTMENT ON:

9/23.

SPECIFICATIONS ARE AS FOLLOWS:

QUANTITY: 1000

COLOR INK: BLUE

SIZE: 2 X 4

YOUR ORDER WILL BE READY ON

9/28.

THANK YOU,
B. MARTINEZ
REPRO. DEPT. MGR.

• •

EXERCISES

1. Write a program that inputs the required information and outputs the form
   below:
   STUDENT NAME: J. RANDY
   I.D. NO.: 65481
   SEMESTER IN COLLEGE: 3
   MAJOR: BUSINESS

2. Write a program that will input the required information and output the form
   below:

TEXT	AUTHOR	CLASS
_____	_____	_____
SKY DIVING	TOM SAYLES	AERO 21
• • • • •	• • • • •	• • • •

BASIC STATEMENTS USED

```
REM
PRINT
END
INPUT
LET
COUNTER
IF/THEN
```

ABSTRACT

The computer can be used to prepare individualized labels, cards, tickets, notices, and so on. This program illustrates how several print statements can be used in a simple algorithm to print out a membership card. The program inputs a name from the keyboard and moves through a series of print statements that print out a formatted card, including the name of the member and a consecutive number. Then, the program loops back to the beginning to input another name. The card number is achieved with a counter written into the program. It starts at 1 and increases by 1 each time the cycle is repeated for another card.

This program illustrates how to do simple graphics and reading in and printing alphabetic variables. At the end of each cycle, it asks the user whether he or she wants to repeat the cycle or terminate the program.

VARIABLE NAMES

C = COUNTER
A$ = NAME
B = Variable used in repeat cycle test

PROGRAM LISTING

10	REM statement identifies program.
20	Sets up counter C and initializes it to zero.
30–60	Request programmer to enter name of member.
70,80	Input variable A$, name.
90	Adds 1 to counter.
100–190	Print upper portion of membership card.
200	PRINT statement includes graphics and name of member.
210–230	Print portion of card.
240	Prints the value of the counter C and signature.
250–270	Complete printing out card and skip two lines.
280,290	Request if programmer wishes to repeat cycle.
300	Inputs B, answer.
310	Branches to statement 50 if answer equals 1.
320–340	Terminate program.

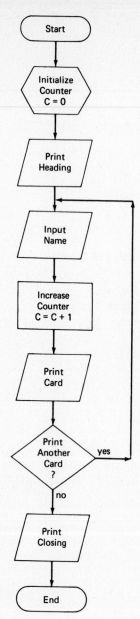

PROGRAM

```
10 REM MEMBERSHIP CARD (MEMCAR)
20 LET C=0
30 PRINT "THIS PROGRAM PRINTS OUT MEMBERSHIP CARDS"
40 PRINT "FOR THE HORSE AND BUGGY CLUB"
50 PRINT
60 PRINT "PLEASE ENTER THE NAME OF A MEMBER"
70 INPUT A$
80 PRINT "THANK YOU"
90 LET C=C+1
100 PRINT
110 PRINT
120 PRINT ".........................................."
130 PRINT
140 PRINT "                    MEMBERSHIP CARD"
150 PRINT "    /XXXXX"
160 PRINT "   /  XXXX            ***********"
170 PRINT " /XXXXXXXXX-       HORSE AND BUGGY CLUB"
180 PRINT " /XXXXXXXXX-          ***********"
190 PRINT " ------------"
200 PRINT "   O     O           "; A$
210 PRINT "                 -------------------------"
220 PRINT "           IS A MEMBER IN GOOD STANDING"
230 PRINT
240 PRINT "   NO. "; C; "         SIGNED:  H. FORD
250 PRINT ".........................................."
260 PRINT
270 PRINT
280 PRINT "DO YOU WISH TO PRINT ANOTHER MEMBERSHIP CARD?"
290 PRINT "ANSWER 1 FOR YES, AND 0 FOR NO"
300 INPUT B
310 IF B=1 THEN 50
320 PRINT "THANK YOU, GOODBYE"
330 PRINT
340 END
```

PROGRAM RUN

```
THIS PROGRAM PRINTS OUT MEMBERSHIP CARDS
FOR THE HORSE AND BUGGY CLUB

PLEASE ENTER THE NAME OF A MEMBER
? GALE JORDAN
THANK YOU
```

```
. . . . . . . . . . . . . . . . . . . . . . . . . . . . . . . . . . . . .

                        MEMBERSHIP CARD

    /XXXXX
    /   XXXX              ***********
/XXXXXXXXX-          HORSE AND BUGGY CLUB
/XXXXXXXXX-              ***********
-------------
    O    O              GALE JORDAN
                    -----------------------------
                IS A MEMBER IN GOOD STANDING

    NO.  1             SIGNED:  H. FORD
. . . . . . . . . . . . . . . . . . . . . . . . . . . . . . . . . . . . .


DO YOU WISH TO PRINT ANOTHER MEMBERSHIP CARD?
ANSWER 1 FOR YES, AND 0 FOR NO
? 1

PLEASE ENTER THE NAME OF A MEMBER
? TOM GILSON
THANK YOU



. . . . . . . . . . . . . . . . . . . . . . . . . . . . . . . . . . . . .

                        MEMBERSHIP CARD

    /XXXXX
    /   XXXX              ***********
/XXXXXXXXX-          HORSE AND BUGGY CLUB
/XXXXXXXXX-              ***********
-------------
    O    O               TOM GILSON
                    -----------------------------
                IS A MEMBER IN GOOD STANDING

    NO.  2             SIGNED:  H. FORD
. . . . . . . . . . . . . . . . . . . . . . . . . . . . . . . . . . . . .


DO YOU WISH TO PRINT ANOTHER MEMBERSHIP CARD?
ANSWER 1 FOR YES, AND 0 FOR NO
? 0
THANK YOU, GOODBYE
```

EXERCISES

1. Design a membership card for your club or student government. Write a program that prints it out with different names.
2. Design a membership card for your club or other organization to which you belong. Include a consecutive counter beginning at number 100.

BASIC STATEMENTS USED

```
REM
PRINT
READ/DATA
IF/THEN
LET
GOTO
```

ABSTRACT

This program prepares a profit report. It will read a group of items from DATA statements, including sales price and net cost. The program calculates the profit in cents and the percentage of profit, based on the sales price. A loop is used to direct the computer through a sequence of statements which read, calculate, and write. The program uses the following logic.

First, the title and column heads are printed. Then, three variables are read from a record. A test is made to determine if it is the last record. This is done by testing the alphabetic variable, A$, to see if it is equal to ZZZZ. If it is not, the computer calculates the profit by subtracting net cost from sales price. Then, the percent of profit is found by dividing sales price into the profit and converting this fraction into a percentage. Finally, the variables are printed out on one line under the column heads. A GOTO statement directs the program back to read another record. When the ZZZZ record is encountered, the program branches to END and execution terminates.

VARIABLE NAMES

A\$ = Item
B = Sales price
C = Net cost
D = Intermediate value, profit B–C
E = Intermediate value, D/B
F = Percentage of profit, E*100

PROGRAM LISTING

10	REM statement identifies program.
20	Prints title.
30–70	Print row of dots and skip lines. Semicolon at end of statement 40 causes the dots in statement 50 to be printed on the same line.
80,90	Print column heads. Semicolon causes all titles to be printed on same line.
100	Skips line. Beginning of loop.
110	Reads in item (A\$), sales price (B), and net cost (C) from a DATA statement.
120	Tests A\$ to see if it is ZZZZ—the last record; control will go to statement 250 if it is.
130	Calculates profit in cents.
140	Calculates ratio of profit to sales price.
150	Converts ratio to percentage.
160	Prints item, sales price, net cost, profit, and percent.
170	Directs control back to statement 100 to repeat loop.
180–230	DATA statements contain data items for program.
240	DATA statement with values indicating it is last record.
250	END statement terminates execution.

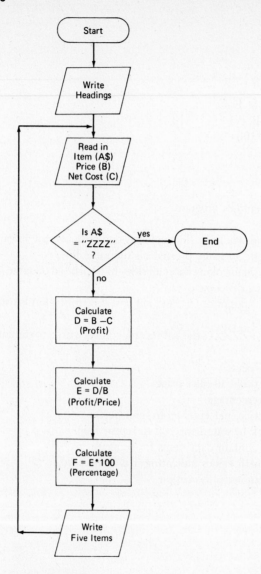

PROGRAM

```
10 REM PROFIT REPORT (PROREP)
20 PRINT "                        PROFIT REPORT"
30 PRINT
40 PRINT "...............................................";
50 PRINT "........."
60 PRINT
70 PRINT
80 PRINT " ITEM     SALES PRICE    NET COST      PROFIT";
90 PRINT "        PERCENT"
```

```
100 PRINT
110 READ A$,B,C
120 IF A$ = "ZZZZ" THEN 250
130 LET D = B-C
140 LET E = D/B
150 LET F = E * 100
160 PRINT A$,B,C,D,F
170 GOTO 100
180 DATA "SOAP",1.39,1.06
190 DATA "SHAMPOO",1.59,1.37
200 DATA "RINSE",1.89,1.65
210 DATA "TOOTHPASTE",2.65,2.42
220 DATA "BLADES",1.49,1.34
230 DATA "RAZORS",2.79,2.51
240 DATA "ZZZZ",99,99
250 END
```

PROGRAM RUN

PROFIT REPORT

. . . .

ITEM	SALES PRICE	NET COST	PROFIT	PERCENT
SOAP	1.39	1.06	.33	23.741
SHAMPOO	1.59	1.37	.22	13.8365
RINSE	1.89	1.65	.24	12.6984
TOOTHPASTE	2.65	2.42	.23	8.67925
BLADES	1.49	1.34	.15	10.0671
RAZORS	2.79	2.51	.28	10.0358

EXERCISES

1. Write a program that will calculate the total number of hours worked and print out the form below:

```
NAME                    DAYS         HOURS         TOTAL
ALEXANDER JOHNSON   5            8             40
. . . . .               . .           . .           . .
```

2. Write a program that will calculate the total amount a salesman earns by adding $10 per diem to his 10 percent commission. Print out the form below:

NAME	SALES	COMMISSION	PER DIEM	TOTAL
SOL HUSTON	289.15	28.9	10.00	38.9
. . . .	. . . .	. .	. . . .	. . .

RATIO
DEMONSTRATION

BASIC STATEMENTS USED

```
REM
LET
PRINT
IF/THEN
GOTO
END
TAB
INPUT
```

ABSTRACT

A mathematical ratio expresses a relationship between two sets of figures or conditions. For example, ratios are often used to find the dimensions of an illustration or photograph when it is enlarged or reduced in size. The relationship of the original size to the new size is expressed as

$$\frac{\text{Original width}}{\text{Original height}} = \frac{\text{New width}}{\text{New height}}$$

Suppose that you have a picture 4×5 inches and want to have it enlarged to fit a picture frame 15 inches high. What should the new width be? The new dimensions can be calculated with the mathematical ratio

$$\frac{4}{5} = \frac{X}{15}$$
$$5 \times X = 4 \times 15$$
$$5X = 60$$
$$X = 60 \div 5$$
$$X = 12$$

Solving for *X,* the new width is 12 inches.

    This program reads in three values and an unknown (9999). A test is made to determine which position the unknown value holds in the ratio. The program will branch to one of four different equations, depending upon this position.

    After calculating the answer, the computer prints out the value of the unknown and the completed ratio. The program includes a test for repeat cycle. A 1, entered in response to the input request, branches the program back to calculate another set of values. Entering a 0 (or any other character) branches the program to END.

    The four formulas used in solving the ratio are all versions of the basic formula

$$\frac{A}{B} = \frac{C}{D}$$

A is unknown: A=C*B/D
B is unknown: B=A*D/C
C is unknown: C= A*D/B
D is unknown: D=B*C/A

VARIABLE NAMES

A = Variable, holds ratio position A
B = Variable, holds ratio position B
C = Variable, holds ratio position C
D = Variable, holds ratio position D
X = Value of unknown variable
Y = Answer to repeat cycle

PROGRAM LISTING

10	REM statement gives title.
20–60	Initialize values of A, B, C, D, and X to 0.
70,80	Skip two lines.
90–110	Print request for data for calculation.
120	Inputs four variables from keyboard.
130–160	IF/THEN statement branches control to respective calculation, depending upon which variable is unknown.
170	Computes ratio when A is unknown.
180	Transfers value of A to X.
190	Sends control to statement 280.
200	Computes ratio when B is unknown.
210	Transfers value of B to X.
220	Sends control to statement 280.
230	Computes ratio when C is unknown.
240	Transfers value of C to X.

250   Sends control to statement 280.

260   Computes ratio when D is unknown.

270   Transfers value of D to X.

280   Skips a line.

290   Prints out value of X, unknown.

300–350 Print out completed ratio, dropping in variables A and C on line 320, and B and D on line 340.

360–380 Request if user wants to repeat cycle.

390   Inputs Y, answer to repeat cycle request.

400   Branches to statement 20 to begin a new cycle, if Y is equal to 1.

410–440 Terminate program.

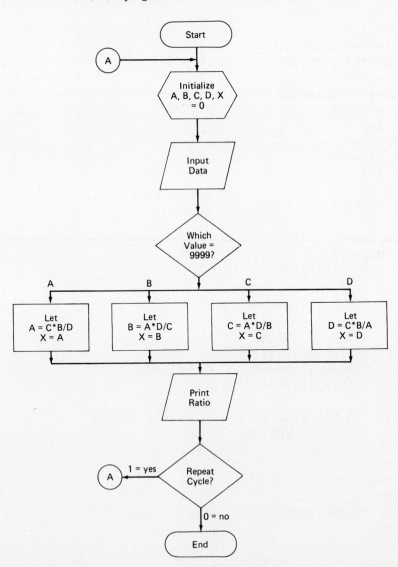

PROGRAM

```
10 REM RATIO DEMONSTRATION (RATDEM)
20 LET A=0
30 LET B=0
40 LET C=0
50 LET D=0
60 LET X=0
70 PRINT
80 PRINT
90 PRINT "PLEASE ENTER YOUR DATA."
100 PRINT "ENTER 9999 AS THE UNKNOWN VALUE."
110 PRINT
120 INPUT A,B,C,D
130 IF A=9999 THEN 170
140 IF B=9999 THEN 200
150 IF C=9999 THEN 230
160 IF D=9999 THEN 260
170 LET A=C*B/D
180 LET X=A
190 GOTO 280
200 LET B=A*D/C
210 LET X=B
220 GOTO 280
230 LET C=A*D/B
240 LET X=C
250 GOTO 280
260 LET D=C*B/A
270 LET X=D
280 PRINT
290 PRINT "YOUR UNKNOWN VALUE IS "; X
300 PRINT
310 PRINT "HERE IS THE RATIO:"
320 PRINT TAB(10);A;TAB(22);C
330 PRINT TAB(10);"-----   :   -----"
340 PRINT TAB(10);B;TAB(22);D
350 PRINT
360 PRINT "DO YOU WISH TO SOLVE ANOTHER RATIO?"
370 PRINT "ANSWER 1 FOR YES, 0 FOR NO."
380 PRINT
390 INPUT Y
400 IF Y=1 THEN 20
410 PRINT
420 PRINT "THANK YOU"
430 PRINT
440 END
```

PROGRAM RUN

PLEASE ENTER YOUR DATA.
ENTER 9999 AS THE UNKNOWN VALUE.

? 2.2,9999,6.4,12.8

YOUR UNKNOWN VALUE IS 4.4

HERE IS THE RATIO:
```
        2.2         6.4
       -----   :   -----
        4.4         12.8
```

DO YOU WISH TO SOLVE ANOTHER RATIO?
ANSWER 1 FOR YES, 0 FOR NO.

? 1

PLEASE ENTER YOUR DATA.
ENTER 9999 AS THE UNKNOWN VALUE.

? 120,360,200,9999

YOUR UNKNOWN VALUE IS 600

HERE IS THE RATIO:
```
        120         200
       -----   :   -----
        360         600
```

DO YOU WISH TO SOLVE ANOTHER RATIO?
ANSWER 1 FOR YES, 0 FOR NO.

? 0

THANK YOU

EXERCISES

1. Write a program that will read a part name and code and output the name in one of four columns depending on the code.

```
1                    2                    3                    4
GEARS
BEARINGS
                     PAINT
                                                               SCREEN
                                          BULBS
```

2. Write a program that will read in a number, perform a short calculation using that number, and then branch to one of two messages depending on the result.

TRUE ANNUAL INTEREST RATE

BASIC STATEMENTS USED

```
REM
LET
PRINT
INPUT
IF/THEN
```

ABSTRACT

This program illustrates simple mathematical operations and interactive programming. The program is designed to calculate the true annual interest rate when the purchase price, interest, down payment, and number of installments are given. True annual interest rate is found with the following formula:

$$r = \frac{2MI}{B(N+1)}$$

Below is an explanation of the quantities represented by the names in the formula and the names assigned to the same values in the program:

PROGRAM	FORMULA	MEANING
T	r	True annual interest rate
12	M	Number of payments in one year
I	I	Total interest paid
B	B	Initial unpaid balance
R	N	Annual rate of interest

The formula looks like this with the names assigned in the program:

$$T = \frac{2*12*I}{B(R+1)}$$

The program begins by initializing the mathematical fields. Then, it asks the operator to input the purchase price and down payment. Next, it asks for the interest rate and number of installments. After inputting these values, the program prints out THANK YOU and proceeds to calculate the true annual interest rate. This rate is printed out together with the amount of the loan, actual interest charges, and total amount repaid. The program then asks if the programmer wishes to repeat the calculations for another set of data. A response of 1 directs the computer back to repeat the program. Any other response will terminate execution.

VARIABLE NAMES

L = Loan
D = Down payment
R = Interest rate
N = Number of installments
B = Unpaid balance ($B=L-D$)
$R1$ = Interest rate changed to decimal ($R/100$)
I = Total interest, $B*R1*(N/12)$
$T1$ = Intermediate value ($T1=2*12*I$)

$T2$ = Intermediate value $T2 =\dfrac{T1}{B(R+1)}$

T = True annual interest rate ($T2*100$) in percent
Y = Test for repeat cycle: 1=yes; 0=no

PROGRAM LISTING

10	REM statement identifies program.
20–70	Initialize mathematical fields to 0.
80–100	Print request for information.
110	Inputs purchase price and down payment from keyboard.
120–140	Print request for information.
150	Inputs interest rate and number of installments from keyboard.
160–180	Print text.
190	Computes balance due (loan − down payment).
200	Converts interest rate from percent to decimal.
210	Computes total interest paid [balance * interest rate * years (installments/12 months)].
220	Computes intermediate value, T1.
230	Computes intermediate value, T2, annual interest rate in decimal.

240   Converts T2 to percentage—true annual interest rate T.
250–310 Print out true annual interest rate, total amount of loan, actual interest
         charge, and amount repaid.
320–330 Print out request to repeat cycle.
340   Inputs Y—answer to request.
350   Tests Y. If Y=1, directs computer to go back to statement 20 to initialize
         and begin a new cycle. If Y is any other character, control drops to next
         statement.
360–390 Print closing and terminate execution.

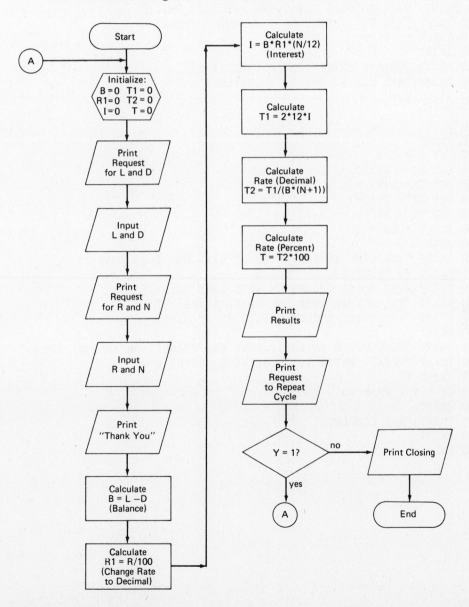

PROGRAM

```
10 REM TRUE ANNUAL INTEREST RATE (TRANIR)
20 LET B = 0
30 LET R1 = 0
40 LET I = 0
50 LET T1 = 0
60 LET T2 = 0
70 LET T = 0
80 PRINT
90 PRINT "PLEASE ENTER THE TOTAL PURCHASE PRICE"
100 PRINT "AND THE AMOUNT OF THE DOWN PAYMENT:"
110 INPUT L, D
120 PRINT
130 PRINT "PLEASE ENTER THE INTEREST RATE"
140 PRINT "AND THE NUMBER OF INSTALLMENTS:"
150 INPUT R,N
160 PRINT
170 PRINT "THANK YOU."
180 PRINT
190 LET B = L-D
200 LET R1 = R/100
210 LET I = B*R1 *(N/12)
220 LET T1 = 2*12*I
230 LET T2 = T1/(B * (N+1))
240 LET T = T2 * 100
250 PRINT
260 PRINT "THE TRUE ANNUAL INTEREST RATE FOR THIS LOAN IS ";
270 PRINT T; "PERCENT."
280 PRINT "THE TOTAL AMOUNT OF THIS LOAN IS: $"; B
290 PRINT "THE ACTUAL INTEREST CHARGES ARE: $"; I
300 PRINT "THE TOTAL AMOUNT REPAID IS $"; B+I
310 PRINT
320 PRINT "TO COMPUTE INTEREST RATE AND CHARGES ON ANOTHER LOAN,"
330 PRINT "PLEASE ENTER 1.  OTHERWISE, ENTER 0"
340 INPUT Y
350 IF Y = 1 THEN 20
360 PRINT
370 PRINT "RUN COMPLETE"
380 PRINT
390 END
```

PROGRAM RUN

```
PLEASE ENTER THE TOTAL PURCHASE PRICE
AND THE AMOUNT OF THE DOWN PAYMENT:
? 600,50

PLEASE ENTER THE INTEREST RATE
AND THE NUMBER OF INSTALLMENTS:
? 6,12

THANK YOU.


THE TRUE ANNUAL INTEREST RATE FOR THIS LOAN IS  11.0769 PERCENT.
THE TOTAL AMOUNT OF THIS LOAN IS: $ 550
THE ACTUAL INTEREST CHARGES ARE: $ 33
THE TOTAL AMOUNT REPAID IS $ 583

TO COMPUTE INTEREST RATE AND CHARGES ON ANOTHER LOAN,
PLEASE ENTER 1.  OTHERWISE, ENTER 0
? 1

PLEASE ENTER THE TOTAL PURCHASE PRICE
AND THE AMOUNT OF THE DOWN PAYMENT:
? 1000,10

PLEASE ENTER THE INTEREST RATE
AND THE NUMBER OF INSTALLMENTS:
? 8,24

THANK YOU.


THE TRUE ANNUAL INTEREST RATE FOR THIS LOAN IS  15.36 PERCENT.
THE TOTAL AMOUNT OF THIS LOAN IS: $ 990
THE ACTUAL INTEREST CHARGES ARE: $ 158.4
THE TOTAL AMOUNT REPAID IS $ 1148.4

TO COMPUTE INTEREST RATE AND CHARGES ON ANOTHER LOAN,
PLEASE ENTER 1.  OTHERWISE, ENTER 0
? 0

RUN COMPLETE
```

EXERCISES

1. Write a program that will convert a percent to a decimal and ask the user if he or she wishes to repeat the loop on another value. Design the program to input and test a variable to control the looping.
2. Write a program that will perform a calculation on a series of data items read in from a DATA statement. Design the program to include a trailer value to limit the read cycle.

STATISTICAL CORRELATION

BASIC STATEMENTS USED

```
REM
LET
READ/DATA
IF/THEN
GOTO
PRINT
Functions
```

ABSTRACT

This program introduces elementary statistical programming. It is unnecessary for a programmer to be a statistician in order to code a formula. He or she must be able only to convert each element in the formula into an instruction the computer can execute.

Business people, statisticians, and others frequently need to know the correlation (relationship) between two sets of variables. They want to know if a change in one set of variables is related in any way to a change in the other set. This test measures whether or not a corresponding change takes place and, if so, how much and in which direction. If a change in one set of variables causes the other set to change in the same direction, it is called a positive correlation. If it changes in the opposite direction, then it is a negative correlation. If no change appears, then no correlation exists. These amounts of change are measured on a scale from -1.0 to $+1.0$. A change of -1.0 represents a 100 percent negative correlation; 0.0, no correlation; and $+1.0$, 100 percent positive correlation. Most statistics books discuss this analytical technique in some detail.

The computer can conveniently calculate correlation using the formula below:

$$r = \frac{N\Sigma XY - \Sigma X\Sigma Y}{\sqrt{[N\Sigma X^2 - (\Sigma X)^2]\,[N\Sigma Y^2 - (\Sigma Y)^2]}}$$

The names in the formula are given below, along with an explanation of what they represent. The names assigned to these same values in the program are also listed.

PROGRAM	FORMULA	MEANING
N	N	Number of variables in each set
X	X	First set of variables
Y	Y	Second set of variables
	Σ	Sum of
R	r	Correlation
A	ΣX	Sum of the first set
B	ΣY	Sum of the second set
C	ΣXY	Sum of the products of each pair
D	ΣX^2	Sum of squared variables of the first set
E	ΣY^2	Sum of squared variables of the second set

The computer is fed two sets of data, each representing a group of observations. The formula above will process the two groups of data and calculate and print out a correlation value between -1.0 and $+1.0$. Below is the formula with the names assigned in the program inserted:

$$R = \frac{(N*C) - (A*B)}{\sqrt{[(N*D) - A^2]\,[(N*E) - B^2]}}$$

This program illustrates a single-pass computation. The computer terminates execution after the correlation for one set of data has been found.

First, the program initializes the mathematical fields. It reads in one value from each set of data (X and Y). Then, it tests X to see if it is the trailer record. If not, it performs several procedures on the two variables and then loops back to read in the next two variables. When the last record has been reached, the program branches to another set of calculations and completes the calculations for correlation. Finally, the answer is printed out as a fraction and the program terminates.

VARIABLE NAMES

N = Number of variables in each set
X = First set of variables

Y = Second set of variables
A = Sum of first set of variables
B = Sum of second set of variables
C = Sum of products
D = Sum of squared variables, first set
E = Sum of squared variables, second set
F = Intermediate value $(N*C) - (A*B)$
G = Intermediate value $(N*D) - A^2$
H = Intermediate value $(N*E) - B^2$
I = Intermediate value $(G*H)$
J = Intermediate value $[SQR(I)]$
R = Correlation value (F/J)

PROGRAM LISTING

10	REM statement identifies program.
20–80	Initialize mathematical fields to 0.
90	Reads in two variables, one from each set (X and Y).
100	Tests X to see if it is last record. (Branches to statement 180 if X= 9999; if not, moves to next statement.)
110	Adds 1 to N. Counter N will count the number of pairs of variables read in.
120	Adds value of variable X just read in to A. Variable A is a running total of all the values in the X set.
130	Adds value of variable Y just read in to B. Variable B is a running total of all the values in the Y set.
140	Multiplies X by Y and adds this product to a running total, C.
150	Squares variable X and adds to a running total, D.
160	Squares variable Y and adds to a running total, E.
170	Directs control back to statement 90 to read in another set of variables X and Y.
180	Computes F, an intermediate value.
190	Computes G, an intermediate value.
200	Computes H, an intermediate value.
210	Computes I, an intermediate value $(G*H)$.
220	Extracts the square root of I.
230	Computes R, the correlation coefficient (F/J).
240–260	Print out the answer and label.
270,280	DATA statements contain X and Y sets of variables. Variables are in alternate positions in the same DATA statement.
290,300	Terminate execution.

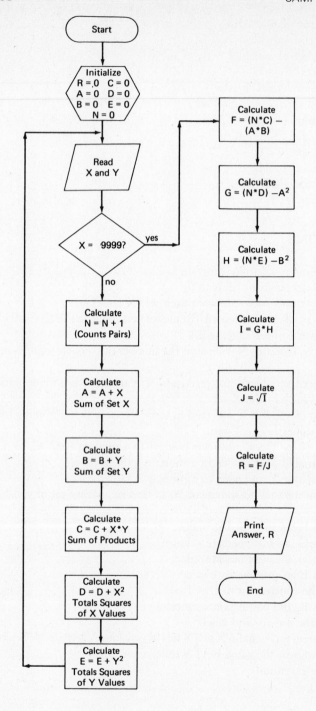

PROGRAM

```
10 REM STATISTICAL CORRELATION (STACOR)
20 LET R=0
30 LET A=0
40 LET B=0
50 LET C=0
60 LET D=0
70 LET E=0
80 LET N=0
90 READ X,Y
100 IF X=9999 THEN 180
110 LET N=N+1
120 LET A=A+X
130 LET B=B+Y
140 LET C=C+X*Y
150 LET D=D+X^2
160 LET E=E+Y^2
170 GOTO 90
180 LET F=(N*C) - (A*B)
190 LET G=(N*D) - (A^2)
200 LET H=(N*E) - (B^2)
210 LET I=G*H
220 LET J=SQR(I)
230 LET R=F/J
240 PRINT
250 PRINT
260 PRINT "THE CORRELATION VALUE FOR YOUR SET OF DATA IS: ";R
270 DATA 9.2,22,26.7,18,32.5,17,31.1,19,49.3,24
280 DATA 62.8,25,73.8,23,86.2,21,9999,9
290 PRINT
300 END
```

PROGRAM RUN

```
THE CORRELATION VALUE FOR YOUR SET OF DATA IS:   .445568
```

EXERCISES

1. Write a program that will read in a series of numbers and compute the mean. Label the output.
2. Modify the program in this example so that the data is entered from an INPUT statement rather than a DATA statement.

LAND POPULATION DENSITY

BASIC STATEMENTS USED

```
REM
PRINT
INPUT
IF/THEN
GOTO
LET
FOR/NEXT
```

ABSTRACT

Pictograms are often used to help visualize statistical and numeric data. This program prepares a pictogram from data entered from the keyboard. The program reads in several parameters: the name of a city, its area in square miles, and its population. The program then prints out a visual pattern of symbols representative of the data.

The algorithm is as follows: First, the computer reads in the city's name, square miles, and population. Then, it branches to one of four tracks depending on the population (P). Each track assigns a different symbol to represent the population density in the pictogram. These range from ". ." for low population density to "**" for high density. Then, the program tests the square miles (M) and branches to one of four tracks depending on the area. Each track assigns a different value to the variable A, which controls the depth and width of the pictogram. The program will print out the assigned symbol (S$) A times across each line for the width. Then, it repeats this line A times for the depth. The value of A ranges from 4 for areas less than 10 miles up to 16 for areas greater than 250 miles.

After printing out the first pictogram, the program asks whether another iteration is desired. Depending upon whether a 1 or a 0 is entered, the program will either repeat the cycle or branch to END.

VARIABLE NAMES

N$ = Name of city
M = Square miles
P = Population
S$ = Symbol to represent population density
A = Variable, representative of square miles, which controls size of pictogram
J = Index in outer FOR/NEXT loop
I = Index in inner FOR/NEXT loop
Y = Test variable for repeat cycle

PROGRAM LISTING

10	REM statement identifies program.
20	Prints request for information.
30	Inputs name of city (N$), square miles (M), and population (P).
40–70	Print title and name of city.
80	Tests P to see if it is less than or equal to 5,000. (If it is, branches to statement 120; if not, goes to next statement.)
90	Tests P to see if it is less than or equal to 15,000. (If true, goes to statement 140.)
100	Test P to see if it is less than or equal to 30,000. (If true, goes to statement 160; if not, goes to next statement.)
110	Directs control to statement 180 when P is greater than 30,000.
120	Assigns symbol ".." when population is less than or equal to 5,000.
130	Directs control to statement 190.
140	Assigns symbol "++" when population is between 5,001 and 15,000.
150	Directs control to statement 190.
160	Assigns symbol "00" when population is between 15,001 and 30,000.
170	Directs control to statement 190.
180	Assigns symbol "**" when population is over 30,000.
190	Tests M to see if it is less than 10. (If true, goes to statement 230; if not, goes to next statement.)
200	Tests M to see if it is less than 100. (If true, goes to statement 250; if not, goes to next statement.)
210	Tests M to see if it is less than 250. (If true, goes to statement 270; if not, goes to next statement.)
220	Tests M to see if it is greater than or equal to 250. (If true, goes to statement 290.) An unconditional branch could have been used here.
230	Assigns the value of 4 to A when the square miles are less than 10.
240	Directs control to statement 300.
250	Assigns the value of 8 to A when the square miles are less than 100.

260	Directs control to statement 300.
270	Assigns the value of 12 to A when the square miles are less than 250.
280	Directs control to statement 300.
290	Assigns the value of 16 to A when the square miles are greater than or equal to 250.
300	Begins outer loop. Directs computer to repeat all statements A times down to line 350. The first time the loop is executed, $J=1$ and the computer prints out the first line. For the next loop, $J=2$, the computer prints out the second line, and so on. When J equals A, the computer will have printed out the line A times and control drops to line 360.
310	Tells computer to move to next print line.
320	Begins inner loop. Directs computer to repeat all steps A times down to statement 340. The first time the loop is executed, $I=1$ and one pattern of S$ is printed out. For the next loop, $I=2$, another pattern is printed on the same line. Then $I=3$ and a third pattern is printed on the same line, and so on. When I equals A, one print line has been completed and control drops to statement 350, which directs the program back to the beginning of the outer loop to print another line.
330	Print statement directs computer to print S$ in packed zone spacing.
340	Increases index for inner loop. Marks end of range.
350	Increases index and marks end of range for outer loop.
360–390	Print out request to repeat cycle.
400	Inputs test variable for repeat cycle, Y.
410	Tests Y. (If $Y=1$, goes back to statement 20 to repeat program; if not, goes to next statement.)
420–450	Terminate program.

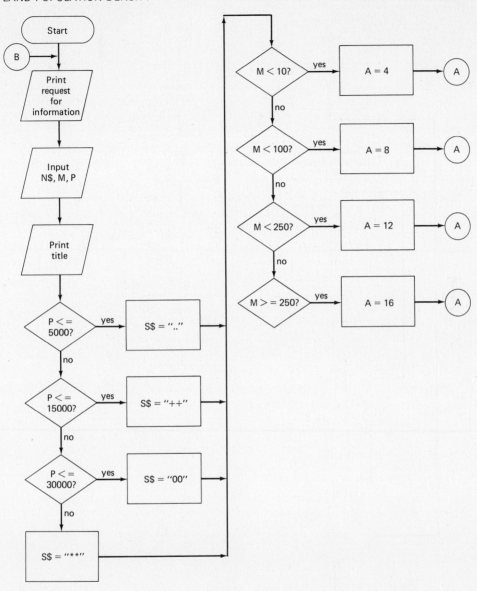

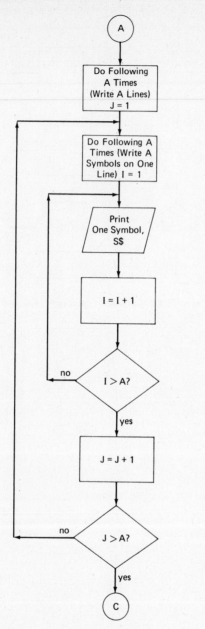

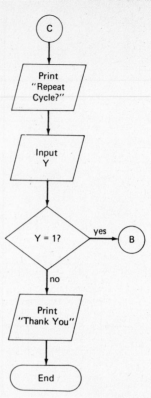

PROGRAM

```
10 REM LAND POPULATION DENSITY (LAPODE)
20 PRINT "PLEASE ENTER CITY, SQ. MILES AND POPULATION"
30 INPUT N$,M,P
40 PRINT
50 PRINT
60 PRINT "HERE IS PICTOGRAM OF "; N$
70 PRINT
80 IF P<=5000 THEN 120
90 IF P<=15000 THEN 140
100 IF P<=30000 THEN 160
110 GOTO 180
120 LET S$ = ".."
130 GOTO 190
140 LET S$ = "++"
150 GOTO 190
160 LET S$ = "00"
170 GOTO 190
180 LET S$ = "**"
190 IF M<10 THEN 230
200 IF M<100 THEN 250
210 IF M<250 THEN 270
220 IF M>=250 THEN 290
230 LET A=4
240 GOTO 300
250 LET A=8
260 GOTO 300
270 LET A=12
280 GOTO 300
290 LET A=16
300 FOR J=1 TO A
310   PRINT
320     FOR I=1 TO A
330       PRINT S$;
340     NEXT I
350 NEXT J
360 PRINT
370 PRINT
380 PRINT "DO YOU WISH TO PRINT ANOTHER PICTOGRAM?"
390 PRINT "ANSWER 1 FOR YES, 0 FOR NO"
400 INPUT Y
410 IF Y=1 THEN 20
420 PRINT
430 PRINT "THANK YOU"
440 PRINT
450 END
```

PROGRAM RUN

```
PLEASE ENTER CITY, SQ. MILES AND POPULATION
? MEADVILLE,5,500000


HERE IS PICTOGRAM OF MEADVILLE


********
********
********
********

DO YOU WISH TO PRINT ANOTHER PICTOGRAM?
ANSWER 1 FOR YES, 0 FOR NO
? 1
PLEASE ENTER CITY, SQ. MILES AND POPULATION
? BROWNTOWN,200,4000


HERE IS PICTOGRAM OF BROWNTOWN


.........................
.........................
.........................
.........................
.........................
.........................
.........................
.........................
.........................
.........................
.........................
.........................

DO YOU WISH TO PRINT ANOTHER PICTOGRAM?
ANSWER 1 FOR YES, 0 FOR NO
? 1
PLEASE ENTER CITY, SQ. MILES AND POPULATION
? SCOTSDALE,50,10000
```

HERE IS PICTOGRAM OF SCOTSDALE


```
+++++++++++++++
+++++++++++++++
+++++++++++++++
+++++++++++++++
+++++++++++++++
+++++++++++++++
+++++++++++++++
+++++++++++++++
```

DO YOU WISH TO PRINT ANOTHER PICTOGRAM?
ANSWER 1 FOR YES, 0 FOR NO

? 1
PLEASE ENTER CITY, SQ. MILES AND POPULATION
? YELLOWROCK,600,20000

HERE IS PICTOGRAM OF YELLOWROCK


```
OOOOOOOOOOOOOOOOOOOOOOOOOOOOOOOOO
OOOOOOOOOOOOOOOOOOOOOOOOOOOOOOOOO
OOOOOOOOOOOOOOOOOOOOOOOOOOOOOOOOO
OOOOOOOOOOOOOOOOOOOOOOOOOOOOOOOOO
OOOOOOOOOOOOOOOOOOOOOOOOOOOOOOOOO
OOOOOOOOOOOOOOOOOOOOOOOOOOOOOOOOO
OOOOOOOOOOOOOOOOOOOOOOOOOOOOOOOOO
OOOOOOOOOOOOOOOOOOOOOOOOOOOOOOOOO
OOOOOOOOOOOOOOOOOOOOOOOOOOOOOOOOO
OOOOOOOOOOOOOOOOOOOOOOOOOOOOOOOOO
OOOOOOOOOOOOOOOOOOOOOOOOOOOOOOOOO
OOOOOOOOOOOOOOOOOOOOOOOOOOOOOOOOO
OOOOOOOOOOOOOOOOOOOOOOOOOOOOOOOOO
OOOOOOOOOOOOOOOOOOOOOOOOOOOOOOOOO
OOOOOOOOOOOOOOOOOOOOOOOOOOOOOOOOO
OOOOOOOOOOOOOOOOOOOOOOOOOOOOOOOOO
OOOOOOOOOOOOOOOOOOOOOOOOOOOOOOOOO
```

DO YOU WISH TO PRINT ANOTHER PICTOGRAM?
ANSWER 1 FOR YES, 0 FOR NO
? 0

THANK YOU

EXERCISES

1. Write a program that will read in a number between 1 and 50. Then have the computer output an equal number of X's on a horizontal line.
2. Modify this program so that the data are entered from READ/DATA statements rather than an INPUT statement.

COMPUTER ART PROGRAM

BASIC STATEMENTS USED

```
REM
PRINT
LET
INPUT
IF/THEN
GOTO
FOR/NEXT
TAB
```

ABSTRACT

There are many graphic techniques that can be used in programming. This program illustrates how symmetrical patterns can be created from various symbols and values input via the keyboard. This program relies heavily upon the TAB command, a valuable extension found on many computers.

First, the program asks the user to enter a symbol and the depth and width of the finished piece of art. The pattern is printed out by PRINT statements (with TAB commands) included in FOR/NEXT loops. The increment (or step) and limit of the loops are determined by manipulating the values input as the depth and width of the pattern.

Here is the logic in the program: Each pattern is divided into three vertical portions. The first section prints out the top of the pattern, from its narrowest point to its fullest width. The third section prints out the bottom of the pattern, where the symbols move from the fullest width back to the narrowest point. The second, or middle, section is used only on long and narrow patterns to print out the lines that do not change width.

First, the program compares the values entered by the user (depth and width) to determine if the pattern will be approximately square, short and wide, or long and narrow. If the pattern is square or short and wide, the program will calculate how many columns the symbols should move apart each time they are printed to reach the fullest width. This value is used as the step in the FOR/NEXT loop, which prints out the symbols. If the pattern is long and narrow, the step is 1—that is, the symbols will move apart one column on each line.

Next, the program determines how many lines are needed to reach the fullest width of the pattern. If the pattern is square or short and wide, the value is found by dividing the depth in half. If it is long and narrow, it is determined by dividing the width in half. Then, the value is multiplied by the step to determine E, the limit in the first FOR/NEXT loop that prints out the top section of the pattern. The program calculates F, the number of lines in the middle section of the long and narrow pattern.

The pattern is printed out by three FOR/NEXT loops. The first outputs the top section of the pattern, printing two symbols on each line. The positions of the symbols are indicated by the TAB command in the PRINT statement. If the pattern is square or short and wide, the tab positions will move two or more columns to the right and left with each pass. If the pattern is long and narrow, the tab positions will move by one column to the right and left each pass.

Next, the program branches, depending on the shape of the pattern. If it is long and narrow, a FOR/NEXT loop prints out the middle section of the pattern. The tab positions do not change. The last FOR/NEXT loop prints out the bottom portion of all patterns. The tab positions move together by the same step value used in the top section and the same number of lines are printed.

Then, the program asks the user if he or she wishes to print another pattern. An answer of 1 returns control to the beginning of the program. Any other answer terminates execution.

VARIABLE NAMES

A = Input variable for repeat cycle
D = Depth of pattern (number of lines)
E = Intermediate value used as limit on first FOR/NEXT loop: number of lines in top portion of pattern multiplied by step
F = Intermediate value: number of lines in middle portion of pattern
I = Index for print cycles, top and bottom sections
K = Index for print cycle, middle section
L = Saves value of I from first FOR/NEXT loop; used as limit in third FOR/NEXT loop, which prints out bottom section
S = Step for FOR/NEXT loops; indicates how far apart symbols will be printed
S$ = Symbol for pattern
W = Width of pattern (columns wide)

PROGRAM LISTING

```
10      REM statement identifies program.
20      Skips line.
```

30–60	Initialize L, S, E, and F to 0.
70–90	Request user to input symbol pattern, depth, and width.
100	Inputs S$ (symbol pattern), D (depth), and W (width).
110	Skips line.
120	Branches to statement 170 if D is less than or equal to W (short and wide or square pattern). If pattern is long and narrow, control drops to next statement.
130	Assigns the value of 1 to S (step).
140	Calculates E (limit for first FOR/NEXT loop).
150	Calculates F (number of lines in middle section).
160	Branches control to statement 190.
170	Calculates S (step for square or short and wide pattern).
180	Calculates E (limit for first FOR/NEXT loop).
190	Begins first FOR/NEXT loop. Directs computer to repeat the following steps, increasing the value of I by S and testing it against E each cycle. When I becomes greater than E, the steps are not performed, and control drops to statement 230.
200	PRINT statement with TAB command. Tells computer to substitute the value of I, evaluate the expression, and use this value as the TAB column indicator. The computer will print S$ in the columns indicated by the TAB commands.
210	Assigns the value of I to L for later use. When the loop is completed, L will be equal to the highest value that I reaches.
220	End of range of FOR/NEXT loop. Directs control back to statement 190.
230	Branches to statement 270 if pattern is square or short and wide.
240	FOR/NEXT loop, which prints out middle section of long and narrow pattern. Directs computer to perform following steps F times.
250	Prints out two symbols per line, using highest value of I from first FOR/NEXT loop. Since the value of I in the TAB command does not change, the symbols will be printed out in the same position each line.
260	End of range of FOR/NEXT loop. Directs control back to statement 240.
270	Third FOR/NEXT loop prints out bottom section of pattern. This uses a negative counter. The initial value of the index is assigned at L (the highest value of I) and the limit at 1. The step (S) will be subtracted from the index each pass, until the limit (1) is reached. At this point, control drops to statement 300.
280	PRINT statement prints out two symbols per line. The value of I in the TAB command will be decreased by the step each pass.
290	End of range of third FOR/NEXT loop. Directs control back to statement 270.
300–330	Print out request for information and skip lines.
340	Inputs A, test variable for repeat cycle.
350	Tests A. If it equals 1, branches control to statement 20. If it is any other character, control drops to next statement.
360–390	Terminate execution.

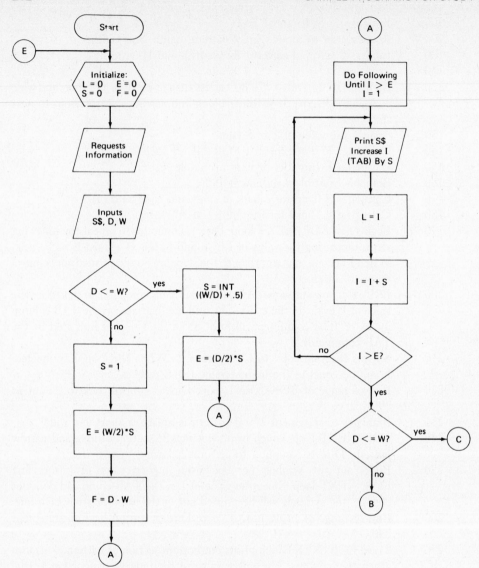

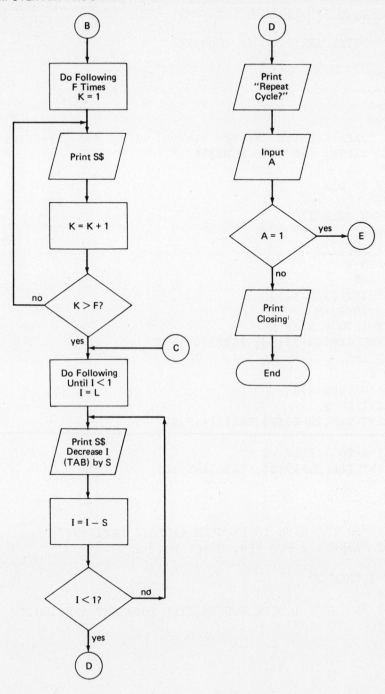

PROGRAM

```
10 REM COMPUTER ART PROGRAM (COMART)
20 PRINT
30 LET L=0
40 LET S=0
50 LET E=0
60 LET F=0
70 PRINT "PLEASE ENTER PATTERN SYMBOL, DEPTH AND APPROXIMATE"
80 PRINT "WIDTH, (IN EVEN NUMBERS)."
90 PRINT
100 INPUT S$,D,W
110 PRINT
120 IF D<=W THEN 170
130 LET S=1
140 LET E=(W/2)*S
150 LET F=D-W
160 GOTO 190
170 LET S=INT((W/D)+.5)
180 LET E=(D/2)*S
190 FOR I=1 TO E STEP S
200    PRINT TAB(20-I);S$; TAB(21+I);S$
210    LET L=I
220 NEXT I
230 IF D<=W THEN 270
240 FOR K=1 TO F
250    PRINT TAB(20-I);S$ TAB(21+I);S$
260 NEXT K
270 FOR I=L TO 1 STEP -S
280    PRINT TAB(20-I);S$; TAB(21+I);S$
290 NEXT I
300 PRINT
310 PRINT
320 PRINT "DO YOU WISH TO PROGRAM ANOTHER PATTERN?"
330 PRINT "ANSWER 1 FOR YES, 0 FOR NO."
340 INPUT A
350 IF A=1 THEN 20
360 PRINT
370 PRINT "          I HOPE YOU ENJOYED YOUR ART SESSION."
380 PRINT
390 END
```

PROGRAM RUN

PLEASE ENTER PATTERN SYMBOL, DEPTH AND APPROXIMATE
WIDTH, (IN EVEN NUMBERS).

? (0),20,10

```
              (0)(0)
             (0)   (0)
            (0)       (0)
           (0)         (0)
          (0)           (0)
         (0)             (0)
         (0)             (0)
         (0)             (0)
         (0)             (0)
         (0)             (0)
         (0)             (0)
         (0)             (0)
         (0)             (0)
         (0)             (0)
         (0)             (0)
          (0)           (0)
           (0)         (0)
            (0)       (0)
             (0)   (0)
              (0)(0)
```

DO YOU WISH TO PROGRAM ANOTHER PATTERN?
ANSWER 1 FOR YES, 0 FOR NO.
? 1

PLEASE ENTER PATTERN SYMBOL, DEPTH AND APPROXIMATE
WIDTH, (IN EVEN NUMBERS).

? <X>,8,30

```
              <X><X>
           <X>        <X>
         <X>             <X>
       <X>                 <X>
       <X>                 <X>
         <X>             <X>
           <X>        <X>
              <X><X>
```

```
DO YOU WISH TO PROGRAM ANOTHER PATTERN?
ANSWER 1 FOR YES, 0 FOR NO.
? 1

PLEASE ENTER PATTERN SYMBOL, DEPTH AND APPROXIMATE
WIDTH, (IN EVEN NUMBERS).

? [*],10,10

                    [*][*]
                   [*]  [*]
                  [*]    [*]
                 [*]      [*]
                [*]        [*]
                [*]        [*]
                 [*]      [*]
                  [*]    [*]
                   [*]  [*]
                    [*][*]


DO YOU WISH TO PROGRAM ANOTHER PATTERN?
ANSWER 1 FOR YES, 0 FOR NO.
? 0

        I HOPE YOU ENJOYED YOUR ART SESSION.
```

EXERCISES

1. Write a program that will input a combination of three symbols and repeat them across a horizontal line.
2. Write a program that will input a combination of three symbols and repeat them down a vertical column.

NUMERIC ARRAY DEMONSTRATION

BASIC STATEMENTS USED

```
REM
DIM
FOR/NEXT
READ/DATA
PRINT
RESTORE
```

ABSTRACT

This program demonstrates how two-dimensional data arrays are loaded and manipulated. Literal text in PRINT statements is used liberally to explain in detail each step and example in the program. Nested FOR/NEXT loops are used to read in and print out data from the arrays. RESTORE statements allow the same data to be used to load three arrays in different ways. The program also illustrates how individual elements in two-dimensional arrays are referenced.

First, the program reserves storage spaces for the three arrays that will be used in the course of execution. Then, the first set of nested FOR/NEXT loops loads array A. Literal text explains the dimensions and indexes of array A. Then, the indexes (subscripts) and data of array A are printed out by PRINT statements. Each element in the array can be referenced individually. Single elements from array A are referenced and printed out with an explanation.

A RESTORE statement makes the same data available again to the program. A set of nested FOR/NEXT loops loads this data into array B, which is 10 rows by 3 columns. The BASIC interpreter prints out arrays five items or more to a line. Since this array has only three columns, each column is called out by its subscript in the PRINT statement. A single FOR/NEXT loop is used to print out the rows automatically.

Next, the data is again restored. This time it is loaded into array C, vertically: the index loading the columns (J) is in the outer FOR/NEXT loop and the index I, which loads the rows, is in the inner loop. This causes the computer to load one column first, then the next, and so on. Nested FOR/NEXT loops print out array C. Since the computer print unit completes one line at a time, the indexes are reversed to output by rows.

VARIABLE NAMES

A = First array; 6 rows, 5 columns, loaded horizontally
B = Second array; 10 rows, 3 columns, loaded horizontally
C = Third array; 6 rows, 5 columns, loaded vertically
I = Index controlling subscripting of rows
J = Index controlling subscripting of columns

PROGRAM LISTING

10	REM statement identifies program.
20	DIM statement reserves storage space for three arrays.
30	Begins outer FOR/NEXT loop. Instructs computer to repeat statements 6 times down to number 70, increasing the value of I by 1 each time. When I is greater than 6, control drops to statement 100.
40	Begins inner FOR/NEXT loop. Instructs computer to repeat statements 5 times down to number 60, increasing the value of J by 1 each time. When J is greater than 5, control drops to statement 70. Each time this loop is completed, one row in the array is loaded.
50	Reads one value into array A, assigning current values of I and J as subscripts.
60	End of range of inner FOR/NEXT loop that directs control back to statement 40.
70	End of range of outer FOR/NEXT loop that directs control back to statement 30.
80–90	DATA statements contain values to be loaded into arrays.
100–140	Print titles.
150–230	Print explanation and description of array A.
240	Prints column headings and index J.
250	Skips line.
260–310	Print out array A with index I shown, each element being called out by subscripts.
320–360	Literal explanation of how to call out single elements.
370–390	Print out single elements A(3,2) and A(5,4) with labels.
400–470	Print out explanation and title for array B.
480	RESTORE statement tells computer to reuse same data in statements 80 and 90.

490   Outer FOR/NEXT loop controls subscripting of rows.

500   Inner FOR/NEXT loop controls subscripting of columns.

510   Reads in one value and assigns it the name B and current values of I and J as subscripts.

520   End of range of inner loop that returns control to statement 500.

530   End of range of outer loop that returns control to statement 490.

540   Loop controls subscripting of rows during printing.

550   Prints out one value from column 1, one from column 2, and one from column 3.

560   End of range of loop.

570–590 Print out heading for array C.

600   RESTORE statement restores data in statement 80 and 90 for reuse.

610   Outer loop controls J index this time—for subscripting columns. Each time this cycle is completed, one column will be filled. When the limit 5 is reached, five columns will be filled. Control then drops to statement 660.

620   Inner loop controls I index—for subscripting rows. This loop will be performed six times, loading one item into each row of the column, and then control will return to the outer loop to move to the next column. Items load vertically.

630   Reads in one value assigning name as C and current values of I and J.

640   End of range of inner loop.

650   End of range of outer loop.

660–680 Print out title of array C.

690   Outer loop controls subscripting of rows. Prints out six rows of array C.

700   Inner loop controls subscripting of columns. Prints out one item from each column.

710   Print statement calls out each item in array, substituting current values of I and J.

720   End of range of inner loop.

730   End of range of outer loop.

740–760 Terminate execution.

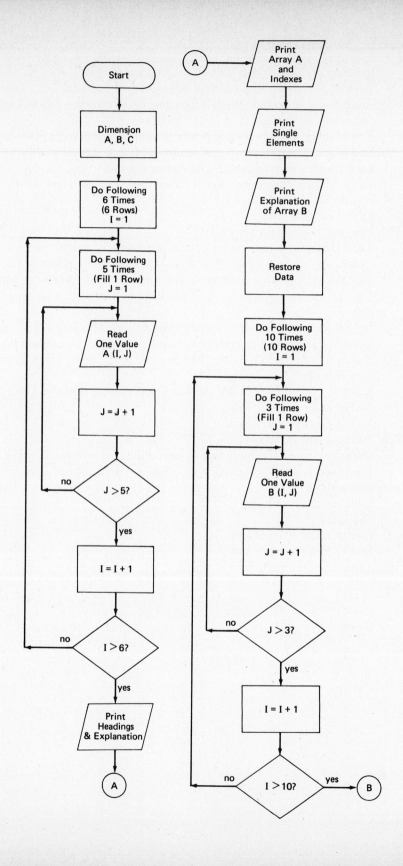

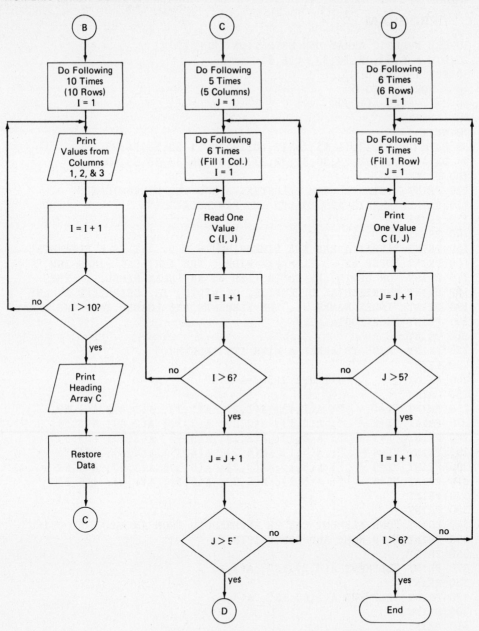

PROGRAM

```
10 REM NUMERIC ARRAY DEMONSTRATION (NUMARD)
20 DIM A(6,5), B(10,3), C(6,5)
30 FOR I=1 TO 6
40   FOR J=1 TO 5
50     READ A(I,J)
60   NEXT J
70 NEXT I
80 DATA 11,12,13,14,15,16,17,18,19,20,21,22,23,24,25
90 DATA 26,27,28,29,30,31,32,33,34,35,36,37,38,39,40
100 PRINT
110 PRINT "THIS PROGRAM ILLUSTRATES HOW TWO-DIMENSIONAL"
120 PRINT "ARRAYS ARE LOADED AND MANIPULATED."
130 PRINT
140 PRINT
150 PRINT "ARRAY A HAS THE DIMENSIONS 6 X 5.  IT IS 6 ELEMENTS"
160 PRINT "DEEP AND 5 ELEMENTS WIDE.  THE VERTICAL DIMENSION,"
170 PRINT "OR DEPTH, IS CONTROLLED BY AN INDEX NAMED I.  THE"
180 PRINT "HORIZONTAL DIMENSION, OR WIDTH, IS CONTROLLED BY AN"
190 PRINT "INDEX NAMED J.  THE ELEMENTS ARE LOADED INTO THE ARRAY"
200 PRINT "HORIZONTALLY."
210 PRINT
220 PRINT "HERE IS ARRAY A WITH ITS INDEXES:"
230 PRINT
240 PRINT "       J=1 J=2 J=3 J=4 J=5"
250 PRINT
260 PRINT "I=1 - "; A(1,1); A(1,2); A(1,3); A(1,4); A(1,5)
270 PRINT "I=2 - "; A(2,1); A(2,2); A(2,3); A(2,4); A(2,5)
280 PRINT "I=3 - "; A(3,1); A(3,2); A(3,3); A(3,4); A(3,5)
290 PRINT "I=4 - "; A(4,1); A(4,2); A(4,3); A(4,4); A(4,5)
300 PRINT "I=5 - "; A(5,1); A(5,2); A(5,3); A(5,4); A(5,5)
310 PRINT "I=6 - "; A(6,1); A(6,2); A(6,3); A(6,4); A(6,5)
320 PRINT
330 PRINT
340 PRINT "ONE ELEMENT CAN BE REFERENCED FROM AN ARRAY BY USING"
350 PRINT "ITS NAME AND SUBSCRIPTS."
360 PRINT
370 PRINT "ELEMENT A(3,2) IS"; A(3,2)
380 PRINT
390 PRINT "ELEMENT A(5,4) IS"; A(5,4)
400 PRINT
410 PRINT
420 PRINT "THE ARRANGEMENT OF ELEMENTS IN AN ARRAY CAN BE CHANGED"
430 PRINT "BY CHANGING ITS DIMENSIONS.  IN ARRAY B, I (DEPTH)"
440 PRINT "IS SET TO 10 AND J (WIDTH) IS SET TO 3."
```

```
450 PRINT
460 PRINT "ARRAY B"
470 PRINT
480 RESTORE
490 FOR I=1 TO 10
500   FOR J=1 TO 3
510     READ B(I,J)
520   NEXT J
530 NEXT I
540 FOR I=1 TO 10
550     PRINT B(I,1); B(I,2); B(I,3)
560 NEXT I
570 PRINT
580 PRINT
590 PRINT "IN ARRAY C THE ELEMENTS HAVE BEEN LOADED VERTICALLY."
600 RESTORE
610 FOR J=1 TO 5
620   FOR I=1 TO 6
630     READ C(I,J)
640   NEXT I
650 NEXT J
660 PRINT
670 PRINT "ARRAY C"
680 PRINT
690 FOR I=1 TO 6
700   FOR J=1 TO 5
710     PRINT C(I,J),
720   NEXT J
730 NEXT I
740 PRINT
750 PRINT
760 END
```

PROGRAM RUN

THIS PROGRAM ILLUSTRATES HOW TWO-DIMENSIONAL
ARRAYS ARE LOADED AND MANIPULATED.

ARRAY A HAS THE DIMENSIONS 6 X 5. IT IS 6 ELEMENTS
DEEP AND 5 ELEMENTS WIDE. THE VERTICAL DIMENSION,
OR DEPTH, IS CONTROLLED BY AN INDEX NAMED I. THE
HORIZONTAL DIMENSION, OR WIDTH, IS CONTROLLED BY AN
INDEX NAMED J. THE ELEMENTS ARE LOADED INTO THE ARRAY
HORIZONTALLY.

HERE IS ARRAY A WITH ITS INDEXES:

```
        J=1 J=2 J=3 J=4 J=5

I=1 -   11  12  13  14  15
I=2 -   16  17  18  19  20
I=3 -   21  22  23  24  25
I=4 -   26  27  28  29  30
I=5 -   31  32  33  34  35
I=6 -   36  37  38  39  40
```

ONE ELEMENT CAN BE REFERENCED FROM AN ARRAY BY USING
ITS NAME AND SUBSCRIPTS.

ELEMENT A(3,2) IS 22

ELEMENT A(5,4) IS 34

THE ARRANGEMENT OF ELEMENTS IN AN ARRAY CAN BE CHANGED
BY CHANGING ITS DIMENSIONS. IN ARRAY B, I (DEPTH)
IS SET TO 10 AND J (WIDTH) IS SET TO 3.

ARRAY B

```
11  12  13
14  15  16
17  18  19
20  21  22
23  24  25
26  27  28
29  30  31
32  33  34
35  36  37
38  39  40
```

IN ARRAY C THE ELEMENTS HAVE BEEN LOADED VERTICALLY.

ARRAY C

```
11          17          23          29          35
12          18          24          30          36
13          19          25          31          37
14          20          26          32          38
15          21          27          33          39
16          22          28          34          40
```

EXERCISES

1. Write a program that will read in data items from a DATA statement and load them into a one-dimensional array. Output the results in a vertical column.
2. Write a program that will read in data items from a DATA statement and load them into a two-dimensional array (4 × 5). Output, labeling rows and columns.

STORE PERSONNEL INFORMATION

BASIC STATEMENTS USED

```
REM
DIM
FOR/NEXT
READ/DATA
PRINT
INPUT
LET
IF/THEN
```

ABSTRACT

This program illustrates one application of arrays. A file of personnel information is stored in three arrays. The first array contains the store numbers; the second array, the number of hourly employees in each store; and the third, the number of salaried employees in each store. This constitutes a data base from which the programmer may retrieve information on each store.

The logic is as follows: A READ statement in a FOR/NEXT loop reads three pieces of data each cycle. It assigns them the same subscript but stores them in different arrays. For example, the first time through the loop, $I = 1$. The first piece of data (store number) is stored in location 1 of array A. The second item (hourly employees) is placed in the first location of array B and the third (salaried employees) in the first location of array C. The next time through the loop, $I = 2$. The next three pieces of data are assigned the subscript 2 and placed in the second location of the three arrays. This continues until information on 10 stores has been loaded and arrayed.

In this program, the store number is the same as the subscript. When the programmer wishes to retrieve information on a specific store, he or she inputs the store number. This is substituted by the program for I (dummy subscript) in the PRINT statements, and the appropriate elements from the three arrays are printed out. The programmer can then repeat the search on another store, or branch to END.

VARIABLE NAMES

A = First array: holds store numbers
B = Second array: holds number of hourly employees
C = Third array: holds number of salaried employees
D = Store number that user needs information on
E = Test variable for repeat cycle
I = Index controlling subscripting of three arrays

PROGRAM LISTING

10	REM statement identifies program.
20	DIM statement reserves storage for three arrays.
30	Repeats the following statements 10 times, increasing the value of I by 1 each pass. (When I is greater than 10, control drops to statement 60.)
40	Reads in three data items from DATA statements 290 and 300. Stores them in arrays A, B, and C, and assigns them the current value of I as their subscript.
50	End of range of FOR/NEXT loop. Returns control to statement 30.
60–80	Print out request for information from keyboard.
90	Inputs D, the store number to be searched for in the file.
100–120	Print message and skip lines.
130	Assigns the value of the store number to the dummy subscript.
140, 150	Print out message containing store number and the current value of I.
160, 170	Print out hourly employees, substituting the value of I to reference the appropriate element in the array.
180–200	Print out salaried employees for the appropriate store. Again the input store number is substituted for the value of I.
210	Prints out the total number of employees in the store.
220–250	Print message asking user if a repeat cycle is wanted.
260	Inputs E, test variable for repeat cycle.
270	Tests E. If E=1, then program branches to statement 60 to repeat the data retrieval cycle. If E equals any other value, control drops to statement 280.
280	Prints closing message.
290,300	Are DATA statements for READ statement 40.
310	Terminates execution.

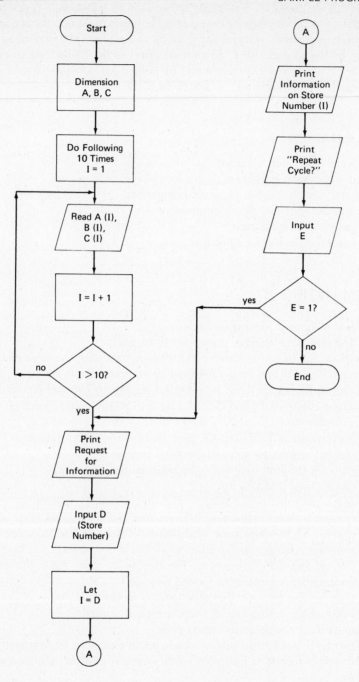

PROGRAM

```
10 REM STORE PERSONNEL INFORMATION (STOPIN)
20 DIM A(10), B(10), C(10)
30 FOR I=1 TO 10
40    READ A(I), B(I), C(I)
50 NEXT I
60 PRINT
70 PRINT
80 PRINT "PLEASE ENTER STORE NUMBER FOR PERSONNEL INFORMATION"
90 INPUT D
100 PRINT "THANK YOU"
110 PRINT
120 PRINT
130 LET I=D
140 PRINT "STORE NO."; A(I); "HAS"
150 PRINT
160 PRINT "     "; B(I); " HOURLY EMPLOYEES"
170 PRINT
180 PRINT "     "; C(I); " SALARIED EMPLOYEES"
190 PRINT "     --------"
200 PRINT
210 PRINT "     "; B(I) + C(I); " TOTAL EMPLOYEES"
220 PRINT
230 PRINT
240 PRINT "DO YOU WISH INFORMATION ON ANOTHER STORE?"
250 PRINT "ENTER 1 IF YES, ENTER 0 IF NO"
260 INPUT E
270 IF E=1 THEN 60
280 PRINT "THANK YOU"
290 DATA 1,23,44, 2,61,18, 3,18,37, 4,25,21, 5,16,42
300 DATA 6,46,32, 7,41,21, 8,16,21, 9,41,34, 10,12,15
310 END
```

PROGRAM RUN

```
PLEASE ENTER STORE NUMBER FOR PERSONNEL INFORMATION
? 5
THANK YOU
```

```
STORE NO. 5 HAS

    16  HOURLY EMPLOYEES

    42  SALARIED EMPLOYEES
    --------

    58  TOTAL EMPLOYEES


DO YOU WISH INFORMATION ON ANOTHER STORE?
ENTER 1 IF YES, ENTER 0 IF NO
? 1


PLEASE ENTER STORE NUMBER FOR PERSONNEL INFORMATION
? 8
THANK YOU


STORE NO. 8 HAS

    16  HOURLY EMPLOYEES

    21  SALARIED EMPLOYEES
    --------

    37  TOTAL EMPLOYEES


DO YOU WISH INFORMATION ON ANOTHER STORE?
ENTER 1 IF YES, ENTER 0 IF NO
? 1


PLEASE ENTER STORE NUMBER FOR PERSONNEL INFORMATION
? 2
THANK YOU
```

```
STORE NO. 2 HAS

    61  HOURLY EMPLOYEES

    18  SALARIED EMPLOYEES
    --------

    79  TOTAL EMPLOYEES
DO YOU WISH INFORMATION ON ANOTHER STORE?
ENTER 1 IF YES, ENTER 0 IF NO
? 0
THANK YOU
```

EXERCISES

1. Write a program that will read in the number of employees over and under 21 years of age who work in each of several stores. Design the program to access the file, printing out the number of employees in each classification when the store code is entered.
2. Modify the example program to print out only the number of hourly employees when the store code has been entered.

BASIC STATEMENTS USED

```
REM
DIM
LET
PRINT
FOR/NEXT
INPUT
IF/THEN
COUNTERS
```

ABSTRACT

This program illustrates a common application for arrays: holding data to be sorted. The program alphabetizes a list of names input by the user. Several FOR/NEXT loops control the data manipulation. The first loop reads in and arrays up to 100 alphabetic strings. A test for last record is included in the loop to branch out of its control if there are less than 100 items in the data set. A counter is also included in the loop to count the number of data items read in.

The BASIC interpreter is designed to assign a numeric code number to each character in the standard character set. Thus, each letter in the alphabet has a numeric equivalent. These equivalents are assigned in consecutive order. The computer can be directed to compare these numeric equivalents to see if one is greater than, less than, or equal to another. If alphabetic strings are rearranged depending on the results of this relational test, they can be easily placed in alphabetical order.

Nested FOR/NEXT loops control the sorting procedure. They restructure the array, placing the elements in alphabetical order, with A at the top of the array and Z at the bottom. The last FOR/NEXT loop prints out the alphabetized list from storage.

The logic used in performing an alphabetic sort is explained below. Since numeric equivalents (not alphabetic characters) are being tested, the same logic is used to sort data input directly as numerals. Basically, the sort program directs the computer to find the smallest of the data elements in the array and place it in the top slot. Then, it looks for the next smallest element and stores it in the second slot, and so on. It does this by comparing the (numeric equivalents of the) name in the first position in the array, A(1), with the name in the second position, A(2). If A(2) has a smaller numeric code than A(1), their positions are reversed. If the name in A(1) is smaller, no change, or transposition, takes place. The name now in A(1) is compared with the name in A(3) and the smaller one is placed in A(1). Then A(1) is compared with A(4), and so on. This continues until A(1) has been compared with all the other names in the array, at which point the name with the lowest numeric code should be in A(1). Finally, the name now in A(2) will be compared with all the other names in the array to find the one with the second lowest numeric code.

This procedure continues until the array has been restructured with all names in alphabetical order. In the program, nested FOR/NEXT loops control the sorting and transposing procedures. The outer loop controls the number of times the computer moves through the entire array and indicates which position in the array is being compared. The first time through the loop, I=1, and the name in A(1) will be compared. The second time through the loop, I=2, and the name in A(2) will be compared.

The inner loop controls the procedure of comparing and transposing the items in the array. It also indicates which is the other position in the array being compared.

Transposing two elements in an array is done by moving the first to a temporary holding slot and the second into the position vacated by the first. Finally, the item in the temporary slot is moved into the position vacated by the second.

The sort procedure can be altered easily to have the array restructured with the largest item at the top. This can be done by placing the larger item in the top slot at each comparison, or by loading the array from the bottom.

VARIABLE NAMES

A$ = Alphabetic array holding names input from keyboard
I = Index controlling subscripting of items in A$
J = Index for inner FOR/NEXT loop
T$ = Temporary holding slot for transposing elements

PROGRAM LISTING

10	REM statement identifies program.
20	DIM statement reserves storage for A$.
30	Initializes the counter N to 0.
40–60	Print request for data to be entered.

70	Directs computer to perform the following steps up to 100 times, increasing I by 1 each pass.
80	Inputs one data item to be stored in A$ and assigns it the current value of I as subscript.
90	Tests the data item just read in to see if it is equal to ZZZZ. (If it is, branches to statement 120; if not, continues to the next statement.)
100	Increases the value of the counter N by 1.
110	End of range of loop. Returns control to statement 70.
120	Begins outer loop. Performs the following steps $N-1$ times, increasing I by 1 each pass. When I is greater than $N-1$, control drops to statement 200.
130	Begins inner loop. Sets the initial value of J at $I+1$ (first cycle, $J=2$). Performs the following steps N times. When J is greater than N, control drops to statement 190.
140	Compares elements in two slots of array (indicated by current values of I and J). (If the condition is true, branches to statement 180; if not, continues to next statement.) (First cycle, $I=1$, $J=2$; the first and second slots will be compared. The condition is not true and control drops to the next statement.)
150	Assigns the value stored in A$(I) to the temporary storage slot.
160	Assigns the value stored in A$(J) to A$(I)
170	Moves the value in the temporary slot into A$(J)
180	End of range of inner loop. Control returns to statement 130.
190	End of range of outer loop. Control returns to statement 120.
200–230	Print out title.
240	Directs computer to do following steps N times.
250	Prints one data item from A$, substituting current value of I for subscript.
260	End of range of loop. Control returns to statement 240.
270	Terminates execution.

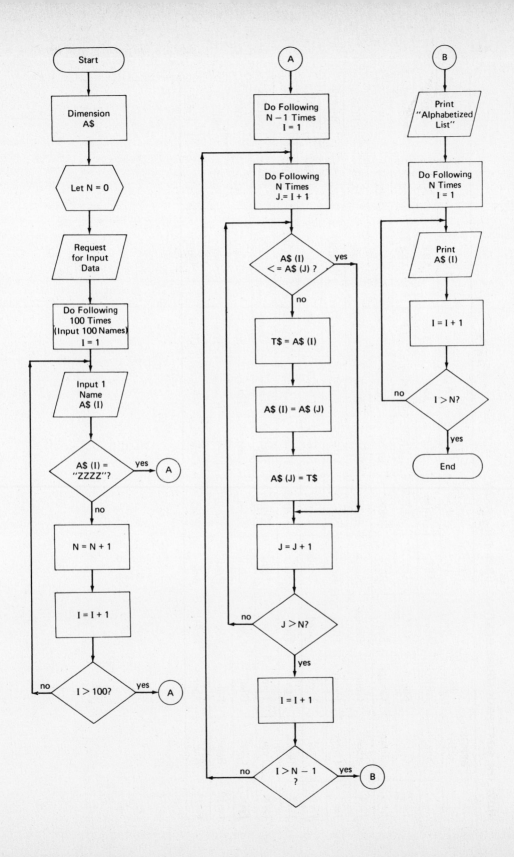

HOW THE SORT PROCEDURE RESTRUCTURES THE ARRAY

	BEFORE SORT	I=1	I=2	I=3	I=4	I=5	I=6	I=7	I=8	I=9	I=10
	Sue	ABE	ABE	ABE	ABE	ABE	ABE	ABE	ABE	ABE	ABE
J=2	Gene	Sue	ALICE	ALICE	ALICE	ALICE	ALICE	ALICE	ALICE	ALICE	ALICE
J=3	George	George	Sue	BEN	BEN	BEN	BEN	BEN	BEN	BEN	BEN
J=4	Alice	Gene	George	Sue	BOB	BOB	BOB	BOB	BOB	BOB	BOB
J=5	Henry	Henry	Henry	Henry	Sue	FRED	FRED	FRED	FRED	FRED	FRED
J=6	Fred	Fred	Gene	George	Henry	Sue	GENE	GENE	GENE	GENE	GENE
J=7	Ben	Ben	Fred	Gene	George	Henry	Sue	GEORGE	GEORGE	GEORGE	GEORGE
J=8	Tom	Tom	Tom	Tom	Tom	Tom	Tom	Tom	GLEN	GLEN	GLEN
J=9	Glen	Glen	Glen	Glen	Glen	Glen	Henry	Sue	Tom	HENRY	HENRY
J=10	Bob	Bob	Bob	Fred	Gene	George	George	Henry	Sue	Tom	SUE
J=11	Abe	Alice	Ben	Bob	Fred	Gene	Glen	Glen	Henry	Sue	TOM

PROGRAM

```
10 REM ALPHABETIZE LIST (ALPLST)
20 DIM A$(100)
30 LET N=0
40 PRINT "LIST THE ITEMS TO BE ALPHABETIZED"
50 PRINT "PLEASE TYPE IN ZZZZ AS YOUR LAST ITEM"
60 PRINT
70 FOR I=1 TO 100
80    INPUT A$(I)
90    IF A$(I)="ZZZZ" THEN 120
100   LET N=N+1
110 NEXT I
120 FOR I=1 TO N-1
130   FOR J=I+1 TO N
140       IF A$(I) <= A$(J) THEN 180
150       LET T$ = A$(I)
160       LET A$(I) = A$(J)
170       LET A$(J) = T$
180   NEXT J
190 NEXT I
200 PRINT
210 PRINT
220 PRINT "HERE IS THE ALPHABETIZED LIST"
230 PRINT
240 FOR I=1 TO N
250    PRINT A$(I)
260 NEXT I
270 END
```

PROGRAM RUN

```
LIST THE ITEMS TO BE ALPHABETIZED
PLEASE TYPE IN ZZZZ AS YOUR LAST ITEM

? SUE
? GENE
? GEORGE
? ALICE
? HENRY
? FRED
? BEN
? TOM
? GLEN
? BOB
? ABE
? ZZZZ
```

HERE IS THE ALPHABETIZED LIST

ABE
ALICE
BEN
BOB
FRED
GENE
GEORGE
GLEN
HENRY
SUE
TOM

EXERCISES

1. Modify Program 12 to print out the unalphabetized list first and then the alpha-betized list.
2. Modify the program to load the array from a DATA statement.

MATRIX DEMONSTRATION

BASIC STATEMENTS USED

```
REM
DIM
MAT READ
MAT PRINT
PRINT
MAT addition
MAT subtraction
MAT scalar multiplication
MAT TRANSPOSITION
DATA
```

ABSTRACT

This program illustrates one of BASIC's most powerful group of statements—the MAT commands. The MAT statement is not available on computers that use Microsoft BASIC. Check your reference manual to see if the MAT statement is available before running this program on your computer. MAT commands allow the programmer to load and manipulate data in matrices (two-dimensional arrays) conveniently and without the use of FOR/NEXT loops. They direct the computer to automatically handle all subscripting necessary when loading data into and out of a matrix or performing matrix arithmetic operations. The arithmetic functions performed by MAT commands follow the rules of algebraic matrix arithmetic. (See the language unit on MAT commands for more details regarding matrix arithmetic and commands.)

This program demonstrates several MAT commands. It directs the computer to perform a MAT function and then to print out the resulting array. First, the program reserves storage for four two-dimensional arrays. Next, a MAT statement commands the computer to load the items from the DATA statements into two arrays, A and B. The computer automatically handles all subscripting, eliminating the need for nested FOR/NEXT loops, indexes, and so on. Next, the computer prints out the contents of the two arrays under the direction of a MAT PRINT statement.

Matrix arithmetic is then demonstrated. The corresponding elements in both arrays are added together to form a new array, D, and the contents are printed out. Matrix A is subtracted from B and the results placed in D. Matrix D is again printed out with the new data. Each element in array A is multiplied by 3 to demonstrate scalar multiplication. The results are placed in matrix D and printed out. Finally, a transposition is performed, which restructures the data from array A. It is loaded vertically into array C, reversing the rows and columns. The transposed array, matrix C, is printed out.

VARIABLE NAMES

A = Mat with four rows and three columns
B = Mat with four rows and three columns
C = Mat with three rows and four columns
D = Mat with four rows and three columns

PROGRAM LISTING

10	REM statement identifies program.
20	DIM statement reserves storage for four matrices.
30	MAT READ command directs computer to load items in DATA statement into matrices A and B, filling A first.
40	PRINT command prints out literal title.
50	MAT PRINT command directs computer to print out all items in matrix A, using packed zone spacing.
60,70	Print out items in matrix B with title.
80	MAT arithmetic statement adds corresponding elements of matrices A and B and places results in matrix D.
90,100	Print out matrix D with heading.
110	MAT arithmetic statement subtracts elements of matrix A from matrix B and places the remainder in matrix D.
120,130	Print out matrix D with heading.
140	Multiplies each element in matrix A by 3 and places quotients in matrix D.
150,160	Print out matrix D with heading.
170	Directs computer to reload elements in matrix A into matrix C, transposing rows and columns.
180,190	Print out matrix C with heading.
200,210	DATA statements contain data items for MAT READ statement.
220	Terminates execution.

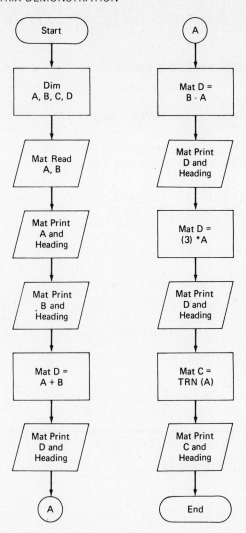

PROGRAM

```
10 REM MATRIX DEMONSTRATION (MATDEM)
20 DIM A(4,3), B(4,3), C(3,4), D(4,3)
30 MAT READ A,B
40 PRINT "MAT A"
50 MAT PRINT A;
60 PRINT "MAT B"
70 MAT PRINT B;
80 MAT D=A+B
```

```
90 PRINT "MATS A AND B HAVE BEEN ADDED TOGETHER"
100 MAT PRINT D;
110 MAT D = B-A
120 PRINT "MAT A HAS BEEN SUBTRACTED FROM B"
130 MAT PRINT D;
140 MAT D = (3)*A
150 PRINT "EACH ELEMENT IN MAT A HAS BEEN MULTIPLIED BY 3"
160 MAT PRINT D;
170 MAT C = TRN(A)
180 PRINT "THIS IS MAT C, THE TRANSPOSITION OF MAT A"
190 MAT PRINT C;
200 DATA 10,11,12,13,14,15,16,17,18,19,20,21
210 DATA 10,12,14,16,18,20,22,24,26,28,30,32
220 END
```

PROGRAM RUN

MAT A
```
10     11     12
13     14     15
16     17     18
19     20     21
```

MAT B
```
10     12     14
16     18     20
22     24     26
28     30     32
```

MATS A AND B HAVE BEEN ADDED TOGETHER
```
20     23     26
29     32     35
38     41     44
47     50     53
```

MAT A HAS BEEN SUBTRACTED FROM B
```
0      1      2
3      4      5
6      7      8
9     10     11
```

EACH ELEMENT IN MAT A HAS BEEN MULTIPLIED BY 3
```
30     33     36
39     42     45
48     51     54
57     60     63
```

```
THIS IS MAT C, THE TRANSPOSITION OF MAT A
   10      13      16      19
   11      14      17      20
   12      15      18      21
```

EXERCISES

1. Write a program that will read in and load items into a 2 × 6 matrix and then print it out.
2. Write a program that will load the same data into a 4 × 3 matrix. Multiply each element by 5 and print out the new matrix.

STORED FUNCTION DEMONSTRATION

BASIC STATEMENTS USED

```
REM
PRINT
INPUT
LET
IF/THEN
Standard functions
```

ABSTRACT

Stored functions perform a variety of mathematical operations and are called into a program by their three-letter name. (They are discussed in some detail in the language unit on standard functions.) This interactive program, consisting of a group of PRINT statements, will illustrate some of the stored functions found in BASIC.

First, the computer requests the user to input a value between 1 and 50. This value, called A in the program, will be manipulated by various functions, for demonstration. The computer calls in SQR and calculates and writes out the square root of A. Then, it calls in COS and writes out the cosine of A. Next, the program offers the user the option of calling in one of three other functions, ABS, LOG, or TAN. The program inputs the three-letter name of the function selected by the user and branches to execute the indicated mathematical procedure on the argument A.

The program then asks whether the user wants to try another function. An answer of 1 directs the computer back to repeat this sequence of instructions. Any other answer directs control to the next sequence. The program asks if the user wants to enter a new variable (A) and repeat the program. An answer of 1 causes a return to the beginning of the program. Any other answer terminates execution.

VARIABLE NAMES

A = Variable input by user for demonstration

X = The answer in a mathematical operation

B$ = Alphabetic string input by user to indicate which function he or she wishes to use

C = Test variable for repeating sequence

D = Test variable for repeating program

PROGRAM LISTING

10	REM statement identifies program.
20–60	Print heading and request for variable.
70	Inputs A, variable used for demonstration.
80–120	Print text describing A.
130–150	Describe and illustrate statement for finding square root.
160	Mathematical statement that calls out square root function.
170–190	Print out answer and skip lines.
200–220	Describe and illustrate statement for calling out cosine function.
230	Calls out cosine function.
240–260	Print out answer and skip lines.
270–310	Print out message to user on how to select another function.
320	Inputs B$, the alphabetic string representing the selected function.
330	Branches to statement 360 if B$ is ABS.
340	Branches to statement 400 if B$ is LOG.
350	Branches to statement 440 if B$ is TAN.
360	Prints out illustrative statement for calling out ABS function.
370	Calls out ABS function.
380	Prints answer.
390	Directs control to statement 470.
400	Prints out illustrative statement for calling out LOG function.
410	Calls out LOG function.
420	Prints out answer.
430	Directs control to statement 470.
440	Prints out illustrative statement for calling out TAN function.
450	Calls out TAN function.
460	Prints out answer.
470–490	Print message asking if user wants to call out another function.
500	Inputs C, test variable.
510	Skips line.
520	Branches to statement 280 if C is equal to 1.
530–550	Ask if user wishes to repeat program with new variable.
560	Inputs D, test variable.
570	Branches to statement 50 if D is equal to 1.
580–600	Terminate execution.

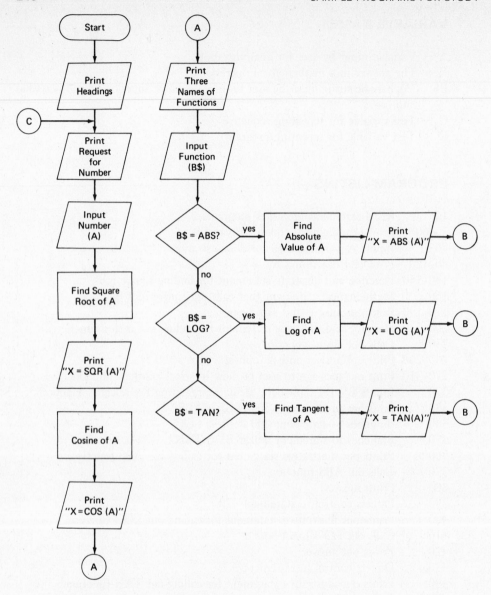

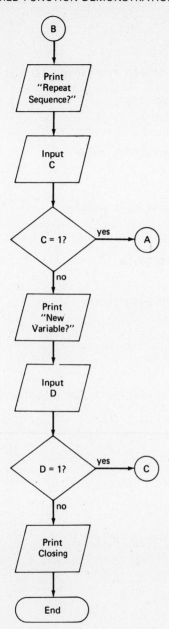

PROGRAM

```
10 REM STORED FUNCTION DEMONSTRATION (FUNDEM)
20 PRINT
30 PRINT "THIS PROGRAM WILL ILLUSTRATE HOW STORED FUNCTIONS ARE USED"
40 PRINT
50 PRINT "PLEASE ENTER A NUMBER BETWEEN 1 AND 50"
60 PRINT
70 INPUT A
80 PRINT
90 PRINT "THANK YOU. THE NUMBER YOU HAVE ENTERED";A;"HAS"
100 PRINT "BEEN ASSIGNED THE VARIABLE NAME A."
110 PRINT
120 PRINT
130 PRINT "HERE IS HOW TO FIND THE SQUARE ROOT OF A NUMBER:"
140 PRINT TAB(15) "LET X = SQR(A)"
150 PRINT
160 LET X = SQR(A)
170 PRINT "     THE SQUARE ROOT OF ";A; " IS: "; X
180 PRINT
190 PRINT
200 PRINT "HERE IS HOW TO FIND THE COSINE OF A NUMBER:"
210 PRINT TAB(15)  "LET X = COS(A)"
220 PRINT
230 LET X = COS(A)
240 PRINT "     THE COSINE OF ";A; " IS: "; X
250 PRINT
260 PRINT
270 PRINT "SELECT ONE OF THE FOLLOWING THREE FUNCTIONS FOR ILLUSTRATION"
280 PRINT "     ENTER ABS FOR ABSOLUTE VALUE"
290 PRINT "     ENTER LOG FOR NATURAL LOG"
300 PRINT "     ENTER TAN FOR TANGENT"
310 PRINT
320 INPUT B$
330 IF B$ = "ABS" THEN 360
340 IF B$ = "LOG" THEN 400
350 IF B$ = "TAN" THEN 440
360 PRINT TAB(15); "LET X = ABS(A)"
370 LET X = ABS(A)
380 PRINT "     THE ABSOLUTE VALUE OF "; A; " IS: "; X
390 GOTO 470
400 PRINT TAB(15); "LET X = LOG(A)"
410 LET X = LOG(A)
420 PRINT "     THE NATURAL LOG OF ";A; " IS: "; X
430 GOTO 470
440 PRINT TAB(15); "LET X = TAN(A)"
450 LET X = TAN(A)
460 PRINT "     THE TANGENT OF "; A; " IS: "; X
470 PRINT
480 PRINT "DO YOU WISH TO CALL OUT ANOTHER FUNCTION?"
490 PRINT "ENTER 1 FOR YES AND 0 FOR NO."
500 INPUT C
510 PRINT
```

```
520 IF C=1 THEN 280
530 PRINT
540 PRINT "DO YOU WISH TO TRY A NEW VARIABLE?"
550 PRINT "ENTER 1 FOR YES AND 0 FOR NO."
560 INPUT D
570 IF D = 1 THEN 50
580 PRINT
590 PRINT "THANK YOU"
600 END
```

PROGRAM RUN

THIS PROGRAM WILL ILLUSTRATE HOW STORED FUNCTIONS ARE USED

PLEASE ENTER A NUMBER BETWEEN 1 AND 50

? 25

THANK YOU. THE NUMBER YOU HAVE ENTERED 25 HAS
BEEN ASSIGNED THE VARIABLE NAME A.

HERE IS HOW TO FIND THE SQUARE ROOT OF A NUMBER:
            LET X = SQR(A)

    THE SQUARE ROOT OF 25 IS: 5

HERE IS HOW TO FIND THE COSINE OF A NUMBER:
            LET X = COS(A)

    THE COSINE OF 25 IS: .991203

SELECT ONE OF THE FOLLOWING THREE FUNCTIONS FOR ILLUSTRATION
      ENTER ABS FOR ABSOLUTE VALUE
      ENTER LOG FOR NATURAL LOG
      ENTER TAN FOR TANGENT

? ABS
            LET X = ABS(A)
      THE ABSOLUTE VALUE OF 25 IS: 25

DO YOU WISH TO CALL OUT ANOTHER FUNCTION?
ENTER 1 FOR YES AND 0 FOR NO.
? 1

      ENTER ABS FOR ABSOLUTE VALUE
      ENTER LOG FOR NATURAL LOG

        ENTER TAN FOR TANGENT

? LOG

            LET X = LOG(A)
        THE NATURAL LOG OF 25 IS: 3.21888

DO YOU WISH TO CALL OUT ANOTHER FUNCTION?
ENTER 1 FOR YES AND 0 FOR NO.
? 1

        ENTER ABS FOR ABSOLUTE VALUE
        ENTER LOG FOR NATURAL LOG
        ENTER TAN FOR TANGENT

? TAN

            LET X = TAN(A)
        THE TANGENT OF 25 IS: -.133527

DO YOU WISH TO CALL OUT ANOTHER FUNCTION?
ENTER 1 FOR YES AND 0 FOR NO.
? 0

DO YOU WISH TO TRY A NEW VARIABLE?
ENTER 1 FOR YES AND 0 FOR NO.
? 1
PLEASE ENTER A NUMBER BETWEEN 1 AND 50

? 8.3

THANK YOU. THE NUMBER YOU HAVE ENTERED 8.3 HAS
BEEN ASSIGNED THE VARIABLE NAME A.

HERE IS HOW TO FIND THE SQUARE ROOT OF A NUMBER:
            LET X = SQR(A)

        THE SQUARE ROOT OF 8.3 IS: 2.88097

HERE IS HOW TO FIND THE COSINE OF A NUMBER:
            LET X = COS(A)

        THE COSINE OF 8.3 IS: -.431376

```
SELECT ONE OF THE FOLLOWING THREE FUNCTIONS FOR ILLUSTRATION
     ENTER ABS FOR ABSOLUTE VALUE
     ENTER LOG FOR NATURAL LOG
     ENTER TAN FOR TANGENT

? ABS
            LET X = ABS(A)
     THE ABSOLUTE VALUE OF  8.3  IS:  8.3

DO YOU WISH TO CALL OUT ANOTHER FUNCTION?
ENTER 1 FOR YES AND 0 FOR NO.
? 0


DO YOU WISH TO TRY A NEW VARIABLE?
ENTER 1 FOR YES AND 0 FOR NO.
? 0

THANK YOU
```

EXERCISES

1. Write a program that reads in a list of numbers, squares each number, and prints out the new list.
2. Write a program that reads in a list of fractions (expressed as decimal numbers) and prints them out as rounded integers.

USER-DEFINED FUNCTION DEMONSTRATION

BASIC STATEMENTS USED

```
REM
DEF
PRINT
LET
TAB
INPUT
IF/THEN
```

ABSTRACT

Even though BASIC contains many standard functions, there are occasions when the programmer needs to repeat a mathematical function (that is not one of the stored functions) several times during his or her program. BASIC has provisions for meeting this need. The programmer can write his or her own function, called a *user-defined function*. This program demonstrates a user-defined function that converts a given number of seconds into days. Functions such as these can be used to convert Fahrenheit into centigrade, feet to meters, and so on.

A user-defined function must be defined and named early in the program with a DEF statement. It is assigned a three-letter name, composed of FN and a letter of the alphabet followed by a dummy argument X. This program demonstrates applications of a user-defined function named FND, which converts a given number of seconds into days.

First, the function is described and printed out. Then, the program uses FND in three different applications. The program requests the user to enter a specific number of seconds for manipulation by FND. The user is given a choice of entering another value of branching to END.

VARIABLE NAMES

S = Seconds
D = Days (result of manipulation by FND)
W = Variable name in arithmetic statement that stands for number of weeks
X = Dummy argument
Y = Test variable for repeating cycle

PROGRAM LISTING

10	REM statement identifies program.
20	DEF statement defines and names user-defined function.
30–60	Print heading.
70–110	Describe and illustrate FND.
120	Assigns the numeric value 1209600 to S.
130–150	Print out explanation to user.
160	Prints out FND within literal text.
170–220	Print out heading for next section of program.
230–250	Print out message describing one way to use user-defined function.
260–280	Print out examples of using user-defined functions.
290–320	Print message on second way to use functions.
330	Prints out example of using function in PRINT statement.
340–370	Print out message describing third usage.
380	Prints out example of FND in a computation.
390,400	Direct computer to carry out computation and print out results.
410–440	Ask user to input numeric value.
450	Inputs S, number of seconds, from keyboard.
460	Skips line.
470	Calculates FND using value input by user, and prints it out within literal text.
480–500	Print message asking if user wants to convert another value.
510	Inputs Y, test variable.
520	Directs computer to branch to statement 410 if Y=1.
530–550	Terminate program.

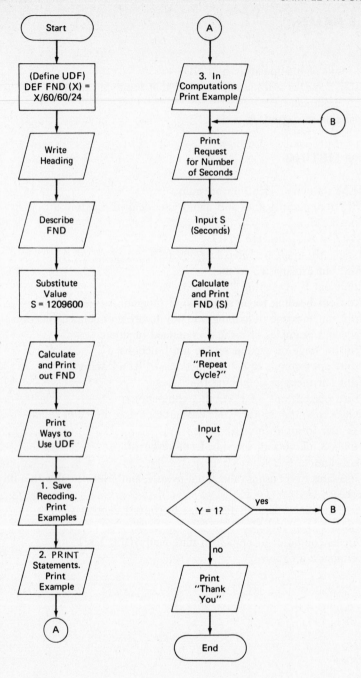

PROGRAM

```
10 REM USER DEFINED FUNCTION DEMO (DEFUND)
20 DEF FND(X) = X/60/60/24
30 PRINT
40 PRINT "USERS CAN WRITE THEIR OWN FUNCTIONS. THESE USER DEFINED"
50 PRINT "FUNCTIONS ARE WRITTEN WITH A DEF STATEMENT."
60 PRINT
70 PRINT "HERE IS A USER DEFINED FUNCTION WHICH COMPUTES DAYS FROM"
80 PRINT "A GIVEN NUMBER OF SECONDS:"
90 PRINT
100 PRINT TAB(19); "20 DEF FND(X)=X/60/60/24"
110 PRINT
120 LET S=1.2096E+06
130 PRINT TAB(20); "IF S=SECONDS, AND WE"
140 PRINT TAB(24); "LET S=1209600"
150 PRINT TAB(28); "THEN"
160 PRINT TAB(10); S; "SECONDS ARE EQUAL TO"; FND(S); "DAYS."
170 PRINT
180 PRINT
190 PRINT
200 PRINT "THE USER DEFINED FUNCTION IS USED IN A PROGRAM"
210 PRINT "IN SEVERAL WAYS:"
220 PRINT
230 PRINT "  1. TO SAVE RECODING A FORMULA USED SEVERAL TIMES"
240 PRINT "IN A PROGRAM:"
250 PRINT
260 PRINT TAB(20); "120 LET D1 = FND(S)"
270 PRINT TAB(20); "200 LET D2 = FND(S)"
280 PRINT TAB(20); "280 LET D3 = FND(S)"
290 PRINT
300 PRINT
310 PRINT "  2. AS VARIABLES IN PRINT STATEMENTS."
320 PRINT
330 PRINT TAB(20); "160 PRINT FND(S)"
340 PRINT
350 PRINT
360 PRINT "  3. AS VARIABLES IN COMPUTATIONS:"
370 PRINT
380 PRINT TAB(20); "LET W = FND(S)/7"
390 LET W=FND(S)/7
400 PRINT TAB(10); S; "SECONDS ARE EQUAL TO: "; W; "WEEKS"
410 PRINT
420 PRINT
430 PRINT
440 PRINT "ENTER THE NUMBER OF SECONDS YOU WISH CONVERTED INTO DAYS."
450 INPUT S
460 PRINT
470 PRINT S; "SECONDS ARE EQUAL TO:"; FND(S); "DAYS."
480 PRINT
490 PRINT
500 PRINT "TO CONVERT ANOTHER VALUE, ENTER 1. OTHERWISE ENTER 0."
```

```
510 INPUT Y
520 IF Y=1 THEN 410
530 PRINT
540 PRINT "THANK YOU"
550 END
```

PROGRAM RUN

USERS CAN WRITE THEIR OWN FUNCTIONS. THESE USER DEFINED
FUNCTIONS ARE WRITTEN WITH A DEF STATEMENT.

HERE IS A USER DEFINED FUNCTION WHICH COMPUTES DAYS FROM
A GIVEN NUMBER OF SECONDS:

```
        20 DEF FND(X)=X/60/60/24
```

```
        IF S=SECONDS, AND WE
            LET S=1209600
                 THEN
   1.2096E+06 SECONDS ARE EQUAL TO 14 DAYS.
```

THE USER DEFINED FUNCTION IS USED IN A PROGRAM
IN SEVERAL WAYS:

1. TO SAVE RECODING A FORMULA USED SEVERAL TIMES
IN A PROGRAM:

```
        120 LET D1 = FND(S)
        200 LET D2 = FND(S)
        280 LET D3 = FND(S)
```

2. AS VARIABLES IN PRINT STATEMENTS.

```
        160 PRINT FND(S)
```

3. AS VARIABLES IN COMPUTATIONS:

```
        LET W = FND(S)/7
   1.2096E+06 SECONDS ARE EQUAL TO:  2 WEEKS
```

ENTER THE NUMBER OF SECONDS YOU WISH CONVERTED INTO DAYS.
? 86400

 86400 SECONDS ARE EQUAL TO: 1 DAYS.

TO CONVERT ANOTHER VALUE, ENTER 1. OTHERWISE ENTER 0.
? 1

ENTER THE NUMBER OF SECONDS YOU WISH CONVERTED INTO DAYS.
? 252000

 252000 SECONDS ARE EQUAL TO: 2.91667 DAYS.

TO CONVERT ANOTHER VALUE, ENTER 1. OTHERWISE ENTER 0.
? 0

THANK YOU

EXERCISES

1. Write a program that calls in a user-defined function two times.
2. Write a program that calls in two user-defined functions two times each.

BASIC STATEMENTS USED

```
REM
PRINT
INPUT
LET
FOR/NEXT
Standard functions
```

ABSTRACT

This program calculates the mean and standard deviation for a group of numbers. The data to be processed are input from the keyboard and the results are printed out in the form of a report.

The computation of mean and standard deviation are common statistical procedures. The mean of a group of numbers is the same as its average. Standard deviation describes how the numbers are distributed around the mean. If all numbers are close to the mean, then the standard deviation is small. If the numbers cover a wide range, then the standard deviation will be larger. Two-thirds of the numbers will always be within one standard deviation below the mean and one standard deviation above the mean.

This program calculates the mean and standard deviation of the diameter of a group of parts. First, it asks the user to enter the lot number and name of the parts. Then, it enters a loop in which it inputs the diameter of the parts. It adds each value to a running total (C), squares each value, and adds the square to a running total (E). When it has read in 30 parts or the trailer value (9999), it calculates the mean and standard deviation. The program prints out these results in the form of a quality control report on the computer.

The mean is calculated by using the following formula:

$$\overline{X} = \frac{\Sigma X}{N}$$

where

$\overline{X}$ = mean (F in the program)
ΣX = sum of the values (C in the program)
N = number of cases (B in the program)

Using the assigned names in the program the formula would be

$$F = \frac{C}{B}$$

The standard deviation is calculated by following the formula

$$s = \sqrt{\frac{\Sigma X^2}{N} - \overline{X}^2}$$

where

s = standard deviation (J in the program)
ΣX^2 = sum of the squared values (E in the program)
N = number of cases (B in the program)
$\overline{X}^2$ = mean squared (G in the program)

Using the names assigned in the program, the formula would be

$$J = \sqrt{\frac{E}{B} - G}$$

VARIABLE NAMES

A = Part diameter
B = Number of cases (1)
C = Sum of values (A+A)
D = Value squared (A^2)
E = Sum of the squared values (D + D)
F = Mean (C/B)
G = Mean squared (F^2)
H = Intermediate value (E/B − G)
I = Array index
J = Standard deviation (SD)
K\$ = Lot name
L = Lot number
M1 = One SD below the mean
M2 = One SD above the mean

PROGRAM LISTING

10	REM statement identifies program.
20	DIM statement tells computer to reserve 30 storage locations for part diameters (A).
30	PRINT statement tells computer to skip a line.
40	PRINT statement directs computer to print out message to user to input values.
50	Requests user to input values K$ (lot name) and L (lot number).
60	Tells computer to skip a line.
70, 80	Print message to user to input part sizes and trailer value.
90–110	Set the initial values of C, D, and E to 0.
120	Begins loop. (Increases I by one each loop and compares value to 30. When I is greater than 30, goes to statement 190.)
130	Reads in up to 30 values of A and assigns each the name A and the current value of I as its subscript.
140	Tests each value of A. (If it equals 9999, goes to statement 200.)
150	Adds current value of A to running total (C).
160	Squares each value of A.
170	Adds squared value to running total.
180	End of range of loop returns control to statement 120.
190	Sends control to statement 220.
200	Sets B equal to I − 1. (One case is subtracted because last value was 9999, not a part size.)
210	Sends control to statement 230.
220	Sets B equal to I if 30 cases were read in.
230, 240	Skip a line and print THANK YOU.
250	Calculates mean.
260	Squares mean.
270	Calculates intermediate value, H.
280	Calls in function SQR to perform last calculation in finding standard deviation.
290	Calculates one SD below mean.
300	Calculates one SD above mean.
310–460	Print out report, dropping in variables on lines 360, 380, 400, and 430.
470	Terminates program.

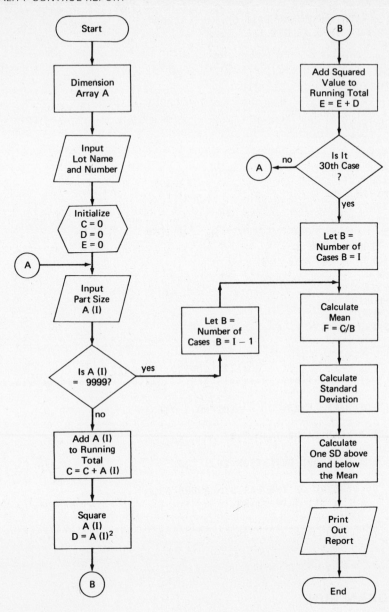

PROGRAM

```
10 REM QUALITY CONTROL REPORT (QUCORD)
20 DIM A(30)
30 PRINT
40 PRINT "PLEASE ENTER LOT NAME AND NUMBER"
50 INPUT K$,L
60 PRINT
```

```
70 PRINT "PLEASE INPUT THE LIST OF PART SIZES"
80 PRINT "ENTER 9999 AS THE LAST ITEM"
90 LET C=0
100 LET D=0
110 LET E=0
120 FOR I=1 TO 30
130 INPUT A(I)
140 IF A(I)=9999 THEN 200
150 LET C=C+A(I)
160 LET D=A(I)^2
170 LET E=E+D
180 NEXT I
190 GOTO 220
200 LET B=I-1
210 GOTO 230
220 LET B=I
230 PRINT
240 PRINT "THANK YOU"
250 LET F=C/B
260 LET C=F^2
270 LET H=E/B-G
280 LET J=SQR(H)
290 LET M1=F-J
300 LET M2=F+J
310 PRINT
320 PRINT
330 PRINT "                    QUALITY CONTROL REPORT"
340 PRINT "***********************************************************"
350 PRINT
360 PRINT "LOT NAME: ";K$;"        LOT NO.: ";L
370 PRINT
380 PRINT "THE MEAN VALUE IS:  ";F
390 PRINT
400 PRINT "THE STANDARD DEVIATION IS:  ";J
410 PRINT
420 PRINT "66 PERCENT OF THE PARTS MEASURE FROM"
430 PRINT "      "; M1; " TO "; M2
440 PRINT
450 PRINT "***********************************************************"
460 PRINT
470 END
```

PROGRAM RUN

```
PLEASE ENTER LOT NAME AND NUMBER
? GEARS,6789
```

```
PLEASE INPUT THE LIST OF PART SIZES
ENTER 9999 AS THE LAST ITEM
? 10.9
? 9.9
? 9.7
? 11.2
? 10.1
? 10.4
? 9.9
? 10.5
? 11.1
? 10.2
? 10.1
? 9999

THANK YOU


                QUALITY CONTROL REPORT
************************************************************

LOT NAME: GEARS        LOT NO.:  6789

THE MEAN VALUE IS:    10.3636

THE STANDARD DEVIATION IS:    .484839

66 PERCENT OF THE PARTS MEASURE FROM
        9.8788  TO  10.8485


************************************************************
```

EXERCISES

1. Write a program that reads in a list of numbers and finds the average and high and low values.
2. Obtain the scores your class received on your last test. Write a program that finds the mean and standard deviation of these scores. Print out the results, labeled.

BASIC STATEMENTS USED

```
REM
DIM
LET
FOR/NEXT
READ/DATA
IF/THEN
GOTO
PRINT
```

ABSTRACT

Another very important algorithm used in programming is the merge routine. In the merge program, two files of data are combined into a new, single file. Before merging, two files are present. Each file is in numerical sequence based upon the data in a specified field. After merging, one file is present with all records in sequence. Merges can be used to combine master and detail files, debits and credits, and so on.

This program reads in two files of numeric data, merges them, and then prints out the new file. Here is the algorithm followed in this program. Storage is set aside for three arrays. Two will hold the detail files and the third will hold the new master file. A FOR/NEXT loop loads the first set of data into the detail file A. A second FOR/NEXT loop loads the rest of the data into detail file B. A variable name is used as the limit for these loops to allow the programmer the option of varying the number of records in the files.

Then the merge begins. The indexes for the three files are set to 1 and therefore point to the first slots in the three arrays. The first record in file A is tested against the first record in file B. The smaller value is moved to the first position in the master file C. The index pointing to the smaller record is increased and now points to position 2 of the detail file. The index for file C is also increased and now points to position 2. Then, the program compares the records in files A and B that the indexes are pointing to. The smaller is again moved to file C. The indexes for C and the one pointing to the smaller detail record are again increased to prepare for the next comparison.

If two records are equal, the one in B moves to the master file first. The value in A will be tested and moved during the next comparison unless, of course, another equal value is encountered in B.

When all records have been compared and moved to the master file, it is printed out under the control of a FOR/NEXT loop.

The reader should be aware that this is a simplified merging routine. In actual practice, the programmer may wish to include error routines to make sure detail files are in sequence, that no numbers above or below the allowed limits are present, and so forth. Other data besides the merge field is usually present on the records being merged. The program must contain provisions for moving this data when records are being transferred from one file to another.

A merging routine might also be written to allow a different number of records in each detail file, to include last record loops, to merge more than two files, and so on. Also, as with most programming procedures, there are several alternate algorithms that can be used to merge files.

VARIABLE NAMES

A = Detail file, to be merged
B = Detail file, to be merged
C = Master file: holds merged detail files
I = Index for file A
J = Index for file B
K = Index for file C
N = Number of records in detail files: sets limit of looping procedures

PROGRAM LISTING

10	REM statement identifies program.
20	Reserves storage for arrays A, B, and C.
30	Sets value of N (number of records in detail files).
40	Directs computer to repeat following step N times.
50	Reads and arrays next data item into A.
60	End of range of loop.
70	Directs computer to repeat following step N times.
80	Reads and arrays next data item into B.
90	End of range of loop.

100	REM statement identifies merge procedure.
110–130	Initialize indexes I, J, and K to 1.
140	Compares value of A to B. Subscripts indicate which records are being tested. If A is equal to or greater than B, control transfers to statement 160. If not, control drops to next statement.
150	Compares value of A to B. Subscripts indicate which records are being tested (as in statement 140). If A is less than B, control transfers to statement 210. (A GOTO statement could also have been used here.)
160	Indicates that B is less than A and thus moves to position in file C indicated by index K.
170	Increases index K by 1 to point to next slot in file C.
180	Tests J index to see if last record in file B has been tested and moved. If it is the last record in B, control drops to statement 310.
190	Increases index J by 1 to point to next slot in B.
200	Indicates that transfer procedure is completed and control is returned to test the next records.
210	Indicates that A is less than B, and thus moves to position in file C indicated by index K.
220	Increases index K by 1 to point to next slot in file C.
230	Tests I index to see if last record in file A has been moved. If it is last record in A, control drops to statement 260. If it is not, control drops to next statement.
240	Increases index I by 1 to point to next slot in A.
250	Indicates that transfer procedure is completed and control is returned to test the next records.
260	Control transfers to this statement after the last record in A has been moved. Transfers the next record in file B to file C. But there are still one or more records left in B.
270	Tests J index to see if the last record in file B has been moved. If it has, control drops to statement 360. If more records remain in B, control drops to the next statement.
280	Increases index J by 1 to point to next position in B.
290	Increases index K by 1 to point to next position in C.
300	Returns control to statement 260 to transfer the next record in B.
310	Transfers the next record in A to C. Control transfers to this statement when the last record in B has been moved. At this point, there are one or more records left in A.
320	Tests I index to see if the last record in file A has been moved. If it has, control drops to statement 360. If more records remain in A, control drops to the next statement.
330	Increases index I by 1 to point to next slot in A.
340	Increases index K by 1 to point to next position in C.
350	Returns control to statement 310 to transfer the next record in A.
360–380	Print out title.
390	Directs computer to repeat following step N*2 times.
400	Prints record from file C, indicated by index.

410   End of range of loop.

420, 430 DATA statements contain numeric values for files.

440   Terminates program.

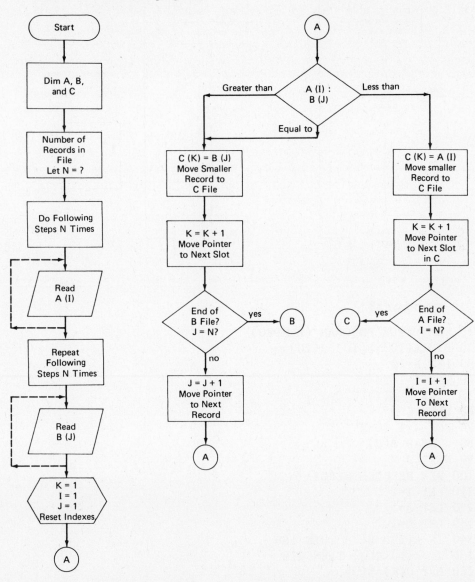

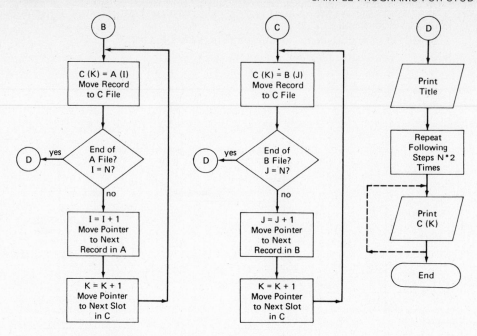

PROGRAM

```
10 REM MERGE PROGRAM (MERPRO)
20 DIM A(10),B(10),C(20)
30 LET N=10
40 FOR I=1 TO N
50    READ A(I)
60 NEXT I
70 FOR J=1 TO N
80    READ B(J)
90 NEXT J
100 REM PERFORM MERGE
110 LET I=1
120 LET J=1
130 LET K=1
140 IF A(I)>=B(J) THEN 160
150 IF A(I)<B(J) THEN 210
160 LET C(K)=B(J)
170 LET K=K+1
180 IF J=N THEN 310
190 LET J=J+1
200 GOTO 140
210 LET C(K)=A(I)
```

```
220 LET K=K+1
230 IF I=N THEN 260
240 LET I=I+1
250 GOTO 140
260 LET C(K)=B(J)
270 IF J=N THEN 360
280 LET J=J+1
290 LET K=K+1
300 GOTO 260
310 LET C(K)=A(I)
320 IF I=N THEN 360
330 LET I=I+1
340 LET K=K+1
350 GOTO 310
360 PRINT
370 PRINT "HERE IS THE MERGED FILE:"
380 PRINT
390 FOR K=1 TO (N*2)
400    PRINT C(K)
410 NEXT K
420 DATA 3,8,26,42,50,74,76,81,90,97
430 DATA 2,10,22,47,48,69,79,81,89,90
440 END
```

PROGRAM RUN

HERE IS THE MERGED FILE:

```
2
3
8
10
22
26
42
47
48
50
69
74
76
79
81
81
89
90
90
97
```

EXERCISES

1. Modify this program so that it will merge two alphabetic lists.
2. Write a program that merges two files of records containing an ID code number and a name. Use the ID number as the test value for the merge. Move the alphabetic field each time a transposition is made.

BASIC STATEMENTS USED

```
REM
DIM
FOR/NEXT
IF/THEN
LET
GOTO
PRINT
INPUT
READ/DATA
```

ABSTRACT

A major advantage of the computer is its ability to rapidly search through a file and locate a specific record. There are several different types of search algorithms used by programmers. In the sequential search, the computer reads in the object being searched for and compares it with each item in the file in sequence. This method of searching is somewhat inefficient, but necessary when a file is in random order.

Another search algorithm, called the *binary search,* is demonstrated in this program. This program reads in a file containing a list of individuals and the departments to which they are assigned. The file being searched must be in sequential order. This file is in alphabetical order in this program.

The binary search is performed by testing to see if the item at the midpoint of the file is the object of search. If it is not, the program determines whether the object is in the upper or lower half of the file. The item at the midpoint of that portion is compared to see if it is the object of search. If not, the program tests to see if the object of search is in the upper or lower half of that portion. Then, the midpoint of this new section is found and tested, and so on, until the object of search has been located.

This program performs a binary search on alphabetic data. The interpreter automatically converts the alphabetic strings into their numeric equivalents and performs the mathematical comparisons on these values. Since the numeric equivalents are assigned according to alphabetic order, the resulting file is in the proper sequence necessary for the binary search.

An error routine is written into the search procedure in case the object of search is not in the file. The computer will print out a message to this effect and then continue processing the next object of search. A counter placed after the calculation that resets the midpoint counts the number of times it is performed. An IF/THEN test branches to the error message when the number of repetitions exceeds one-half the number of records in the file. Without this safeguard, the computer could enter an endless loop and use up many processing units before the programmer or operator became aware of the problem.

VARIABLE NAMES

D$ = Department name
H = Subscript that sets upper limit of portion of file being searched
I = Index in FOR/NEXT loop that assigns subscripts to D$ and N$
K = Counter for error routine
L = Subscript that sets lower limit of portion of file being searched
M = Subscript that sets midpoint of portion of file being searched
N$ = Name of individual
P$ = Department being searched for
X$ = Object of search; name being searched for
Y = Test variable for repeat cycle

PROGRAM LISTING

10	REM statement identifies program.
20	Reserves storage for N$ and D$, files of names, and corresponding departments.
30	Directs computer to perform following steps up to 100 times.
40	READS in one value of N$ and D$. Assigns each the current value of I as subscript.
50	Branches to statement 90 if N$(I) is the trailer record (ZZZZ). If not, continues to next statement.
60	End of range of loop.
70	Initializes the value of H (upper limit) to I, the number of records read in.
80	Branches control to statement 100.
90	Control branches to this statement if less than 100 records are read in. Sets the value of H (upper limit) to I − 1 (1 is subtracted from the record count to avoid including the trailer record in the file being searched).
100	Initializes the error routine counter K to 0.
110–140	Print message requesting object of search be entered on keyboard.
150	Inputs X$, object of search, from keyboard.
160	Skips line.
170	Sets value of L (lower limit) at 1.
180	Compares X$ to value stored in first position of file. If they are the same,

control branches to statement 290. If not, control continues to next statement.

190 Compares X$ to value stored in highest position of file. If they are the same, control branches to statement 310. If not, control continues to next statement.

200 Calculates midpoint of portion of file to be searched; M is used as a subscript.

210 Increases counter K by 1. Counts number of times statement 200 is repeated for each object of search.

220 Branches control to statement 420 if K is greater than one-half I (I is the number of records). If such is not the case, drops to next statement.

230 Compares X$ to value stored in the middle position of the portion of file being searched. If they are the same, control branches to statement 330. If not, control continues to next statement.

240 Tests to see whether X$ is in upper or lower half of portion being searched. If X$ is greater than value stored at the midpoint, then it is in the upper half and control branches to statement 270. If X$ is less than the value stored at the midpoint, it is in the lower half and control drops to the next statement.

250 Indicates that since object of search is in the lower half, the old midpoint now becomes the new upper limit.

260 Branches control to statement 200 to calculate the new midpoint.

270 Indicates that since object of search is in the upper half, the old midpoint now becomes the new lower limit.

280 Branches control to statement 200 to calculate the new midpoint.

290 Control branches to this statement when the value stored in position one of the file is the object of search. It transfers the department name stored in the corresponding position of the D$ file to the slot named P$.

300 Transfers control to statement 340.

310 Control branches to this statement when the value stored in the highest position of the file is the object of search. It transfers the department name stored in the corresponding position of the D$ file to the slot named P$.

320 Transfers control to statement 340.

330 Control branches to this statement when the value stored in the position indicated by the subscript M is the object of search. It transfers the department name stored in the corresponding position of the D$ file to the slot named P$.

340 Prints individual's name (X$) and department (P$).

350–370 Print out message asking if user wishes to repeat search.

380 Inputs test variable for repeat cycle.

390 Branches control to statement 470 if Y is equal to 0.

400 Control passes to this statement if user wishes to repeat cycle. If I (record count) is less than 100, it directs computer back to the proper initializing statement for H. Otherwise control drops to the next statement.

410 Directs computer back to the proper initializing statement for H, since I must be equal to (or greater than) 100.

420–450 Control branches to these statements if statement 200 is repeated more than I/2 times. Object of search is not in file and an error message is printed.

460   Directs control back to statement 370 to repeat another cycle.

470,480 Print message.

490–540 DATA statements contain information for N$ and D$ files.

550   Terminates program.

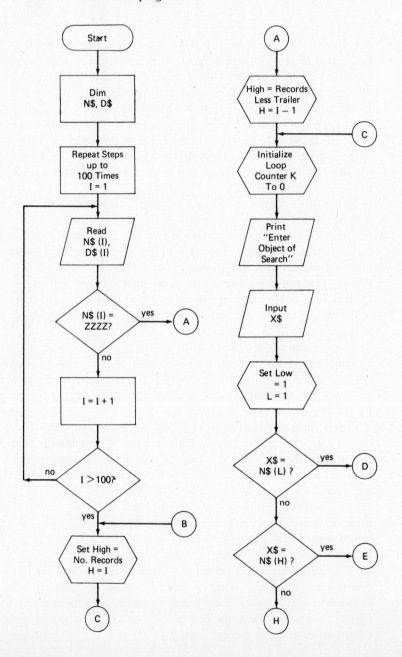

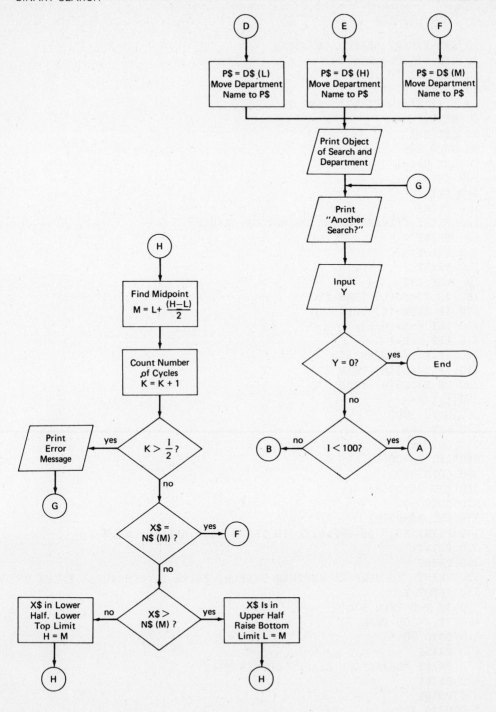

PROGRAM

```
10 REM BINARY SEARCH (BINSEA)
20 DIM N$(100),D$(100)
30 FOR I=1 TO 100
40    READ N$(I),D$(I)
50    IF N$(I)="ZZZZ" THEN 90
60 NEXT I
70 LET H=I
80 GOTO 100
90 LET H=I-1
100 LET K=0
110 PRINT
120 PRINT
130 PRINT "PLEASE ENTER OBJECT OF SEARCH"
140 PRINT
150 INPUT X$
160 PRINT
170 LET L=1
180 IF X$=N$(L) THEN 290
190 IF X$=N$(H) THEN 310
200 LET M=L+(H-L)/2
210 LET K=K+1
220 IF K>I/2 THEN 420
230 IF X$=N$(M) THEN 330
240 IF X$>N$(M) THEN 270
250 LET H=M
260 GOTO 200
270 LET L=M
280 GOTO 200
290 LET P$=D$(L)
300 GOTO 340
310 LET P$=D$(H)
320 GOTO 340
330 LET P$=D$(M)
340 PRINT X$;" IS EMPLOYED IN THE ";P$;" DEPARTMENT."
350 PRINT
360 PRINT
370 PRINT "TO PERFORM ANOTHER SEARCH, ENTER 1, OTHERWISE ENTER 0"
380 INPUT Y
390 IF Y=0 THEN 470
400 IF I<100 THEN 90
410 GOTO 70
420 PRINT
430 PRINT "OBJECT OF SEARCH NOT IN FILE"
440 PRINT
450 PRINT
460 GOTO 370
470 PRINT "THANK YOU"
480 PRINT
```

```
490 DATA "BENSON","SALES","CARLE","PRODUCTION","DIAZ","SHIPPING"
500 DATA "DOBSON","SHIPPING","KENT","MERCHANDISE"
510 DATA "LEONARD","SALES","ROBERTS","SALES"
520 DATA "SELIG","PRODUCTION","THOMAS","SHIPPING"
530 DATA "UNRUH","RESEARCH","VICTOR","PRODUCTION"
540 DATA "YATES","MARKETING","ZZZZ","ZZZZ"
550 END
```

PROGRAM RUN

PLEASE ENTER OBJECT OF SEARCH

? BENSON

BENSON IS EMPLOYED IN THE SALES DEPARTMENT.

TO PERFORM ANOTHER SEARCH, ENTER 1, OTHERWISE ENTER 0
? 1

PLEASE ENTER OBJECT OF SEARCH

? DIAZ

DIAZ IS EMPLOYED IN THE SHIPPING DEPARTMENT.

TO PERFORM ANOTHER SEARCH, ENTER 1, OTHERWISE ENTER 0
? 1

PLEASE ENTER OBJECT OF SEARCH

? YATES

YATES IS EMPLOYED IN THE MARKETING DEPARTMENT.

TO PERFORM ANOTHER SEARCH, ENTER 1, OTHERWISE ENTER 0
? 1

```
PLEASE ENTER OBJECT OF SEARCH

? SMITH


OBJECT OF SEARCH NOT IN FILE


TO PERFORM ANOTHER SEARCH, ENTER 1, OTHERWISE ENTER 0
? 1


PLEASE ENTER OBJECT OF SEARCH

? SELIG

SELIG IS EMPLOYED IN THE PRODUCTION DEPARTMENT.


TO PERFORM ANOTHER SEARCH, ENTER 1, OTHERWISE ENTER 0

? 0
THANK YOU
```

EXERCISES

1. Modify this program to search for numeric data.
2. Write a program that performs a binary search on file records containing three alphabetic strings. Use one string as the search field. Design the program to print out all three fields when the object of search has been found.

APPENDICES

APPENDICES

FLOWCHARTING

WHAT ARE FLOWCHARTS?

Most programmers begin organizing a program for the computer with a careful analysis and examination of the problem to be solved. Then, they develop a plan for computer solution of the problem. This plan is put down on paper in the form of a flowchart.

Flowcharts are graphic aids that illustrate the logic used in a computer program. They are composed of symbols and lines organized to create a picture of the relationship of each step in a program. Figure A.1 is an example of a simple flowchart.

The meaning of each symbol in a flowchart is determined by two things: its shape and the text or message written within it. Together these convey the nature of each step in the logic flow.

FLOWCHART APPLICATIONS

Flowcharts are used for many reasons. They enable the programmer to see the entire program in a condensed, graphic form. They serve as communications devices to explain a program to others who may study or use it. And they provide a quick, convenient way of experimenting with different examples of program logic.

Since logic flow is clearly visualized in flowcharts, they are a very efficient means of detecting errors in logic. They simplify and speed up coding, which is the conversion of steps in a program into language statements acceptable to the computer. Since the flowchart is an outline, it facilitates the conversion of each step into BASIC. To be of greatest use, the flowchart should be drawn early in the programming cycle, long before the problem is coded or the programmer sits down at the computer.

In planning a computer program, one or more flowcharts may be drawn to suggest

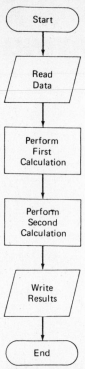

FIGURE A.1 Flowchart

various methods of solving the problem. Hence, each flowchart will represent an alternative design or an improved version.

After the programmer selects the most satisfactory approach, a detailed flowchart is drawn for coding, or for use at the computer. This flowchart shows each step in sequence and in sufficient detail to facilitate coding.

After the program has been coded and runs satisfactorily on the computer, the programmer prepares a *documentation file*. The function of this file is to gather together in one place the major items related to the program. It includes a listing of the program, flowcharts, sample data, and so on.

The documentation file is helpful in making changes and revisions in a program at a later date. It can also be an aid to other users of the program. The flowchart is always a major element in the file. It provides an overview of the program and illustrates at a glance the logic used.

HOW DETAILED SHOULD A FLOWCHART BE?

The level of detail involved and the time used in preparing a flowchart vary with the nature of the program and the needs of the programmer. A program that reads three numbers into computer storage, sums them, and outputs the results is relatively simple. Figure A.2 illustrates a flowchart of sufficient detail for this kind of problem.

More complex programs, involving intricate steps and many calculations, need more extensive flowcharts. Figure A.3 illustrates such a flowchart. A programmer could easily

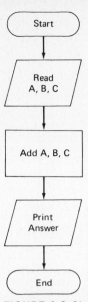

FIGURE A.2 Simple flowchart.

become confused and make errors and omissions while coding a sophisticated program such as this without the aid of a flowchart.

The technical quality maintained in a flowchart depends upon many factors, including time, costs, permanency of the program, number of users, and so on. Simple flowcharts can be drawn freehand in pencil. But flowcharts kept in a permanent documentation file should be carefully drawn in ink, with text or description typed in each box. The end use of the flowchart largely determines the level of neatness and detail with which it is drawn.

STANDARD FLOWCHART SYMBOLS

A group of about 25 symbols for preparing flowcharts have come into widespread use in the data processing industry. These symbols indicate a variety of operations, from reading data from a card to storing data on magnetic tape, data transmission links, and so on. The reader will find that only five or six of these symbols are needed for most common programming jobs. A plastic template facilitates drawing neat symbols. The template in Fig. A.4, available from RapiDesign, shows the flowchart symbols approved by the American National Standards Institute (ANSI). A similar template is available from IBM Corporation (Form X20-8020). The more important symbols the reader should learn to use are illustrated in Fig. A.5 and are discussed below.

Terminal

The beginning and end points of a program are represented by the terminal symbol, an oval. The words START and END are written in it to mark the beginning or end of the program. Terminal symbols are the first and last ones shown in a flowchart.

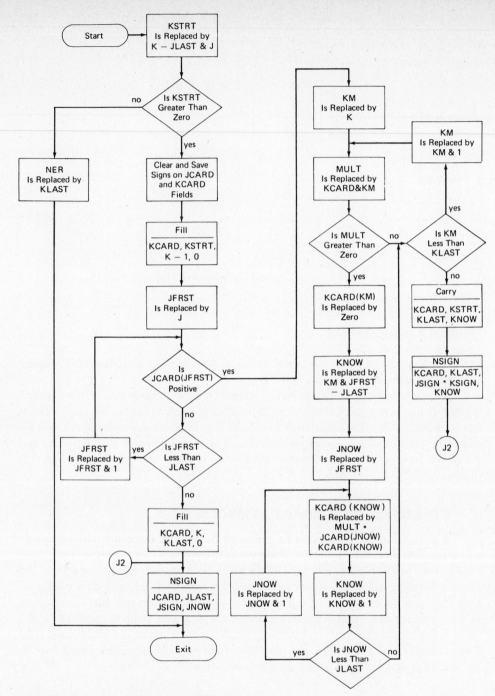

FIGURE A.3 Complex flowchart. (IBM Corporation)

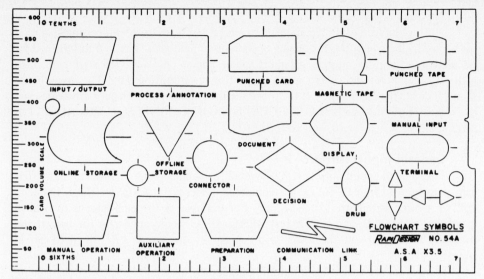

FIGURE A.4 Flowcharting template. (RadiDesign Corporation)

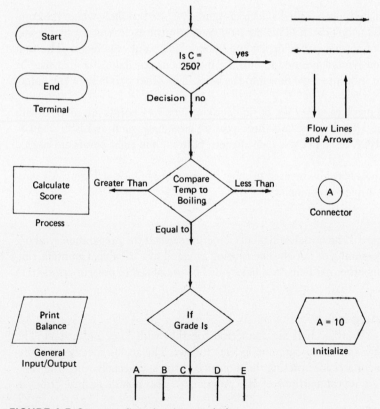

FIGURE A.5 Common flowcharting symbols.

Process

The process symbol is a rectangular box and is used to indicate a processing operation performed by the computer. Processing operations include such tasks as transferring data, calculating, setting up counters, assigning values, and so on. These steps are performed within the computer and do not involve inputting or outputting data. The programmer should indicate the exact nature of the process within the symbol with appropriate descriptive words or phrases, such as CALCULATE PROFIT, FIND SQUARE ROOT OF A4, COUNTER=A + 10, and so forth.

General Input/Output

The general input/output (I/O) symbol, a parallelogram, is used to show that data is to be read into or out of the computer. Descriptive words for the I/O operation are written within the parallelogram. For example, if the computer is to read in quantities called A, B, and C, the text READ A,B,C would appear in the box. If the computer is to print out the result of a calculation, the words PRINT SUM would appear.

More specific symbols for input and output may be used to indicate data is being read from a punch card or being printed out on a document, among others.

Decision

A diamond-shaped block, called a decision symbol, is used to show where the computer makes a decision or branch. This decision usually involves testing a variable and then selecting one of several paths, depending upon which value was found. The four points of the decision symbol are used to indicate the various possible paths that may be taken. The top point indicates logic flow into the block. The other points show the outgoing paths.

If the branch involves only a yes or no decision, then two points are marked with the words YES and NO. If there are three possible branches, such as LESS THAN, EQUAL TO, or GREATER THAN, then the left, bottom, and right points are labeled accordingly.

Decision symbols may also be used to show four or more branches. Figure A.5 illustrates how to draw a five-way branch.

Initialize

A six-sided figure is the initialize symbol (sometimes called the preparation symbol). It indicates that a beginning or initial value is being assigned to a variable. Counters, running totals, and many other mathematical fields must be initialized to prevent errors from old data in storage.

Lines and Arrows

All symbols on the flowchart are connected together with lines and arrows. The lines indicate the path that the programming logic follows. The arrows specify the direction. This custom facilitates interpreting the sequence of steps, especially when the computer is to branch or repeat portions of the program. It also guards against errors in logic.

Connectors

Another way to show program logic flow following branches and repetition of steps is to use connector symbols instead of lines and arrows. These symbols are small circles with an identifying name or number inside (such as A or 100).

One connector is drawn at the point where the logic flow stops and another where it resumes. Both connectors have the same label for identification. Short lines and arrows join the connectors to the other symbols and indicate the direction of flow. Use of these symbols becomes very helpful in programs with multiple branches and loops. Otherwise, flow lines may intersect and become confusing to follow. Connectors can also be used to show that logic flow moves from the symbol at the bottom of the page to one at the top of the page.

Programmers will sometimes use statement numbers as the connector label, such as GOTO 100, GOTO 64, and so on, enclosed within the circle. These cross-reference particular points in program logic flow to the specific instructions in the program.

HOW TO DRAW FLOWCHARTS

Several simple rules should be observed in drawing and developing flowcharts (see Fig. A.6):

1. Indicate flow from the top of the page down, and from left to right.
2. Insert descriptive text and material within each symbol.

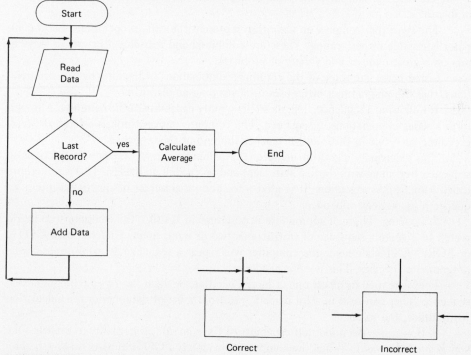

FIGURE A.6 Rules of flowcharting.

3. When decision symbols are used, label each branch or leg clearly.

4. Connect each symbol with a line and arrow (or use a connector) showing the direction of data flow.

5. Only one line should enter a given symbol. When it is necessary to show several lines entering a symbol, have them point to the line leading to the box. Do not draw several lines entering a symbol at different points.

6. Use a template and ink for permanent flowcharts.

7. Label each box in the flowchart with a statement number. This statement number should key the flowchart to the program. This facilitates tracing the program and relating it to the flowchart.

COMPUTER LOGIC AND ALGORITHMS

A computer cannot be instructed to FIND THE ANSWER, or CALCULATE THE BALANCE. It must be given much more detailed instructions than that. A computer is relatively limited in the operations it can perform. It can compare values, perform arithmetic calculations, branch, count, make a simple quantitative decision, or repeat a sequence. Consequently, a programmer must build his or her plan to solve a problem based upon these rather elementary building blocks.

The prescribed group of operations that will solve a problem is called an *algorithm*. It is a series of steps that will carry out the logic or plan for the solution of the problem. There are often several different plans or algorithms that can be used to solve a given problem.

The steps that compose an algorithm represent the various operations that a computer is capable of performing. These are combined and rearranged in various ways to process a great number and variety of problems.

Listed below are some of the common combinations of building blocks, or operations, that the programmer often uses in developing an algorithm.

1. Following a sequence. The most elementary capability of the computer is to perform a series of operations in sequence. The computer moves through a series of steps, executing each one in turn until it reaches the end of the sequence.

This elementary algorithm requires the computer only to execute instructions in sequence, beginning with the first statement and proceeding to the last. This is sometimes called a *single-pass execution*. It is used when the programmer desires to execute a sequence of operations only once.

2. Looping. Through appropriate instructions in BASIC, the computer can be directed to execute a sequence of instructions two or more times. Directed by a GOTO or FOR/NEXT statement, the computer will repeat a sequence as many times as the programmer specifies. This is calling *looping.*

Loops are used to repeat one or more operations without having to reprogram each sequence. They can read in a list of data, print out a list of data, perform a calculation many times, and so on.

3. Branching. An important capability of the computer is its ability to branch. One way is *unconditionally*. When the computer encounters a GOTO instruction in the program, it will automatically begin to execute the statement named in this instruction. The branch is made unconditionally, each time the computer encounters the GOTO.

The computer can also branch *conditionally.* It can test a value and branch to one of several paths or sequences within the program, depending on the result of the test. This is done by inserting an IF statement into the program.

The computer can be directed to read in and test a value, for example, TEMPERA-TURE. If the value of TEMPERATURE is 100° or above, it may be directed to branch to a sequence that prints out the words CAUTION, ABOVE BOILING. If the TEM-PERATURE read in is below 100°, it can branch to another sequence directing it to print out BELOW BOILING.

This ability to test a value and branch to various points in a program, depending upon that value, can be used by the programmer to build some useful algorithms.

4. Counting. A useful operation that the computer can perform is counting. By including appropriate BASIC statements in the program, the programmer can direct the computer to set up a counter and add or subtract to it each time a statement is executed.

This device allows the programmer to direct the computer to count how many numbers have been read into storage. Conversely, he or she can direct the computer to subtract one from the counter each time a number is read out of storage. The value of the counter can be printed out on the terminal or used for mathematical calculations. Counters can be used to limit loops, trigger branches, facilitate reading in and naming long lists of variables, and perform many other valuable tasks.

5. Performing mathematical calculations. The foundation of the computer's claim to usefulness rests on its ability to perform arithmetical calculations quickly and accurately. The computer can perform thousands of additions, subtractions, multiplications, exponentiations, and so forth, in a second. It is this powerful mathematical capability, far superior to man's, that makes a computer so invaluable to modern technology and society.

6. Storing data. Most modern computers have a storage system enabling the machine to read in thousands of numbers or characters and save them for processing. The results of intermediate calculations, or final values, can be stored for further processing. This capacity is indispensable to many of the algorithms used in programming computers.

SIMPLE PROGRAM ALGORITHM EXAMPLES

Let us use some of the building blocks described above to develop some practical algorithms. These building blocks can be used, either singly or in combinations, to construct complex, sophisticated programs. Below are some commonly used programming techniques. They can be used by the reader immediately in his or her programming activities.

1. Single-pass execution. The most elementary program logic, the single-pass execution, is flowcharted in Fig. A.7. The program is designed to calculate the net pay for an employee.

The first symbol indicates the beginning of the program. The next step is for the computer to read in the number of hours worked, the pay rate, and deductions. The general I/O symbol, next in the flowchart, has text describing this step. The computer calculates gross pay by multiplying the number of hours worked by the hourly rate. Deductions are then subtracted from gross pay to find net pay. All these steps are shown in a single process box. A more detailed flowchart might break them down into separate boxes. Finally, the computer prints out the net pay, as indicated by the next general I/O symbol. The flowchart concludes with an END terminal symbol.

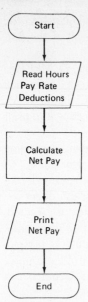

FIGURE A.7 Single-pass execution.

As the program is set up, the computer will proceed through the sequence of operations only once. If several employees are to be processed, the programmer must run the program through the computer several times, since no provision is included here to repeat the sequence automatically.

2. Interactive calculation. Figure A.8 is a flowchart for a single-pass execution with interactive data entry. In this program, the computer is directed to calculate a checking account balance. The algorithm involves several steps. First, the computer requests the programmer to input the amount of the old balance on the keyboard. Then, it requests him or her to input the amounts of the deposits made. These steps are shown in general I/O boxes.

Next, the computer calculates the intermediate balance in the account. It then requests input of the amounts of checks and other withdrawals made. The machine processes the data and calculates the new balance. It outputs this figure on the printer. Again, the flowchart begins and ends with the terminal symbol.

3. Combination INPUT and READ. The algorithm flowcharted in Fig. A.9 illustrates an interactive program in which the data is entered in two ways: from the keyboard, using an INPUT instruction; and from the program, using READ/DATA statements.

This program searches out the price of an item listed in a table and calculates the total price for multiple units of that item. The computer first reads in values for an inventory table, entered from the program. This table contains several hundred items, including the number in stock for each item and the selling price per unit. After the table has been entered, the program requests more input from the keyboard by printing a ?, which indicates that it is waiting for more data. The programmer then enters the name of the item he or she wishes to price and gives the quantity ordered.

The computer first looks up the item in the table in storage to locate the price per unit. It multiplies this price by the number of units purchased to find the total selling

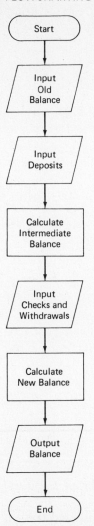

FIGURE A.8 Interactive single-pass execution.

price. This is shown in several process blocks. Finally, the machine prints out the total selling price as shown in the last general I/O symbol.

This type of algorithm is often used to enter a large amount of fixed data first. The programmer can then query the computer about the data in storage or input new data to update prices, check inventory controls, add new items, and so on.

4. Decision. Another common algorithm employs the decision, or branch, statement. This requires an IF instruction. In the program flowcharted in Fig. A.10, the computer reads in and processes information to print out a payroll. First, it reads in the number of hours worked, the hourly rate, the deductions, and a classification code.

An IF statement is used to test the classification code. If the code indicates that a salesperson works out of town, the computer branches to the left leg and calculates an additional travel allowance before computing net pay. It then prints out the result. If the

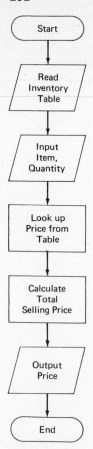

FIGURE A.9 Data entry via INPUT statement and program.

code indicates that a salesperson is local, the machine branches to the right leg, calculates net pay without adding a travel allowance, and prints out the total.

This program differs from the one shown in Fig. A.7, the single-pass execution, in that it contains a branch. This program requires the computer to test a value (classification code) and select one of two alternate paths depending upon the result.

Algorithms such as these are used to perform different calculations or operations on data depending upon a given set of conditions. The program is also a single-pass execution, since each branch leads to a terminal statement and no provision has been made to branch back to the beginning of the program.

5. Simple loop. The flowchart in Fig. A.11 represents a modification of the single-pass execution. In the simple loop, the computer is directed back to the beginning of the program to execute the statements again. In this instance, the program reads in number of hours worked, hourly rates, and deductions. Then, it calculates net pay and prints out the results. It differs from the program in Fig. A.7 since control is directed back to the beginning of the program to repeat the cycle. This is done with a GOTO statement. The instruction can direct control to almost any point in a program.

Simple loops are used to eliminate reprogramming procedures that are performed

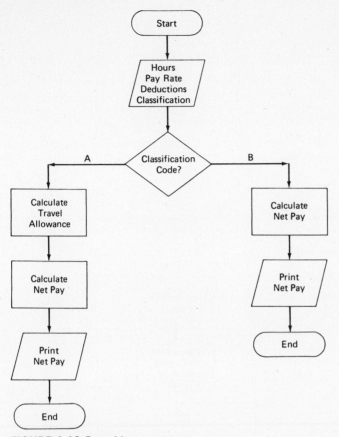

FIGURE A.10 Branching.

many times within a program, to process many sets of data without having to reenter a program each time, and so on. No provision has been made in this example to limit the number of times the cycle will be repeated. The computer will therefore continue looping and processing until it runs out of data.

6. FOR/NEXT loop. Figure A.12 is a flowchart illustrating a modification of the simple loop. This program performs the same read-calculate-write steps shown in Fig. A.11. Upon completing the printout, the computer will automatically branch back to the beginning of the program. However, in this program, a GOTO statement is not used to direct control. Instead FOR/NEXT instructions are inserted in the program to cause the computer to repeat a sequence of instructions. The FOR/NEXT statements allow the programmer to specify the number of times the loop is to be executed. After repeating the loop the specified number of times, the computer will drop down to execute the next instruction in line—in this case, the END statement.

7. Loop with input test. Another modification of the simple loop is shown in the flowchart in Fig. A.13. In this program, the computer is to perform the same sequence of steps—calculate net pay and output results—as in the previous example. This time, however, the programmer takes advantage of the interactive capabilities of the computer

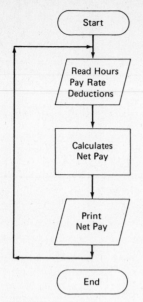

FIGURE A.11 Simple loop.

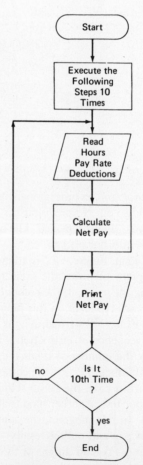

FIGURE A.12 FOR/NEXT loop.

to control looping. He or she directs the computer to print out a request asking whether he or she wants to repeat the cycle.

If the programmer enters the number 1, the computer branches back to the beginning of the program and repeats the cycle for another employee. If he or she types in 0, the computer branches control to END. This sequence can be repeated over and over, as long as the programmer types in 1 on the terminal at the end of each cycle.

This type of algorithm is usually used when the programmer wants the machine to perform a given sequence of processes on data input. He or she uses the input test to indicate to the computer whether or not there will be more data.

To program the algorithm, an IF statement similar to the one in Fig. A.10 is used. This statement tests a value (1 or 0) and branches accordingly. A YES or NO can also be used as the test quantity on some systems.

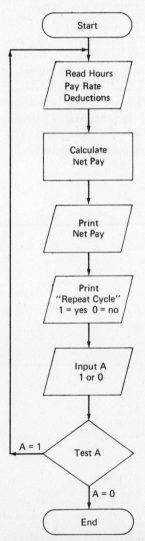

FIGURE A.13 Loop with INPUT test.

8. Loop with test for end of file. It is preferable when writing a program with loops to include one of several techniques which automatically indicate to the computer that it has processed the last piece of data in a file. In some systems, the computer will terminate a program when it finds that there are no more data to be processed. If this occurs before all the steps of the program have been executed, it can prevent the program from running properly.

Several techniques have been developed to indicate to the computer that it has reached the end of the file. In Fig. A.14, the flowchart illustrates an algorithm similar to the previous examples, which calculate net pay. Here, only one of the techniques for indicating end of file—the trailer record—is included.

The computer will read in a list of data under the control of a loop. It has been directed to test each of the pieces of data named HOURS, as it is read in, to see if it equals 9999. If it does, the computer branches to END and terminates the program. If it does not, the computer will continue processing.

The trailer record may be included in the data written into the program or entered as the last item of data input from the keyboard. Any value may be selected as the test value, as long as it will not normally be found in the data set. On some systems, an alphabetic variable may be tested as well, such as IF NAME = "ZZZZ" GOTO END.

The programmer directs the computer to perform the last record test by placing an IF statement after the READ statement. A GOTO included after the PRINT instruction directs control back to the beginning of the loop.

This technique can be used to branch to points in the program other than END.

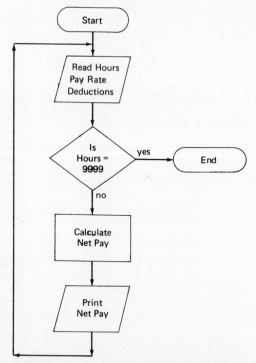

FIGURE A.14 Loop with test for end of file.

For example, a group of data can be read in under a loop and tested for the end of file. When the trailer record is reached, control can be directed to a series of calculations.

EXERCISES

1. Summarize the functions of a flowchart.
2. Study the flowchart symbols given in Fig. A.5. Be able to identify their functions by their shapes.
3. Obtain a flowchart template. Identify each of the symbols and practice drawing them.
4. Draw a simple flowchart that reads data, performs a calculation, and prints out the answer. Be sure to include START and END symbols.
5. Flowchart an interactive program that reads in a number from the program, inputs a number from the keyboard, sums them, and outputs the results on the printer.
6. Draw a flowchart of a program that reads in student ID numbers. Print out all evening-student numbers (below 20,000) in one column and day-student numbers (above 20,000) in a second column.
7. Flowchart a program that inputs a value from the keyboard, performs three calculations on it, prints out the results, and then gives the programmer the option of repeating the steps on another value or branching to END.
8. Draw a flowchart of a computer algorithm that performs a simple interest calculation for one or more sets of values.
9. Suppose a file with 20 records is stored on a disk. Draw a flowchart of a program that will read a value from each record and add it to a running total. When the end of file is reached, write out the total.
10. Draw a flowchart of a program that will calculate the average cost from a list of prices read in. Include a test for last record.

PROGRAM DEBUGGING AND DOCUMENTATION

"What's wrong with this machine? It adds 3.00 and 5.75 and gets 3201.63892!"

The most common reaction of a new programmer when he or she experiences a first programming error is to blame the machine. Unfortunately, though, for the human ego, almost without exception the fault lies not in the equipment but in simple human programming error. And, in addition, no matter how carefully a programmer writes his or her instructions, the chances of making one or more errors increase greatly with the length and complexity of the program. Even the novice programmer writing programs with only a few statements should expect one or more errors.

Obviously, programs that contain errors, or give erroneous results, serve little practical value. The procedure for eliminating errors and error conditions from a program is a normal and important part of the programming process.

Errors in programming are called *bugs,* and the process of eliminating them from the program is called *debugging.* Programming errors fall into three groups:

1. typing or keyboarding errors
2. data-entry errors
3. errors in logic

The first two groups are called clerical errors. They result from miskeying one or more characters or from entering the wrong kind of data to the program. Alphabetic data may have been keyed in when the program was expecting numerics or a value may have been left off, for example.

The third group of errors, mistakes in program logic, are often harder to detect than the first two. Examples are program statements that direct control of the computer to the wrong statement number or to one with an incorrect formula, a program that adds values or performs calculations on quantities before they are actually input, and so on.

DEBUGGING METHODS

The best method of handling errors is, of course, to avoid making them in the first place. It is always much easier to prevent errors than to spend programming and computing time later trying to find them. Here are a few hints that will be of help in avoiding or reducing errors.

1. Define your problem. Before programming a problem, analyze and define it carefully. Plan each step in the program so that it follows a logical sequence leading to the solution. Programs that have been hastily written usually result in many errors. Determine exactly what form and type of input are needed, what output results are desired, and what steps must be taken to reach them.

2. Flowchart the problem. Use flowcharts to help organize your thinking. They are a graphic description of the algorithm and provide an excellent means of spotting logical errors. Any program containing more than a few steps, or involving branches or loops, should always be flowcharted.

3. Study the BASIC reference manual and follow the rules it lists. Any deviation from these rules or changes in syntax or spelling will introduce difficulties.

4. Keep each statement simple. As a rule, the novice programmer should write statements as uncomplicated as possible. This may mean using two or more separate commands to perform a procedure that could have been programmed in one complex statement. It may take more storage space and make the program a bit longer, but it is easier to follow. Sophisticated programming techniques shorten a program and speed up execution, but they can seriously complicate debugging.

5. Build your program in modules. Whenever possible, construct programs in blocks or modules that can be run and tested independently. This greatly simplifies programming, helps to prevent errors, and facilitates debugging. Complex programs with interlocking steps may be interesting and fun to design, but they increase the possibility of bugs and are best left to the more experienced programmer.

6. Build essentials first and adorn them later. If your program contains many branches, conditions, or calculations, write a skeleton program first, containing only the minimum number of steps necessary to get the program running. Later, expand the steps, add refinements, include graphic touches, and so on.

7. Account for all branches. Each alternative path created by branches in your program must have a way of returning to the main program flow or to normal program termination.

8. Include sufficient REM statements in each program to help you follow program flow. Place REM statements before major branches, major sequences, calculations, input and output routines, and so forth. This is especially important for the novice programmer who can soon become lost in a maze of programming commands. (The example programs in this text seem to break this rule—they contain only a minimum amount of REM statements. But additional REM statements were felt to be unnecessary, since the programs are so well documented. They would also require more memory, which may not be available on some machines.)

9. Initialize variables. Initializing means including a statement in a program to assign an initial value to a variable. This prevents errors in several ways. Data left in the computer's storage system from a previous program will sometimes interfere with the present program. Assigning a new value to the appropriate location avoids this situation. Errors will often occur in programs involving looping if variables are not reinitialized each cycle. (Conversely, looping back to an initializing statement at the wrong point in the program can be a source of error also.)

10. Assign names that relate to, and help identify, the quantities in storage. Names should be selected for easy association with the quantities they represent. For example, a program involving amount, principal, interest, and balance might use A, P, I, and B rather than A, B, C, and D assigned names. It is a good idea to prepare a written list of assigned names and the quantities they represent. A list will also help one avoid accidentally assigning the same names to two variables.

11. Enter data via the program with a READ statement rather than from the keyboard with an INPUT statement when testing. This decreases the chances of errors. Each time the program is run, you are sure that you are using the same set of data. If you input the data via the keyboard, you introduce the possibility of entering a different data set each time the problem is run, thereby making bugs much harder to detect. Program execution is also faster when the machine doesn't have to wait for data entered via the keyboard.

12. Write out your statements carefully on a coding sheet or paper and check them for errors before keyboarding. Print in capital letters. Use plenty of space between lines. Indent FOR/NEXT loops and keep margins neatly aligned.

13. Keyboard carefully. Take time to keyboard each line with care. This rule may seem easy to follow, but programmers often fall into bad keyboarding practices and rely on the "forgiveness" of the computer to correct errors. If you make a mistake on an ordinary typewriter, you must erase the error (or apply whitener), backspace, and strike the correct character. On the computer keyboard, you can delete an error simply by striking the left arrow key or by deleting the entire line. (See Part One, Chap. 3.) But since you can type more quickly and correct errors more easily on a computer keyboard, sloppy typing habits result and the chances for more errors increase.

HOW ERRORS ARE DETECTED

Because even the best of programmers will make errors, several techniques and methods of detecting and eliminating bugs have been developed. Obvious errors such as misspellings and incorrect punctuation are often easily spotted by the programmer during a quick review of the program. Other, more subtle errors may require a more systematic, intensive method of detection.

Three methods commonly used are discussed below.

1. Error detection by interpreter. Interpreters systematically scan and check each programming statement as they translate it into machine language. They look for errors in spelling, syntax, form, and conformity to the rules of the language. Statements containing errors cannot be executed.

Some computers will check and interpret each statement as it is keyboarded. If an error is found, the computer will immediately respond by printing a communication, called a diagnostic message. Figure B.1 shows examples of such messages. The interpreter indicates the kind of error that is present.

Other computers begin detection of errors only after the whole program has been keyboarded and run. These systems print out diagnostic messages at the end of the program listing. See Fig. B.2. The computer gives the line number of the error and the kind of error present in the statement. Some systems list one error and wait for a correction to be entered, then they list the next error and wait, and so on. Others print out all errors at one time.

Most reference manuals include a list of the error messages generated by that system. Figure B.3 is an example. The manual gives a description of the kinds of errors, but the programmer has the responsibility of detecting the exact changes that are needed.

After all errors have been corrected, the program is ready for execution. At this point, many other clerical or logical errors may appear. Figure B.4 shows examples of several clerical errors that are not detected until execution time. These include entering alphabetic data when the program specifies numeric, entering too few, or too many, variables, inserting incorrect line numbers in GOTO statements, and even making typographical errors.

2. Manually trace data through all branches of program. A second method of detecting errors in a program is to prepare a set of data and manually trace it through the steps

```
10 REM DIAGNOSTIC EXAMPLE
20 READ AGE
SYNTAX ERROR
30 IF AGE =21 THEN GOTO END
TROUBLE AFTER IF
BAD NUMBER
30 IF A=21 THEN 70
40 IF AGE<21 LET X=MINOR
TROUBLE AFTER IF
45 LT X=A
SYNTAX ERROR
50 PRNT AGE,X
SYNTAX ERROR
60 END
```

FIGURE B.1 Diagnostic error messages—during keyboarding.

```
10 REM DIAGNOSTIC EXAMPLE
20 READ AGE
30 IF AGE=21 THEN GOTO END
40 IF AGE<21 LET X=MINOR
50 PRNT AGE, X
60 GOTO 20
70 END
170 DATA 19,24,15,27,23,21,19,20

RUN

INCORRECT FORMAT   IN 20
ILLEGAL RELATION   IN 30
ILLEGAL RELATION   IN 40
INCORRECT FORMAT   IN 50
```

FIGURE B.2 Diagnostic error messages—at end of listing.

Message:	FOR/NEXT OUT OF SEQUENCE
Cause:	A NEXT statement appears at a point where no incomplete FOR loop exists
Action:	Execution is inhibited.
Message:	INVALID ARRAY DECLARATION
Cause:	An array name appears in a DIM statement after the name has been implicitly or explicitly declared.
Action:	Execution is inhibited.
Message:	INVALID ARRAY REFERENCE
Cause:	The line contains an array variable with a different number of subscripts than the first reference to the array.
Action:	Execution is inhibited.
Message:	INVALID LITERAL CONSTANT
Cause:	The line contains a literal constant without a final boundary character.
Action:	Execution is inhibited.
Message:	INVALID MATRIX OPERATION
Cause:	Matrix inversion or transposition in place has been attempted, or matrix multiplication has been specified where the product matrix is the same as a multiplier or multiplicand matrix.
Action:	Execution is inhibited.
Message:	INVALID MATRIX REFERENCE
Cause:	The line contains a matrix reference to an undefined or a one-dimensional array.
Action:	Execution is inhibited.
Message:	INVALID NUMERIC CONSTANT
Cause:	The line contains a numeric constant whose absolute value is too large for the machine, and/or the constant has an incorrect syntax.
Action:	Execution is inhibited.
Message:	INVALID USER FUNCTION
Cause:	A user function has been defined more than once.
Action:	Execution is inhibited.

FIGURE B.3 Error messages—partial list.

of the program. These data should be selected so that they will test all branches written into the program and other possible conditions that might be encountered in the run. This is an excellent means of detecting logical errors that are not obvious from reading through the statements.

3. Running program with known test data. The third means of error detection is to run the program through the computer by using a set of data for which the answers are known. Computer printouts look deceptively official and accurate, and it is easy to believe that if the program runs at all, the results are probably correct. But a programmer shouldn't assume that everything the computer prints out is perfect. If an important variable is left out of the mathematical calculations, if a step is skipped, or if other logical errors are made, the results can be meaningless.

For this reason, the programmer should manually calculate results for a set of data, using the original formula. He or she should then compare these answers with the computer-generated output for the same set of data. If results agree, chances are that the bugs are gone. (Of course, any set of data for which the answers are known is suitable for this step.)

```
10 REM DIAGNOSTIC MESSAGE TEST
20 READ A$,B,C,D$,E
30 IF A$= 0   THEN 110
40 LET T=B+C(E/4)-3^2
50 PRINT A$
60 PRINT D$,T
70 GOTO 20
80 DATA SMITH, 169, 28.2, 16
90 DATA GARCIA, 314, 29.6, N694, 83
100 END
RUN
 UNDEFINED LINE REF AT 30


30 IF A$= 0   THEN 100
RUN
 BAD DATA IN READ AT 20


80 DATA SMITH, 169, 28.2, G367, 16
RUN
SMITH
G367               160
 SUBSCRIPT ERROR AT 40


40 LET T=B+C*(E/4)-3^2
RUN
SMITH
G367               272.8
GARCIA
N694               919.2
 END OF DATA AT 20
```

FIGURE B.4 Clerical errors.

Each programmer soon learns other techniques and methods of his or her own to help debug programs. Some programmers rely heavily upon the machine to detect errors—running a program over and over, making slight changes, until they remove all bugs. Others will spend many hours studying one printout, trying to detect the errors. Good practice lies somewhere in between.

Below are some hints for locating errors. Since all programs are a little different, the debugging techniques used will differ from one to another.

1. Get a listing. After you have keyboarded the program, get a listing from the computer. Some programmers prefer to run the program first and then get a listing only if they encounter trouble. But since most programs contain bugs in the beginning, a correct listing will be essential anyway. Study a listing carefully. Look for keyboarding and spelling

```
10 REM PRINT TRACE
20 READ A,B,C
30 LET D=A+B
35 PRINT "    TRACE D ="; D
40 IF D=> 50 THEN 70
50 LET E=D*C
55 PRINT "    TRACE E ="; E
60 GOTO 80
70 LET E=D*10
80 PRINT "THE ANSWER IS "; E
90 PRINT
100 GOTO 20
110 DATA 5,7,20,30,30,15
120 DATA 60,10,20,1,5,40
130 DATA 4,5,6,30,2,5
140 END
```

```
    TRACE D = 12
    TRACE E = 240
THE ANSWER IS  240


    TRACE D = 60
THE ANSWER IS  600


    TRACE D = 70
THE ANSWER IS  700


    TRACE D = 6
    TRACE E = 240
THE ANSWER IS  240


    TRACE D = 9
    TRACE E = 54
THE ANSWER IS  54


    TRACE D = 32
    TRACE E = 160
THE ANSWER IS  160

Out of DATA in 20

10 REM PRINT TRACE
20 READ A,B,C
30 LET D=A+B
40 IF D=> 50 THEN 70
50 LET E=D*C
```

```
60 GOTO 80
70 LET E=D*10
80 PRINT "THE ANSWER IS "; E
90 PRINT
100 GOTO 20
110 DATA 5,7,20,30,30,15
120 DATA 60,10,20,1,5,40
130 DATA 4,5,6,30,2,5
140 END
```

```
THE ANSWER IS   240

THE ANSWER IS   600

THE ANSWER IS   700

THE ANSWER IS   240

THE ANSWER IS   54

THE ANSWER IS   160

Out of DATA in 20
```

FIGURE B.5 PRINT trace statement.

errors. Check to see that all variables have been used correctly. Watch that statements follow rules of form. And so forth.

2. Check each error message generated by the computer. The language manual is of great help here. You can probably determine the cause of most errors by looking up the message or by carefully reviewing the statement.

3. Recheck your logic and flowchart. The program may run, but output may still be erroneous. Have you left out steps? Have all branches been accounted for?

4. Insert PRINT trace statements. Many errors can be detected by placing extra PRINT statements in the program. See Fig. B.5. Temporary PRINT statements in loops, at points where intermediate results are calculated, and so forth, enable you to check these values, which are not normally printed out as the program runs. Once the program has been debugged, delete the extra PRINT statements. Numbering temporary PRINT statements differently from the other programming statements makes them easier to spot. For example, use only line numbers ending in 5 (15, 25, 35) or in 1 (81, 91).

5. Run separate modules. If you cannot get your program running after following all the methods described, run only parts of the program. This can be done by inserting GOTO statements to skip over sequences or by deleting some statements. Sometimes it is best to build up the program in modules. Don't add a new block until the previous one checks out on the computer.

6. Discuss the program with others. Sometimes errors are not detected because the programmer is "too close" to the program. It may be necessary to put the program aside

for a day or so and come back to it with a fresh outlook. Sometimes, just discussing it or explaining the algorithm to another person will help you uncover errors.

SOME COMMON BUGS
AND HOW TO ERADICATE THEM

The following examples illustrate some of the more common errors made by novice programmers.

1. Errors in data. Figure B.6 illustrates an error condition in which the programmer desires to read in four quantities, the first two alphabetic and the last two numeric. However, the data in statement 140 is not correctly entered. The third quantity, "CHARLIE", is to be read in under a numeric name, but it contains alphabetic information.

Figure B.7 illustrates another error in data. The program reads in three quantities, A, B, and C. However, in DATA statement 120, the values are separated by spaces instead of commas. Since the computer ignores spaces, it will read in 3 14 89 as one variable and print out an error message that it has run out of data.

Another input error condition is shown in Fig. B.8. There are three INPUT statements in the program and each reads in one variable. However, the programmer has entered all three quantities on the same line. The computer responds that too much data has been entered and requests the programmer to retype it correctly.

The program in Fig. B.9 illustrates another error condition. The program inputs two quantities, one alphabetic and one numeric. However, the programmer has entered two alphabetic pieces of data.

2. Errors in logic. A common logical error made by novice programmers is shown in Fig. B.10. The program reads in and prints out the name of a customer and the balance due. The programmer has mixed up the sequence of operations (either through a clerical error of reversing line numbers or a logical error) and asks the computer to print out a value before it is read in (or calculated). The program will run as written, but the results will be erroneous.

```
10 REM PROGRAM READS ALPHA AND NUMERIC DATA
20 READ N$, A$, C, D
30 PRINT N$, A$, C, D
140 DATA "JOHN","SAM","CHARLIE",28
150 END

RUN
Syntax error in 140

140 DATA "JOHN","SAM","CHARLIE",28
140 DATA "JOHN","SAM",4,28
RUN
JOHN           SAM              4              28
```
FIGURE B.6 Data error.

```
10 REM PROGRAM READS NUMERIC DATA
20 READ A
30 READ B
40 READ C
50 PRINT A, B, C
120 DATA 3 14 89
130 END

RUN
Out of DATA in 30

120 DATA 3,14,89
RUN
 3                14               89
```
FIGURE B.7 Another common data error.

```
10 REM THIS PROGRAM READS THREE VARIABLES
20 PRINT "PLEASE ENTER ELEMENT, WEIGHT, AND NUMBER"
30 INPUT E$
40 INPUT W
50 INPUT N
60 PRINT E$, W, N
70 END

RUN
PLEASE ENTER ELEMENT, WEIGHT, AND NUMBER
? ZINC, 65, 30
?Redo from start
? ZINC
? 65
? 30
ZINC              65               30
```
FIGURE B.8 INPUT error.

Another common logical error is made in the program shown in Fig. B.11. The program is supposed to read in and add the values of X to a running total (T) until the total is equal to, or greater than, 100. At this point, it branches to END and the program terminates. When the programmer attempts to run the program, an error message is printed out stating that the computer has run out of data. Before the next run, the programmer inserts a PRINT statement at line 45 to trace the value of T. This shows that the total (T) is not accumulating the values of X. A careful review of the program reveals an error in line 60. The program loops back to statement 20, which initializes T to 0 each cycle, thus erasing the values of X previously read in. Statement 60 is corrected to read GOTO 30 and the program runs without error.

```
10 REM PROGRAM READS ALPHA AND NUMERIC DATA
20 PRINT "PLEASE ENTER NAME AND AGE"
30 INPUT N$, A
40 PRINT N$, A
80 END


RUN
PLEASE ENTER NAME AND AGE
? RALPH, NINE
?Redo from start
? RALPH, 9
RALPH            9
```
FIGURE B.9 A second type of INPUT error.

```
10 REM DIAGNOSTIC MESSAGE TEST
20 READ A$
30 PRINT A$, "BALANCE DUE - $"; T
40 READ T
50 DATA JOHN, 16
60 END


RUN
JOHN            BALANCE DUE - $ 0


30 READ T
40 PRINT A$, "BALANCE DUE - $"; T
RUN
JOHN            BALANCE DUE - $ 16
```
FIGURE B.10 Logical error.

PROGRAM DOCUMENTATION

Program documentation involves the preparation of a permanent file to accompany a program. Documentation should be considered an essential step in the planning, development, and construction of computer programs.

It is particularly important for the programmer to keep complete documentation files for each program he develops. Programming skills are gained through a learning process based upon experience. Old programs offer ideas, techniques, and algorithms for building new programs. Programming details, algorithms, and logic are also easily forgotten once a programmer has not worked with a program for awhile.

Documentation files contain several items, depending upon the needs of the programmer and the application of the program. The most common items in the file are (see Fig. B.12):

1. Flowchart. Graphic illustration of program logic.
2. Program listing. The file should contain an accurate listing of the program. This

```
10 REM PROGRAM ADDS A NUMBER TO A RUNNING TOTAL
20 T=0
30 READ X
40 LET T=T+X
50 IF T>=100 THEN 70
60 GOTO 20
70 PRINT "     THE TOTAL IS:"; T
80 DATA 6,8,10,9,5,9,50,14,25
90 END

RUN
Out of DATA in 30

45 PRINT "TRACE T:"; T
RUN
TRACE T: 6
TRACE T: 8
TRACE T: 10
TRACE T: 9
TRACE T: 5
TRACE T: 9
TRACE T: 50
TRACE T: 14
TRACE T: 25
Out of DATA in 30

60 GOTO 30
RUN
TRACE T: 6
TRACE T: 14
TRACE T: 24
TRACE T: 33
TRACE T: 38
TRACE T: 47
TRACE T: 97
TRACE T: 111
     THE TOTAL IS: 111
```

FIGURE B.11 Another common logical error.

listing should include adequate REM statements so that the program can be easily followed by others.

3. Written narrative. The programmer should explain in one or more paragraphs the nature of the algorithm and the logic followed in the program. Such a statement is especially helpful to others who use the program.

4. Description of input data. An essential part of the documentation file is the de-

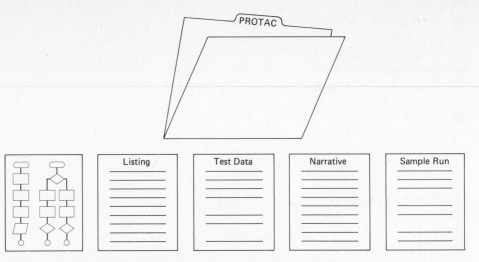

FIGURE B.12 Documentation file.

scription of the form and type of data used in the program. The sequence, amount of data, and type required should be clearly indicated.

5. Sample run and output. It is very useful to include in the documentation file a sample run of the program with the test data used. This should be a clean copy of the printout, illustrating all branches of the program.

PROGRAM DEVELOPMENT

Programs often go through several stages of preparation in their development, which can cause some confusion. It is not uncommon for a programmer to experiment with a number of different algorithms, revisions, or versions until the program is perfected. Even after the program is running properly, he or she may make additional changes or alterations.

If some systematic means is not used to keep track of these changes, the programmer may soon be hopelessly lost in pages of printouts, each showing a different version of the program or dozens of unlabeled disks.

The programmer should get in the habit of numbering and labeling each version of a program he or she develops.

A convenient method of identifying programs is to assign a name and number to each version of the program developed. First, a six-letter mnemonic name or title should be assigned for reference. For example,

Financial Analysis Program: FINAPR
Program for Storing Math Test: PRFSMT
Calculates True Interest Rate: CATINR

This mnemonic name should be included in the first REM statement of the program. It should be written in large letters on the top of each printout, on all tapes, and on any documents referring to that program.

A numbering system should be developed to account for changes and alterations made in the program. One convenient system is composed of the mnemonic name, the date, and a sequential number to represent the different versions developed. The first version is labeled 1, the second 2, and so on. For example,

CATINR   32673–1
CATINR   32673–2
CATINR   32673–3

EXERCISES

1. List the ways in which errors are detected in a program.
2. How can PRINT statements be used in debugging?
3. Prepare a written narrative for a running program you have developed.
4. Write a data input description for a running program.
5. Prepare a program documentation file on a running program.
6. Set up a physical file box to hold program tapes. Label each tape with a six-letter mnemonic title.
7. How are REM statements used in program documentation?
8. Find the logic error in the program below.

```
10 LET C=A+B
20 LET A=10
30 LET B=20
40 PRINT C
50 END
```

9. Find the errors in the program below.

```
10 COMMENT TEST PROGRAM
20 READ ACME, F, G
30 OUTPUT ACME, F,G
40 END
```

10. What would you look for if you obtained the following error messages?
    a. FOR WITHOUT NEXT
    b. LINE TOO LONG
    c. SYNTAX ERROR
    d. DATA EXHAUSTED
    e. DIVISION BY ZERO
    f. NO LINE AT--
    g. PROGRAM CONTAINS NO LINES
    h. WHAT?

INDEX

83 84 85 86 7 6 5 4 3 2 1